To Go Beneath the Water

K L MILLER

Disclaimer: This is a work of non-fiction. Names and specific places have been changed. Witness 'truths' appear as they were presented at the time of writing or the time period discussed. All scripture references unless otherwise stated are from the New World Translation of the Holy Bible published by The Watch Tower Bible and Tract Society, New York. This book seeks to acknowledge that we all have the right to examine what truth is, and are at liberty to engage in deeper enquiry as part of our freewill as intelligent, free-thinking human beings. In the words of Ronni Abergel, founder of the Human Library and writer of the foreword, the book also seeks to 'pave the way for a much-needed discussion about the way we treat each other' based on what we have either been led or have chosen to believe about each other. For the purposes of deeper enquiry, some of the subject matter in this book is of a deeply sensitive and, at times, unpleasant nature which some readers may find difficult.

ISBN: 978-1-7399711-0-6

To Go Beneath the Water

'At once a prison diary and a thrilling escape story, the author tells how she summoned the courage to break away from the intellectual, emotional and psychological bondage of the Jehovah's Witness community. She doesn't hide her anger for the church that stole her childhood and nearly her life; yet at the same time she shows an understanding of her oppressors. For others who find themselves trapped as she was – and of course it's not just Jehovah's Witnesses who entrap children in the name of faith – the message of this brave and important book is: If something, anything, is trapping you, change it or escape.'

Nicholas Humphrey, emeritus professor of psychology, London School of Economics, author of *Soul Dust: the Magic of Consciousness* and 'What Shall We Tell the Children?'

'The author of this wonderful and shocking book has found the courage, after years of silence, to share a story that needs to be heard. She lifts the lid on the Jehovah's Witnesses, a religion I had previously thought was harmless but a bit odd. She reveals the blatant manipulation of minds, right from childhood, and the deep fear of questioning a single word of what she was taught. Every human being on Earth has the human right to a personal voice, a viewpoint, without fear of rejection. This emotive, powerful piece of writing will change the way you view every belief you have, and every single person you encounter and how you treat them.'

Neil Wilkie, psychotherapist,
author, relationship expert and creator
of The Relationship Paradigm

'This powerful and important book echoes my strong belief that we are all capable of being an ally to someone in distress, and we are all capable of change.'

Ronni Abergel,
founder of the Human Library

'The more honest, sensitive work on the Witnesses we can get out there, the more chance we have of affecting people's lives for the better.'

Dan Kokotajlo,
writer and director of *Apostasy*

'This extraordinary book has offered a view of the world unknown to me. It has challenged some of my more engrained assumptions. It has already changed me.'

Duncan Brown,
author of *Reintroduction*

To my mother, for whom my love knows no bounds.
To my daughters, you beautiful, funny girls,
and source of pure joy.

Acknowledgments

My fellow ex-JWs, we share a special kind of kinship.

Dan Kokotajlo for the film *Apostasy* and for your immediate support for this work.

Ronni Abergel, founder of the Human Library, for the foreword, for your deep desire to connect the world through talking, and your belief in the message of this book.

Joanna Ezekiel, for your encouragement when *To Go Beneath the Water* was a draft that became an assignment that became the book.

Sarah, for sharing your home, garden and kedgeree unreservedly.

Maeve, for your tender care and making me laugh most unexpectedly.

Hannah, my spiritual sister, for the times you gathered me up when I wasn't okay, and for just being the most beautiful, gentle, hilarious soul.

To all those who read early drafts and urged me on.

To the miracle of the human spirit for its indomitable will to survive.

My Thanks

Alice Kennedy from Glow Designs Ltd for the stunning cover design. www.glow-designs.co.uk

Clint MacDonald for the invaluable publishing advice and speedy work in getting this book uploaded.
www.mac-nificent.co.uk

The Title of this Book

The title *To Go Beneath the Water* was chosen for several reasons.

It was chosen to represent the full-body immersion in water in the form of adult baptism, the metaphorical cleansing of a body of its previous sinful state, and the outward symbol of commitment to a lifetime of faithful service to God.

It was chosen to capture the sense of drowning under the weight of a religion from which, as a child, I had no possible means of escape.

It was chosen to symbolise the act of diving beneath the surface of belief, what it means to us to believe, and what lies waiting to be discovered, and challenged, if we are brave enough to look.

Construct of the Book

To Go Beneath the Water has been put together in two parts.

The first part is predominately about the period prior to leaving the Witnesses, followed in part two by the torturous, wonderful recovery after leaving. Both are a flashback to my child's-eye view of my confusing Witness world, my teenage years trying to work it all out, an adult at odds with what I was told was the only truth, and the excruciating, necessary learning along the way. They are not written in a linear fashion, but rather dip in and out of those flashbacks as the greater enquiry of truth and belief unfolds.

I finally left the Witnesses 2 January 2001.

'Today I choose compassion over intolerance, sympathy over hatred, and love over fear.'

– L.J. Vanier

About the Author

This is the author's first work, borne of an unadulterated love of learning, an intense curiosity about humankind and our beliefs, and the absolute conviction we are all able to challenge those beliefs if we choose to.

She lives and writes and runs her self-publishing agency between Spain and the UK.

Foreword

All people seek a meaning to their life. Some find it early, while others are first led astray before they reach the path that is right for them. The author of this book is such an individual.

Paving the way for a much-needed discussion about the way we treat each other, how we engage and relate to groups in our community that have different beliefs, views or lifestyles, and in essence understanding this, will help us all confront our own biases and safely challenge what we thought we knew.

This powerful and important book echoes my strong belief that we are all capable of being an ally to someone in distress, and we are all capable of change.

Ronni Abergel
Founder of the Human Library
https://humanlibrary.org

Prologue

You will sense anger here, and sadness and shame too. But this book was not written with fist-shaking resentment or judgment, or to attract sympathy or even to self-flagellate, it was written as a prompt for the conversations we must now have about what we believe about each other. It was written to examine why we choose to believe in a thing at all, or not as the case may be, and from both sides of what that feels like. It was written to shed light on belief when it diminishes souls and damages lives.

Whether you are an ex-Jehovah's Witness, or a JW who longs to leave, or anyone at all held captive by your beliefs or culture, stay open to how these words feel, for they were written with great intent.

To parents, we know what we teach our wide-open, beautiful children as they learn to navigate this world is critical to their psychological development, so, some of the points raised in this book, they're not that easy.

And to the greater world, what we believe about each other either segregates or gathers together, alienates or unites. I do not shrivel from analysing both in words that might not feel comfortable at times.

There is no doubt that the world is a broiling mass of opinions and perspectives; and there is no doubt that listening to each other might just help us to make sense of each other, even if we don't agree. But in order to do so, we must want to do so. More importantly, *we must be free to do so*. So don't close this book, or allow another person to close it for you, stay open and acknowledge how you feel – are you fearful of what you might read? curious about what might be revealed? – and allow yourself to examine the length and breadth of what it is to be a believing, or an unbelieving, human being.

For Socrates an examined life was a thing of beauty, the thing that married wisdom with humility. Should we want for anything less?

PART ONE

What are we to do with the combative playground of childhood, full of best friends and name-calling, skipping and spitefulness? For whether there are swings or a roundabout is irrelevant, as it is the interactions themselves, in any which place, that shape and misshape.

I could hang upside down from the top rung of the climbing frame and use my arms to catapult my body to the cracked concrete below – no soft friendly coloured bouncy stuff in my playground – and land precisely in the same spot, upright and smiling, every time.

For a time I was like that about everything: about relocating to a town where I didn't understand the accent when Mum married a pale, thin postman; about the untethered discipline from this man, who didn't care and didn't dare 'spare the rod and spoil the child'. I even landed upright and smiling despite the kids on our estate calling me 'loser' (no TV), 'saddo' (no birthdays), 'weirdo' (no Christmas), 'murderer' (no blood transfusions). Being a child in a family of Jehovah's Witnesses you had to be good at smiling. And landing on unforgiving surfaces.

My younger brother wasn't. He was bashful and blue-grey-eyed, like our mum, and as blonde and chubby as I was dark and thin. He always fell off walls and out of trees and into bodies of water, and suffered worst at the hands of the postman. So, my brother, he needed me. We would play in his cold bedroom, on the nasty blue Linoleum that snapped, crackled and popped if you jumped on it. We shared chocolate, when Mum could afford it. We'd buy those fake cigarettes from the corner shop by the chip shop with our pocket money, and 'smoke' them cross-legged on the Linoleum. We shared (forbidden) swearwords and chickenpox, giggling at the sound of the word fuck and comparing spots that hurt like fuck. Me and him, our own little twosome team.

"Dear Jehovah[1]," I'd pray later, in my most serious nine-year-old voice, "I'm sorry I said those words and smoked. I know you don't like those things in your kingdom. Please forgive me and let me be in paradise. I'm sorry, through Jesus'ses' name, amen."

I am six years old and sat between my mother and a woman with fidgeting hands. We're at a Bible study meeting in a room that is too hot. The carpet is bright 1970's mustard and purple with pattern. There is the turning of Bible pages, wafer-thin, and a study book's rasping of thicker, cheaper paper. An elder speaks, instructing another elder to read from the study book. My neck is sticky, like hot custard skin, but I have ice cubes in my bones.

The adults are discussing Armageddon, the war where all the sinners and those who don't believe in Jehovah will get killed, and the crows that will eat the bodies of those who are killed, and I'm really so frightened of this, and I really want to leave the room.

I glance at my brother. He's asleep on our nan's lap in his red Noddy pyjamas. I wish I was three and not six.

[1] Jehovah is the name used by Jehovah's Witnesses for the god of the Bible, the modern version of the Hebrew 'Yahweh' (the god of the Israelites), and from the original tetragrammaton YHWH.

I look at the door. *How far is it? What if I can't walk that far?* Mummy! *Why is my whisper not working?*

I stand up and vomit into the middle of the swirls on the carpet. The smell, and the hands across mouths and noses, and the glances at my mother as she pulls me from the room are simultaneous.

"Why didn't you tell me you felt sick?" she asks.

"I didn't know," I reply.

I did.

I become obsessed with sin.

"So *why*?" I ask again.

My mother peers around her hair. I've distracted her yet again from her yellow-orange crocheting.

"Why what?"

"Why have I sinned?"

"Well, we're all sinners."

"Why?"

"Because Adam and Eve ate the fruit from the tree that Jehovah said not to eat from, remember?"

"But I'm only six. I haven't done any sins! Or eaten any naughty fruit!"

"No…you haven't, that's true."

"Well, *why then*?"

I am as outraged and terrified as a six-year-old can be at the thought of being a sinner. I know it means I might get punished, or God won't love me, or I won't live in the paradise after the Armageddon war, and I might get killed because I'm not good enough and the crows will eat me and, actually, I don't even know what a sin is to not do one, apart from not eating fruit that Jehovah doesn't want me to eat. But how will I know? He hasn't told me!

My mother pulls me into her arms, but I stay stiff. "That's why we pray to Jehovah, so that he can forgive us. And when you get bigger, you know you can get baptised to wash away your sins."

I contemplate this. I like swimming. I'm back bouncing on the hard surface and smiling. "Go under the water? Like Auntie Jo?"

"Yes, like Auntie Jo."

I smooth her kaftan whirls. "Can I wear my goggles?"

The crochet hook slides from the yellow-orange loop as she laughs. "You might not need them when you're older."

"But, Mummy, the *chlorine*!"

This time I let her hug me.

Eventually I learnt the difference between adult Jehovah's Witness baptism versus the world's[2] infant baptism. It isn't the making amends for having sex on a Sunday morning instead of going to church; the hope that a bit of a christening will be just the ticket with God (to God) for the resultant oblivious infant. No, for Jehovah's Witnesses it's the conscious, adult decision to be fully submerged in water, symbolic of the cleansing of former sin, thus entering into a lifetime of service to Jehovah God. So I did. So help me God.

I wasn't thinking about sin at all though when I was baptised in the freezing public swimming baths hired for the

[2] Anything or anyone not part of the Witness faith is considered part of 'the world', the seething mass of humanity who don't worship God in the correct manner.

purpose. I was thinking about how my boobs looked in my black modest swimming costume, and the tanned hairy arms of the elder who baptised me. It was only later I thought that perhaps I should have been paying more attention; and, wow, now I had started my whole life as a baptised Witness all wrong; and how on earth – I wouldn't have said how the hell? (or worse) at this time – was I going to make amends for that?

I tried. I really did. I went door to door with the *Watchtower*, the bi-monthly magazine published by the Witnesses to spread the 'good news of the Kingdom' – Jesus Christ's kingdom, as established in heaven and soon to be established on Earth. I didn't swear (anymore) or smoke (anything). I studied my Bible, so hard, poring over the texts and constructing arguments for an argument I didn't dare cause arguments about. I watched all of my childhood friends get baptised, and married, and teach their children about crows and Armageddon and sin, and thrash them, often and hard in some cases, so they wouldn't be ostracised for 'sparing the rod and spoiling the child'. And all the time the hot custard neck and the ice cubes.

We've climbed into the top bunk, me and my brother, off the cold blue Linoleum. We're watching the fireworks from his bedroom window as it's Guy Fawkes Night, which we don't 'do', like birthdays, because John the Baptist got his head chopped off at a birthday party in the Bible because…do you know, I can't even remember the because. He's a bit scared of fireworks so, whilst we're watching, I distract him, like a good big sister.

"Do you believe in the Truth[3]?" I ask him.

"The what?"

"The Truth? You know, about paradise and..." – and I admit I'm showing off a bit here, because I'm nearly ten – "that Jehovah will 'wipe out the tears from their eyes, and death will be no more', like in Revelation in the Bible?"

"No."

"But you know we need to believe in it, because everybody else in Satan's world doesn't, and we don't want to die like them. I don't want you to die!" My heart is hurting, and my hands are cold.

"I'm not gonna die."

"Why?"

"Cos I'm Batman! Na-na-na-na-na-na-na-na-na-na... *Batman*!"

"What about the crows?"

"What crows?"

"The ones that eat the bad people."

He looks at me. Starts laughing.

"That's stoopid."

"It's not!"

"Tiz!"

"Not!"

A huge firework explodes. We press our foreheads to the window. As the coloured fizzles pop and bang, I wonder if I will ever write my name with sparklers, if I will ever get married and have a TV, if it's true about the Truth, and what happened to my real dad.

Dear Jehovah, I pray in my most serious nearly ten-year-old head, *please don't kill my brother. He's only seven and he doesn't*

[3] The Witnesses vehemently believe their belief system is the only truth about our existence and purpose on Earth, therefore it is called 'the Truth'.

understand. Please let him be in paradise. I'm going to try harder to teach him the Truth. Through Jesus's name, amen.

The final sparks empty out in soft arches.

Imagine if all you knew became a cage, with wraparound rules a mile thick. Rules about sex: no sex before marriage, no sex outside of marriage, no oral sex, no masturbation. Rules about things which made no sense: no beards on the men, no trousers on the women, no standing up for the National Anthem, no saying the Lord's Prayer in school assembly. Imagine the desire to take a screwdriver to the rules, to stab them and the men who made them. Imagine sitting in a room in front of three men, elders, who will decide in a couple of hours whether your baptism was a sham and you must be expelled from the cage because you've just returned from a holiday in Greece, on your own, where you happily stabbed your way through a whole row of rules.

I was twenty-three and still high from riding pillion on Dimitri's motorbike, helmetless and with bare legs, from drinking ouzo and holding on to the sun-smell of him.

I was defiant as Elder No.1 asked, "Did you have sexual intercourse in Greece?" *Yep.* "With whom?" *A guy.* "How many times?" *I lost count.*

Elder No.2: "Did you enjoy it?" *What?*

Elder No.1: "Were you in any way remorseful whilst engaging in sexual relations with this man?" *It was great.*

Elder No.3: "So you have no remorse for your actions?" *It was great.*

Elder No.2: "Have you asked Jehovah for forgiveness?" *No.*

Elder No.1: "So you haven't prayed for forgiveness?" *No.*

Elder No.3: "Why?" *Because I'm not sorry.*

This went backwards and forwards for a while, while they tried to extract a modicum of regret from a girl still smiling from all the rule-stabbing.

I was then asked to leave the room, whilst they prayed to Jehovah to help them decide that my baptism *was* a sham, that I had no real grasp on the gravity of my flouting of the rules, and they must remove me from the purity of God's congregation.

As I awaited my fate, I recalled another elder, who just two days previously had sat in front of this same panel of elders and lied, and lied some more. I went to Greece because I loved him, and he loved me, and I thought he might follow me. We shouldn't have loved each other like that, of course, but I was half-demented with grief after miscarrying my first baby and he'd been so kind. He later comforted me by sliding his foot between my legs on the London Euston train, and kissing me to the wall in the underpass at Trafalgar Square whilst my husband and his wife wandered above and wondered where we were. He wrote poems to me – '*I saw you today, eyes far and wide, hair blown by the wind, and I sighed for us…*' – and how I adored him. And when he was asked all the questions – did you two touch each other intimately? did you two kiss often? do you love each other and want to be together? – he'd said no-no-no; but I'd said yes-yes-yes (on top of my confessions from Greece).

I was called back into the room and disfellowshipped.[4]

[4] Disfellowshipping is the Witnesses' way of keeping the congregation clean of sin, and sinners. When a brother or sister is disfellowshipped it is announced at their local Kingdom Hall and all contact must cease immediately with that person, whether family or friends. The disfellowshipped person may still attend meetings if they wish, but must sit at the back of the hall and not attempt to communicate with anyone.

The elder with the tanned hairy arms who baptised me lied and got to stay. I told the truth and was expelled.

When an otherwise fine employee is guilty of wrongful conduct in the workplace more often than not they are called into an office for an initial chat, where their boss will look at a whole ream of reasons why the misconduct may have occurred and possible solutions to avoid reoccurrence: What's happening at home? Are you happy working here? What can we do to help? This constructive approach may win the employee's trust that their boss cares about them, build their faith in the company, and make them take a hard look at why they did what they did in the first place. The approach is respectful of the whole picture, and only if the misconduct continues is further action taken.

It's not that I didn't understand why I had been disfellowshipped: I was utterly unremorseful. But I was honest, and broken, and actually just wanted one of them to say, "We're so sorry about the baby, and we understand how relationships can develop in difficult circumstances, and thank you for being so honest with us, and is there anything we can do to help…?" But they didn't believe me, they believed him when he said a) it hadn't happened at all, and b) I had misread his concern for his Christian sister as romantic interest. The man wrote me poetry and said he loved me! And as wrong as that was, and we were, I believed him. But had I been remorseful, and they had not disfellowshipped me, I would still have had to endure the humiliation of a 'public reproval' from the platform in the Kingdom Hall, with an elder announcing, "And finally, we must inform the congregation that Sister K X has been reproved before a body of elders," for which I was obligated to attend, and which would have 'marked' me as a bad association. My friends would then have ignored me, I wouldn't have been invited to any social events, and I would have to have sat shamed and shunned at the back of the hall. They would have gossiped about what it was I had been reproved for, and watched my every move, analysing and conferring, looking for clues. Eventually, though, all those who had hugged and shrieked with excitement when I'd told them about the baby would filter back over; they may even have asked how I was feeling, and if I was praying enough to help me get over my loss. And I would have said no, and they would have been very concerned about my lack of faith in the healing power of prayer to Jehovah, and filtered away again.

In a way, being disfellowshipped was a blessing.

I remember the walk back across town to my mother's – I was staying with her because my Witness husband couldn't have a sinful wife in the house – my heart, soul, mind and body emptied of all life. I remember the pack of cigarettes I bought, the flick of the lighter, the revolting taste (these were definitely not made of candy). I remember the tall, black guy with beautiful piano-playing hands standing in the hallway, a friend of my brother's, on the way to the silence of my room. And then there was a time when I didn't remember much at all.

♪ *We're Jehovah's Witnesses; we speak out in fearlessness; ours is the God of true prophecy; what he foretells comes to be.* ♪

I am standing in a stadium of eighty thousand people, roaring this into the pouring rain, believing it with most of my whole heart. Feel the power of that; sense its cellular effect. It's one of the 'Kingdom Songs' (the Witnesses do not sing traditional hymns; they compose bespoke songs that are sung at meetings and all-day assemblies) written by a bunch of guys in the Most Holy of Holies – back then an expensive piece of real estate in Brooklyn, New York, and the Witnesses' headquarters – who consider themselves God's sole spokesman on planet Earth. These men – as far as I know, women are still not permitted to enter this gentleman's club of religiousness – are responsible for writing every song, every article in the *Watchtower* and *Awake!*[5] magazine, every pamphlet, and every study book. They are adamant that what they write is 'inspired of God and beneficial for teaching, reproving and setting things straight', (2 Timothy 3:16, NWT[6]), and they are to be revered and feared, for it is their words, directly translated from Jehovah God himself, that shape every single second of your life as a Witness. And you are not, *absolutely not*, to doubt or question a solitary word that issues forth from these men onto paper.

So imagine there's a little part of you that does doubt and question. What if, as you sing heartily that 'what he foretells comes to be', you see that it hasn't? What if it's 1985 and certain big mighty dates earmarked by the Governing Body[7] for big mighty things have come and gone, by a lot?

Take 1914. This year was a monster biggie for the Witnesses; the supposed end of the Gentile Times (the oppression of God's

---

[5] A more topical magazine covering anything from orange-lipped conch snails, to the nutritional benefits of an avocado, to stories of faith service from brothers and sisters across the globe.

[6] The New World Translation, completed in full in 1961 by Clayton J. Woodworth and George H. Fisher and said to be 'the posthumous work of Mr Charles Taze Russell', the founder of the original Bible Students (later the Jehovah's Witnesses), is the only translation of the Bible the Witnesses will use. It will become clear why.

[7] The title the gathered men in Brooklyn call themselves, along with 'the Society' and 'the Organisation', and under the banner of The Watch Tower Bible and Tract Society. https://www.jw.org/en/jehovahs-witnesses/faq/governing-body-jw-helpers/

chosen people by non-Israelites); the end of the time, times and half a time[8] from the fall of Jerusalem to the Romans in 607 BCE, when God's chosen people (at the time) were released from captivity. It signified Jesus Christ being crowned as king in heaven, his first task to oust Satan and his demons – an unspecified number of other renegade angels who'd decided to join Satan in his rebellion against Jehovah – so they could wreak their havoc on Earth. This invisible celestial event, they in Brooklyn said, would mean the whisking away to heaven of God's anointed ones[9] – them – from where they would rule over the non-anointed 'common' Witnesses, or Bible Students as they were called back then, of which there were around 50,000. It must have been rather embarrassing when, come 1915, they were still at their desks.

And I remember the illustrations in the Society's publications in the early seventies, leading up to 1975, the next monster biggie because the self-appointed anointed were very much still on Earth and not in heaven, so events had had to be rejigged (more on this later) to state that God's destruction of evil mankind was probably going to happen then, or soon. I recall the tumbling buildings and the lightening, the ground opening up to 'swallow its dead', the unbelievers running as if towards the reader, terror sketched into their faces.

I remember excitable elders stating from platforms that more than the usual number of crows were present that year, a

[8] This is understood (by the Witnesses) to be 1,260 days (or 42 months based on the 360-day Jewish year) translated into years and based on the 1+2+0.5=3.5 algorithm which commenced at the destruction of Jerusalem and terminated in 1914 CE (based on Daniel 9:24-27 and the 'day for a year' formula.

[9] Part of the remaining 144,000 mentioned in Revelation 7:4 and 14:1, 3 who would be heirs to Christ's heavenly kingdom, and who were specifically selected as his (and his father's) spokesmen whilst on Earth.

bumper crop if you like, and how miraculous it was that Jehovah had provided exactly what was needed at exactly the right time, and observing the nodding nods and smiling smiles of *Ah, how lucky we are to have such a wonderful god…*

There were images in the magazines of crows feasting on the dead, and I remember looking around at my classmates when I was back at school on Monday morning and imagining their stomachs and eyes all pecked out, and feeling the sickness… but it was tinged with a sort of self-righteousness, because they didn't worship Jehovah like me.

As a newly baptised honorary member of the JWs, imagine you're wondering about 1914, and you're wondering about 1975 too, because you're ten years the other side of Armageddon supposedly happening in the autumn of that year. You are aware too that you are cornered in the cage of rules, the number one rule of rules being: thou shalt not doubt nor discuss thy doubt for fear of being cast out.

You look around you, at your world, at the tens of thousands of your brothers and sisters. You see your immediate family in long rows to your left and right; you see your childhood friends here, there and everywhere. Outside in the streets you hear Satan's world honking their car horns and swearing, and banging and crashing through their non-Witness lives; you hear your fear of them pounding at your temples. But louder is the voice that stirs the hot custard skin and rattles the ice cubes: everything is not as it appears.

Under normal circumstances you would feel free at that point to tune in to your instinct, the gut feeling, the visceral whisper, and have a look at why it has prodded you. But these are not normal circumstances, and there is a reason why, as a Jehovah's Witness, acknowledgement of this reaction is not encouraged.

There is much discussion about right versus left brain processing and response[10], and what is happening on a physiological level when we encounter something that just doesn't feel right. Without digressing into far more detail about the various functions of specific regions of the brain, the right brain processes in pictures, senses and emotions. It communicates things which the left brain, which processes in language and logic, is inclined to overrule, categorising the intricate, multi-faceted second-by-second collage of sensory inputs into 'files'. The left brain has many, many files, which it adores and clings to like a cerebral comfort blanket. It uses these files as a constant point of reference for the present and the future. It doesn't really like listening to the right brain, which it considers to be ineffectual at processing life.

So when the right brain breaks you out in a sweat and churns your stomach to let you know you need to pay attention, the left brain cuts in and says *For goodness' sake get a grip. You're all about the emotions, and that's no way to make a decision. We've got it all sussed this side: A = B = C, because that's what we've been told, and that's how it is, and that's how it's always going to be.* So the right brain goes quiet.

But A = B = C is never always true, and disregards the ultra-sensitive, intuitive right brain whose job it is to warn you so. But as a Witness, A = B = C is it. There is nothing else. There is no D, and certainly not an E or F. So this primal, instinctive reaction

[10] One of the most remarkable books on the subject is *My Stroke of Insight* by neuroscientist Jill Bolte Taylor, written after her colossal stroke, when she literally witnessed her left brain going offline. Her astonishing TED talk on the subject can also be found here: https://www.youtube.com/watch?v=PezzZ_ccgQ

to a thing that doesn't feel right is programmed out from before the moment you're even aware it exists, and certainly before you might choose to examine what it is and why it is. But it's the voice that still says *Get the hell out*! when you sense something is not quite as it appears.

Watch a baby, or a small child, when they encounter someone new. Their left brain is nowhere near developed enough to get all logical and say *Look, we know you don't like the look of this person staring into your pram, but they're a friend of the family, so you must give them the benefit of your doubt and not scream the place down.* Their right brain just screams the place down. But as the child grows, it is told to be nice, to smile, to shake hands, and thus the instinct is programmed out.

There's a reason for the programming, of course, as we can't move through life howling like a baby every time we encounter someone we don't take a shine to; we have to learn to analyse and rationalise and make a conscious choice to be polite even if we don't particularly like a person. Only when we sense real bad, a bad that won't go away despite all the analysing and rationalising, are we forced to overrule and say no, we really are getting the hell out this time.

But I was told, over and over again, that A = B = C when it came to 1914 and 1975, and Satan's wicked world, and that being a Jehovah's Witness was the only way I could please God the way he wanted to be pleased so I would survive Armageddon.

I was programmed to believe that any doubts I had about any of this came from Satan himself[11], and that if I dared to

[11] https://wol.jw.org/en/wol/d/r1/lp-e/2011524

voice them I was 'mentally diseased'[12], as good as an apostate[13], and he would claim me as his own.

I was bound by a group of men in Brooklyn Bethel for whom fear of exposure of not being who they so vehemently claimed to be – God's only true representative on Earth – was greater than the fact itself. And so they continued to write great sweeping truths about doubt being Satan's tool for getting into our minds. Education was also presented as another of his specific methods, and that reading outside of the Society's publications, particularly material about the Witnesses, was tantamount to apostasy and a disfellowshipping offence. It goes without saying then that any sense, or gut feeling, or right-brain prod that what I was being told was not the absolute truth was quickly silenced before it became a question voiced out loud, that became the fear of being cast out.

And so I sang, 'all he foretells comes to be', and tried to believe it with most of my whole heart for fear of being cast out.

I was most astonished when I came home from school one day to see a TV on the sideboard. It was 1975, the year Armageddon was supposed to come[14], and the year of Robin Ellis's Ross Poldark. I'd never seen my captivating mother so captivated; but even to my untrained eight-year-old eye, the postman wasn't a patch on Ross.

[12] https://wol.jw.org/en/wol/s/r1/lp-e?q=mentally+diseased&p=par&r=occ

[13] Apostasy is defined as 'A standing away from true worship, a falling away, defection, rebellion, abandonment' in the 2019 book *Shepherding the Flock of God*, written specifically for elders by the Governing Body and not available for regular Witnesses. Note the audacious reference to '*true* worship'.

[14] The significance of which is quite something, seeing as we were not supposed to be doing anything other than preparing to be saved or killed, not watching *Poldark*!

I was only allowed to watch *Poldark* when the postman was out – he didn't have any mates who he met for a pint on a Sunday night, so he'd make 'shepherding visits'[15] with another elder – and it was our little secret, me and Mum, because no doubt the TV would have been removed at the speed of light if he'd found out.

I will never forget us in our night clothes, cuddled in the crocheted blanket in silence and awe as we watched Ross's love for Demelza and Elizabeth, all tangled and passionate, and the galloping, and the crashing waves and, oh, it was beautiful.

And my beautiful mother's eyes would fill with tears and how I would wonder about her.

When is it we notice that this mother, the one who cleans and feeds and mends and moulds us, is another behind the call to the efficiency and order motherhood demands? For underneath the bath-times and bedtimes is a woman, a real woman. Have you seen yours too? Mine had friends, back then, who'd visit, and she'd bake and make tea and there would be a whole lot of chatting, and sometimes she'd be looking through the visit at the light changing in the garden, where she couldn't be because she'd be there, with them.

She sang sometimes, when she played her beat-up old Beatles albums; and she'd dance too, laughing and doing something called jiving. But the singing and the dancing and the laughing would go quiet when the time came around for the postman to return home from work.

She had eyes that filled with tears whilst watching *Poldark*. And I longed to ask her: Who are you?

---

[15] Shepherding visits, a play on a shepherd tending his flock, were calls made on brothers and sisters in their homes to build them up spiritually (by praying for their failings).

"Let's make them kiss."

"Take his weights off first."

My brother obeys and we manoeuvre Deep Sea Diver Action Man and Ballerina Sindy so that their plastic smiles snog.

"Now what?" he asks, concentrating hard on the kiss.

"Do they love each other, do you think? Real love?"

"I dunno. That's girls' stuff."

"Poldark loves Elizabeth *and* Demelza, and he's a man, so love is for men too." Quickly: "I read it at school."

"Well, they'll have to get married, then, I s'pose."

"No, let's not. They can love each other anyway." (I have a whole Poldark-shaped new story in my head and I love it.)

My brother has no arguments there, wrenches his Action Man from the kiss, and starts undressing him.

"Take her clothes off too," he says.

"Why?"

"Well, they can do it now, can't they, if they *lurv* each other."

What have I started? And how does he know about 'doing it', he's only six! And, oh no, here's the hyper-active voice in me saying No! they can't do it without getting married! they'll die! and I'll die for making them! Can toys get punished, though? I look at them. They haven't got brains, so they don't know about the Truth, therefore they don't know what they're doing, therefore they can't be killed. Jesus said, 'Forgive them, they know not what they do', as he hung from nails, stabbed in the side and dying for everybody's sins, so it would all be okay. But I'd still be the one making them do it, so would I be like Eve making Adam eat the fruit? I promise you, this is how my brain worked.

I carefully remove Sindy's white lacy tights and pink leotard and prepare to change the innocent play of childhood for all time through toy-sin, thinking deeply about this and how it may feel afterwards. Action man is already naked and ready.

Afterwards, we discuss whether Sindy may now be pregnant, and I am honestly in awe of my brother's knowledge of such matters. Who does he hang out with when he's not with our JW friends, acting out Bible dramas and playing 'Bible-Word Scrabble'? I'll maybe have to get Mum to sew her some loose clothes if she is pregnant, but not tell her why. And I can make the baby a crib, easily, from cardboard, and add cotton wool for a mattress.

I slowly redress Ballerina Sindy, smooth her hair and sit her prettily; Deep Sea Diver Action Man is still naked, lying face down on the bed, as my brother has now moved on to the Lego.

'Stay alive to Seventy-Five'… Not the age, the year.

I was still playing pregnant Sindy dolls, and colouring in in my pristine colouring books, and making chocolate-covered cornflake cakes. Mum had just told me that she was pregnant too, and that the baby was due in September. Wasn't that when we were all supposed to die or live, depending on Jehovah's opinion of us at the time? My head was full of hope of paradise on Earth, when I wouldn't get poorly anymore because I'd be made perfect again like Adam and Eve were before they sinned and ruined everything, and of rainbows and waterfalls and playing with lions and tigers, because those were the other images on the *Watchtower* covers and in the study books; but my heart was all ice-cubey and, somehow, when I looked at the pictures I wasn't sure I was going to be there, or whether it was true, or what my mum would do if she was there and I wasn't, because of the smoking and swearing

– and, oh no! the Sindy and Action Man sex! – and what about my brother and him thinking it was all stoopid?

Oh, the fabulous speeches from many platforms in Kingdom Halls or stadiums across the world in the preceding years (publication's bold):

> 'Well now, as Jehovah's Witnesses, as runners, even though some of us have become a little weary, it almost seems as though Jehovah has provided meat in due season. Because he's held up before all of us, a new goal. A new year. Something to reach out for and it just seems it has given all of us so much more energy and power in this final burst of speed to the finish line. And that's the year 1975. Well, we don't have to guess what the year 1975 means if we read the Watchtower. And don't wait 'till 1975. The door is going to be shut before then. As one brother put it, '**Stay alive to Seventy-Five**'.[16]

And how these were repeated. And repeated.

It scared me, that bit about the door being shut, and I used to imagine sobbing whichever side of the door I was on, separated from my family and friends, and how I wished my brain would stop working, or that I didn't have one at all. Or maybe I could change brains and grow up without the Truth and meet a Poldark and be his Demelza? But then I rather preferred Elizabeth's fine clothes and beautiful jewels to tin mugs and calloused hands, so I must go to the library and find a book about country houses and ball gowns. And where was my

[16] https://www.jwfacts.com/watchtower/1975.php

real dad, anyway? Had anybody found him and told him about the Truth? If I found him, I could tell him…but if he thought it was stoopid too, maybe he might be able to hide me from Armageddon? Maybe he lived in a country house already, with horses, instead of on a stinky estate where people ate food that made their houses smell like food, all the time, and said high-pitched things with too many vowels. And why did we have to leave *shire? He must still be there somewhere?

But life around me geared up for The End not the life of my imagination, the one with big houses and horses and hero dads. I remember all the flurry, all the excitement. We had this 'new goal', a 'new year' to get all self-righteous about, and you're going to love the maths that led to the whole 1975 furore (on top of the Gentile Times story); something about it being the six thousandth year since Adam's creation in 4026 BCE (or six biblical creative days of 1,000 years), and God resting on the seventh day, the Sabbath[17], so he could go right ahead and plan the destruction of all those who didn't follow his ways, and tee up Jesus's thousand-year reign of peace on Earth (or something like that):

> 'Are we to assume from this study that the battle of Armageddon will be all over by the autumn of 1975, and the long-looked-for thousand-year reign of Christ will begin by then? Possibly, but we wait to see how closely the seventh thousand-year period of man's existence coincides with the sabbath-like

[17] The seventh day, or biblical Sabbath, was traditionally observed as a rest day, a day dedicated to worship where even food preparation was not permitted because it was considered 'work' and therefore breaking the rules; it was okay, though, to engage in mass murder of unfaithful humankind and set up kingdoms.

> thousand-year reign of Christ. If these two periods run parallel with each other as to the calendar year, it will not be by mere chance or accident but will be according to Jehovah's loving and timely purposes…'[18]

What do you think about that as a piece of prophecy you could stake your odds on? The language they would use, those men in Brooklyn – 'assume', 'possibly', 'if' – when there was no evidence whatsoever that a single word of this was a) grounded in actual biblical teaching (aside from convoluted cross-referencing between the Old and New Testament, much like the 1914 maths) and b) grounded in any actual truth of any kind at all!

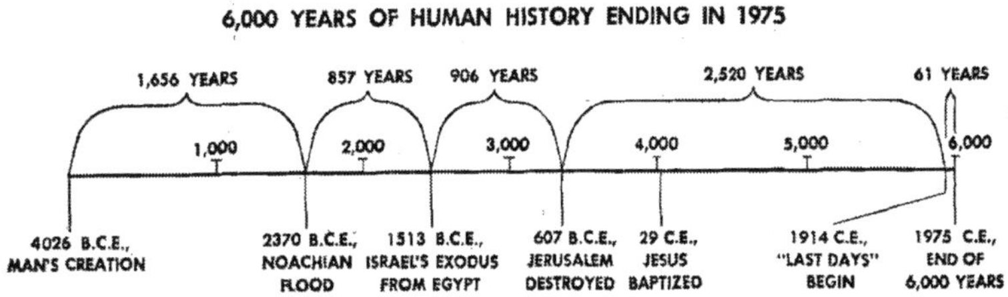

I'm not about to launch into a BCE-CE account of whether the dates were right or not – although clearly they were not, because at the time of writing it's 2019 – but invite you to take a look at the sheer audacity of claiming these dates were accurate, of presenting them as fact, of using them as proof that the Witnesses were right and set apart from the rest of the world's 'false' religions.

These *truths* changed people's lives.

[18] https://www.jwfacts.com/watchtower/1975.php

The years preceding '75 were a Witness carnival of house-selling, cancelling life insurance policies and vital surgical procedures (because we would be living forever so our families wouldn't need life insurance pay-outs, and all illnesses and ailments would be cured in paradise), giving up jobs, not having children and not bothering with education because secular qualifications would not be required in the New System.[19] Even my grandfather, an intelligent and shrewd businessman, abandoned his lifelong work with medicine, and his business, and went to work part-time in a hospital pharmacy so he would be ready for Armageddon and not distracted by his 'worldly' career.

The reasons presented in the pages of many *Watchtower* articles for making decisions like these, decisions that would prove to Jehovah we were 'awake' and fully his for whatever he needed us to do, went something like this: We wouldn't need jobs, as we would soon be working for Jehovah building the New System and establishing Jesus's kingdom on Earth after Armageddon; we shouldn't have kids, because wartime is not a time to raise children, and it would be so much harder for those with young children and babies to dedicate long hours to rebuilding the Earth; we absolutely should not embark on further education, as this would keep us away from our real and only mission – preaching about 'the last days'[20] and God's

[19] Another name for the post-apocalyptic Witness-only paradise, also referred to as the 'New Order'.

[20] When 1975 didn't happen, we were provided with wordy explanations about the possible 'new meaning' of the last days of this system of things, with no specified end date, just that Jehovah knew best… No explanation or apology accompanied these new meanings; and the confusion and disappointment and, in many cases, the catastrophic financial and health implications of faithful brothers and sisters were never directly acknowledged by the Governing Body.

imminent war against unbelieving mankind – and would be worthless in paradise anyway.

The last point, about education, I have never, ever forgotten. I loved learning, I was good at it, and as I got older I desperately wanted to do more. But imagine wanting to do that in a world where you were told this (publication's bold; my underline):

> 'Many schools now have student counselors who encourage one to pursue higher education after high school, to pursue a career with a future in this system of things. Do not be influenced by them. <u>Do not let them "brainwash" you with the Devil's propaganda to get ahead, to make something of yourself in this world.</u> **This world has very little time left!** Any "future" this world offers is no future! Wisely, then, let God's Word influence you in selecting a course that will result in your protection and blessing. Make pioneer service, the full-time ministry, with the possibility of Bethel or missionary service your goal. This is a life that offers an everlasting future!'[21]

This went on way after 1975 had come and gone, embarrassingly, which made way for a whole swathe of 'new truths' about the truth of the end of the world, and I remember the conversations with some of my friends, sat around all horny and listening to worldly seven-inch vinyl singles we should not have been listening to.

"Are you going to pioneer?" Daniella asked me, her dark fringe hovering over her hazel eyes.

---

[21] https://www.jwfacts.com/watchtower/1975.php

"Well, I–"

"She's gonna come to Ecuador with me and her bro, and serve where the need is great[22]," Ben assured her, his wishful thinking far more real than the reality I wouldn't.

"I'd like to pioneer, and I want to, but I also want to go back and do my A-levels…" I could feel Ben's eyes on me.

"Me too," Dani agreed. "My dad wants me to."

"What would you study?" I asked her, as Ben poo-pooed and informed her school was for losers and my brother agreed with him.

"English, maths and biology. What about you?"

"English, sociology and art."

"Why?" the boys asked, loudly.

Dani smiled. "I want to study medicine, so–"

"*Medicine*! We're not going to need any *medicine*!" Ben mocked. "What good's that gonna serve in the New System?"

"We're not going to be perfect straightaway!" Dani countered. "It'll take years, so we'll still need doctors. And people will still have injuries–"

"What about you? What pointless thing do you want to be?" he interrupted, turning to me, fully in his critical stride now.

"I'd like to be a writer, or a journalist…but I also love sociology, which is the study of how people interact in societies, cultures and religions, so–"

"We're all going to be one religion, and one people, so we won't need any of that stuff, either. And the Society write all the publications!" Ben said.

And there it was.

---

[22] Which entailed preaching in parts of the world where there weren't many Witnesses, also called 'missionary service'.

> 'If you are a young person, you also need to face the fact that **you will never grow old in this present system of things**. Why not? Because all the evidence in fulfillment of Bible prophecy indicates that this corrupt system is due to end in a few years. Of the generation that observed the beginning of the "last days" in 1914, Jesus foretold: "This generation will by no means pass away until all these things occur."-Matt. 24:34. Therefore, as a young person, **you will never fulfill any career that this system offers**. If you are in high school and thinking about a college education, it means at least four, perhaps even six or eight more years to graduate into a specialized career. But where will this system of things be by that time? It will be well on the way toward its finish, if not actually gone.'[23] (Society's bold)

Truths like this formed the backdrop to my entire life: "[…] as a young person, *you will never fulfill any career that this system offers.*"

I cried when I reread this over thirty years later; cried for the wasted decades and all the things I'd so badly wanted to do. We were programmed into believing we would never get old. We were programmed to consider learning as 'the Devil's propaganda'. From childhood, we had been saturated in fear of certain failure, even death, if we did anything other than follow the advice in the *Watchtower* and *Awake!* with respect to our futures. It was all fear. Fear of death, fear of God, fear of the world, fear of anything outside the cage of rules, fear of speaking

[23] https://www.jwfacts.com/watchtower/1975.php

up, fear of the funny, intelligent, kind friends in Satan's world we weren't allowed to be friends with... Fear of pretty much everything.

We'd been told often, and in no uncertain terms, that the only career for a servant of Jehovah was his service – the kingdom service[24] – and that anything else was at best abandoning our Christian duty, and at worst allowing the Devil into our minds and hearts. *Why the hell did I believe this?* Even the postman didn't believe this, I don't think, because he was furious when I abandoned my A-levels for pioneering – or devoting a minimum of sixty hours a month preaching about Jehovah's imminent New System – and got a part-time job in a backstreet café where fat from the fryers congealed on the kitchen ceiling and dripped on me when it got hot. I absolutely hated it but, God, the pressure to pioneer was so great. It was considered the ultimate career; the thing that would make you an exemplary Witness; a bastion of faith; a joy to your parents and congregation and Jehovah. So why was the postman angry with me? I thought it would make him proud of me if I pioneered, particularly as he was now an elder?

But then I wasn't sure what I would have done if I had finished my A-levels anyway. If it was frowned upon to do A-levels, attending university was tantamount to abject rebellion and rejection of Jehovah's will. And what would I have said to everybody, and how would I have coped? I had no idea who I was aside from Sister K X, the faithful servant of Jehovah, and it was torture not to be able to debate the

[24] The 'kingdom service', or 'field service/ministry', or 'ministry' are some of the phrases used to describe fulfilling the God-instructed command to go door to door to spread his word and the good news of his son's coming reign over Earth.

length and breadth and depth of everything that fascinated me because I had so little to say. I spoke the only language I was familiar with, the only language I'd ever known: the Witness language. And then there was the whole thing of "How will Jehovah view you when it comes to choosing those he wants in his kingdom, and you're at college instead of out on the ministry?" followed by the long pause while the intent of the question seeped in and sank you.

But I've jumped about a bit.

It was 1975, and the year that Sindy and my mother were pregnant and we had a TV. I often wonder what was going on in my parents' minds at this time: a baby and a TV (for the first time), in the year our faith in and loyalty to Jehovah would be judged as worthy of life or death? Was this some kind of blatant rebellion, maybe? A rare moment of marital solidarity against a regimen that even my parents saw as ludicrous? Despite despising his relentless shouting and bullying, the postman was an intelligent man, and a damaged one, I suppose, in today's parlance; a man, by all accounts, who had been bullied by his father whilst his older, taller brother had accrued much favour. Was having a child with my mother and getting us a TV his way of sticking it to 1975 and the men who invented it?

I never did ask him.

I am wearing a pink shift dress and carrying a broken heart, watching from the sidelines where I'm safe as my most favourite teacher marries his fiancée, and I wish I was she and not me. In a wedding dress the size of the eighties she is this pretty little thing, all post-breakfast champagne and in love with her northern man and what they are and what they will be.

I imagine them having sex tonight, like I've imagined having sex with him every night since he walked into our fourth-year biology class two years ago. We've dissected rats together, and worms, and a pig's heart, just me and him, because there was never anybody else in that room, not ever. They may have been clattering and chattering, my classmates, and asking questions about valves and arteries, but they were distance learning compared to me, because that's where I wanted them to be.

His light brown eyes and flopsy brown hair; his dimples and that irresistible Durham accent. He's going off to train to be a dentist, like his wife, after their honeymoon in Mauritius.

I don't want him to go.

I want him to hug me again on the fifth-floor landing of our horrid comprehensive school where he read the poem I wrote for him.

I want to stop dying.

As the wedding reception unfolds, I fold in further still. This is the world. This is what they do, all drinking and smoking and laughing, and why was I even allowed to come here? What magic did my mother perform so the postman said yes instead of no? (I don't want to know.) I am a stray atom, separated, adrift between worlds. Speeches. Toasts. (I've been primed not to raise my glass because Witnesses are not permitted to say Cheers! I don't know why.)

How do you know the bride and groom? What a pretty dress! Have you got a light? My voice isn't working again, and I feel sick. But something worse than that room is happening, and I don't know what it is. My heart thumps in time with some kind of ache, and I need my bed the moment I leave it, and all sound pops and warps and hurts, like being at the bottom of the deep end.

My brother has been caught smoking – and stealing to get the funds for the cigarettes as our pocket money doesn't stretch to the real thing. I don't think I can handle this; all the hushed talk and my mother weeping at the kitchen table. What will they do with him? He's still a kid? The brothers and sisters are all kind and "Poor you, poor you" because they know how close we are. I get invited to things I never got invited to before, with all the older teenagers, and those in their early twenties, the ones who drive and seem so sure. About themselves. About the Truth. About life. But here, too, I'm the stray atom, caught between being sixteen and nineteen or twenty-two, which may as well be five million years. I didn't know then that some of these older Witness friends would become real friends, for a time, and boyfriends; that I would kiss most of them and marry one of them; but also that they would all, without exception, turn their backs on me when this life, any life, simply wasn't what I wanted anymore.

I remember Sam, who was in his twenties, inviting me over to his parents' house for the evening, ostensibly to study the designated *Watchtower* article for Sunday morning. A brother called Charles was there too, and the aforementioned Ben, my brother's Yamaha-riding friend – although he wasn't allowed to associate with my brother now that he'd been caught smoking. Leah, a super-confident, sexy Norwegian sister who terrified me, was seated cross-legged on a bean bag in the corner; and Mattia and his sister Izabella were visiting from a nearby congregation. They helped run their non-Witness father's Italian restaurant and they were so, so smart, talking about food like the others talked about *The Meaning of Life* and *Jaws III* and the Police and Queen. I'd raised my head at the mention of 'the meaning of life', and lowered it again when Ben launched into '*Every sperm is sacred…'* Charles dropped me home, on account of being an older and reliable brother. I barely knew him, but it seemed he was trusted by my parents to take care of me, and they were right to. But I shouldn't have been there. I was so stupid compared to them, pretending to know about movies and music I'd never even heard of, just like I was now at this wedding.

I wave with the rest in my pink dress. The tin-can thing, and the shaving foam and lipstick on the windows of the Rolls Royce as they are driven away. I'd never seen a thing like that before. Witness weddings were all 'Don't forget the threefold cord – Jehovah – in your marriage and his blessing on your God-given gift of sexual union', which was about as conducive as having your mum (sorry, Mum) orchestrate proceedings. This biology teacher of mine. He was the first grown-up from the world to see me; to see beyond my dimples and the humour I used to field the interrogations and mask the debilitating terror of life.

Why don't you celebrate Christmas? they would ask me. *Because who needs it, when life is a lifelong Christmas Day of tinsel and baubles and geography homework?*

Why do you leave assembly when we say the Lord's Prayer?

I don't wish to insult you, but have you heard how drony you lot are?

Why don't you have sex before marriage? *This body belongs to the Lord, and I will only allow my husband and lord to enter the gates of my virginity.*

He was the first grown-up from the world I wasn't afraid of, who cooled the custard skin and melted the ice cubes. We would go into town in his car, an old blue thing – I still remember the registration number – to buy chips and the *Beano* comic and eat and read side by side, giggling and reading bits out to each other. (It was the eighties; we did stuff like that.) He would ask me about me: What food do you like? Where would you like to travel? Do you think you'll get married and have kids? Do you think you'll ever meet your real dad? Do you think you'll always be a Witness?

But he was gone. Married. And wouldn't be returning in September to teach O-level biology to the next lot of fourth formers. But do you know something? For a time he wrote to me, telling me about his studies, about anatomy and anaesthesia and life in a university city. He sent me photos of his cats, and apologised for dropping a tomato he was eating onto the writing paper. And, for a time, I felt real.

Think of the thing you are most afraid of. Snakes? Bats? Spiders? What is it about this thing that sends you to the world of irrationality and fear – because we all know these fears are irrational – and has you clawing to get space between you and the thing? Do you know where it comes from? Does it make any difference how many times you tell yourself it's irrational? It seems not, because the very next time an arachnid dashes across the rug you're up, every cell screaming.

What if the thing you fear is deeper, though, borne of life experience that has embedded long before you were even aware you were aware[25], triggering reactions simply beyond your control?

My chubby, smiling, blonde angel of a brother would become demented at the age of six months at the sight of tall men with dark hair; and I would hum or sing and become completely unreachable if a man, any man, even my gentle,

[25] There is a vast amount of evidence to support cell 'memory' of this nature.

beautiful grandfather, would walk into the room. Our real father was loud, vicious, six feet five inches tall, and had dark hair. I'd found out we had to leave *shire because of him. No further explanation necessary.

So as we grew older, in fear now of men in suits preaching from platforms, of the postman, of God, my brother smoked and stole money to smoke and I resorted once more to unreachableness. I would hum and sing just like I did as a little girl, but silently, and go deep, deep inside, where tall loud men and vomiting at Bible study meetings and Armageddon couldn't harm me. I would bounce on the hard surface of the Truth, the discipline, the rules, the teasing, a veritable fielder of new fears and secretor away of the ones that had already made it inside.

We each have our way of managing the unmanageable.

The fear bred as a Jehovah's Witness creates many types of individuals. There are those who operate in piety to mask the fear, their virtue manifested in such untouchable holiness that who are we to think we can match them scripture for scripture, act of reverence for act of reverence? But even these are split into two camps: the genuinely pious, in the true sense of the word, whose devotion knows no bounds and who actually wish no harm; and the heinous pious, whose self-aggrandising proselytising serves only to serve themselves and diminish others.

There are those who live a world of secrecy, and you never really know what they're thinking or doing behind the scenes when they're raising their hand to answer up[26] during the *Watchtower* review, or gushing about how Jehovah's gifts to his servants are so bountiful.

[26] Answering up – or raising your hand to make a comment – was a way of a) providing evidence you had pre-studied the publication or *Watchtower* article we were reviewing and b) showcasing your knowledge of and faith in its truth.

There are those who withdraw, slipping away into a safe place, whether seated next to you at the Kingdom Hall or standing by your side on a doorstep on the ministry. When you look at them, you're not sure where they've gone, you just know there's a reason they've gone there.

And there are those who live in a constant state of semi-rebellion: So what if I drop the odd blasphemy, kiss this brother or sister (or both), finish the bottle of gin… I rather liked these types, I have to say.

But how ever the fear manifests, of one thing there is no doubt: it splits personalities down the middle; it creates division of the deepest part of who we are to the point where we no longer know whether we are acting from fear or faith, fear or integrity, fear or love.

And in a closed-off closed-in world such as the Witnesses, every single word and look and action is analysed and judged: she's too flamboyant; he's too weak; she's a strong sister, but she suffers from depression; he says all the right things, but I've heard he likes a drink. On and on and on. But it's not just your fellow brothers and sisters who are watching. God, too, is observing. Every moment of every day in his omnipresent, omniscient way, because that's the only way he can tell whether you are as worthy of life in paradise in private as you are in public. This used to haunt me as a child and then as a young woman, when now there were breasts and periods and pubic hair. As a child I'd go under the bed covers and imagine his eyes looking right in, like an x-ray, right to where my brain was hating him for looking at me all the time. As a teenager, I'd shower and look up through the steam, through the ceiling. I'd sit on the loo and look out of the skylight window, up at where he might be peering in. I'd cover myself with my hand when I was putting clean knickers on, realising that was stupid, because he could see straight through my hand. But could he really see me? And what was he judging, anyway?

Fear breeds only more fear.

I recall the children who wore their smart clothes without complaint, who sat tidily and quietly at never-ending endless meetings and held on to *Watchtower* magazines and Bibles like they really were the Truth.

I recall the children who were full of rageful questions and anxiety about our lives, present and future, tortured by thoughts of sin, eternal judgment, survival or death.

I remember my blue-grey-eyed brother, who had gone from smoking candy in his bedroom with his big sister to tobacco with his friends.

And then there was the little girl who would sing out loud so she could hide behind her tunes, who became the teenager who sang inside her head to hide inside.

I have one question: Is this really any way to live?

It's the early nineties and I'm dressing the window in our local department store encouraging unbending arms into some sweater or other. The Witnesses have stopped coming into this branch, so terrified are they that I will taint them with my sin since being disfellowshipped. A few have walked in unwittingly over the last couple of weeks, however, not knowing I work here, and their reaction needs to be broken down into freeze-frames so swift is their departure. These people have known me since I was seven years old.

I smoke now too, since coming back from Greece and being disfellowshipped, because I can – even though I absolutely detest it, and even though I know that pretending to smoke a lighted cigarette is not really smoking – and I delight in the rebellion of it. And I'm planning on committing lots more adultery as soon as I can too, as Charles and I are still married (yes, we got married, three years after I was invited into their terrifying older fold) for as long as no papers get signed, and it would really seal the deal on my sin. As I pin the sweater at the back to make it appear smooth at the front, I'm thinking about the black guy with the piano hands standing in the hallway at Mum's.

There is a green 3-series BMW parked outside, with a conversation going on inside, but I don't know this.

"I'm gonna marry that girl, man."

"That girl is my sister."

"You kid me, man?"

"No, man. That's my big sister."

"Then I'm definitely going to marry her. She Kate Bush."

"Sure. Just don't sleep with her first."

There are voices from the kitchen when I get back to Mum's after work. My brother's and a rich, slow-roast-coffee movie star voice: I am face to face with the piano-hands guy. My brother wanders off to answer the phone, and this long-fingered, handsome black man and I consider each other, and the possibilities for conversation, and then begin.

When we return to considering each other, silenced by the realisation of our ease together, he eventually says, "You know we have to see each other again?"

In response I play 'Lovely Day' by Bill Withers on seven-inch on the stereo in the lounge, and return to the kitchen to be kissed.

Charles. My bendy-thumbed guitar-playing estranged Brummie husband. It was a sunny day when we got married, and the ice cubes were there, but I did like him so very much. I want him to hold my hand again as we walk down the street, and in the car in between changing gear, and as we fall asleep. I remember his horrified face when I burnt his horrible grey 'elephant' corduroy trousers (on account of being wrinkled and baggy) in the garden when we were first married, and him loving my roast dinners, and the songs he would write for me. But I went to Greece. I rode pillion, bare-legged, and slept with the guy we'd hung out with, and I'm so glad I did, but I so wish I hadn't. The shame of that, and how it hurt Charles.

The postman bought Charles's old guitar for me when I was fifteen, and I mimed to John Williams's 'Cavatina' because playing the chords from the *Beginners Guide to Guitar Playing* hurt my hands. My brother asked if he could play it when the miming got boring and the guitar lay prostrate like a summary of my lack of enthusiasm. By the end of the afternoon he had written his first song.

His voice was soft and young, and the song full of sadness and love. Just as with his six-year-old knowledge of sex, where had this thirteen-year-old ache of trying to find a girl whose footsteps were all 'covered with snow' come from?

Charles started coming over after that, and together they would play Eric Clapton and Simon and Garfunkel, my brother learning the lead and the rhythm as easy as that. Charles taught him to harmonise, too, and Mum would have those tears again, but by now I knew a little of why. He encouraged me to sing – they all did – but I would shrivel inside one of the places I'd constructed for when I wasn't confident or comfortable. But Charles, he had this way of making everything safe and quiet and, when I wasn't in one of my inside places, I would go places with him, until he and I became us, with rings and hopes.

I go to one of those places now as the man with the piano fingers removes my clothes, and I remove his, under a blanket on a settee in an untidy house I don't like in a part of town that scares me. I have consciously decided to do this; but I have consciously removed myself from the scene.

In Jehovah's Witness homes all over England the Tuesday night book study meeting will just be finishing, and there will be amens, and then tea and biscuits will be served. I want to go back. I want my friends, as duplicitous as they are. I want the love, as conditional as it is. I am alone here. And stoned. And about to commit the extra adultery I wanted. But I want Charles. I want to hear his guitar in tune and in time with my brother's, and have him tell me off (still) for not singing with them.

I cover my face with a cushion as the adultery begins.

I have nothing in place to understand what I have become.

If you plant and grow your son or daughter in an environment such as the Witnesses, you lay the foundation for a frightened child, a floundering youth, an adult drowning in the world of the only world you have insisted it belong to or else it will die.

But it's dying anyway.

Its beautiful innocence you have filled with crows pecking the flesh of sinners, a man hanging from nails for the world's sin, of prayers and apologies and supplications for its personal sin.

Its wonderful, natural curiosity and myriad questions you have silenced with a scriptural admonishment or a good hiding.

Its desire to understand how other people feel and love and believe, so it can form its own opinions and picture of the world, you have closed down.

Its creativity you have replaced with a long list of nos, because it means associating with people in Satan's world: no to drama club; no to tennis club; no to art club. Because it will mean being with children who 'don't love Jehovah' beyond the absolute necessity of a basic education. These children might be bright, and well-mannered, and talented and kind, but they don't love Jehovah, so always no.

Are you okay with this? Are you okay with stifling the life out of your child so you can sit it next to you in a Kingdom Hall in a little suit or a pretty dress and be praised for raising a child 'strong in the Truth'? be admired for being an exemplary example of a Christian parent? be commended for encouraging your beautiful, open, intelligent, curious child to cleave only to Jehovah, because that's the only way to live an acceptable life, or else it will die? telling it all their little schoolmates are going to die because they don't love Jehovah? showing it images in the Society's publications of people being struck down dead, their mouths gaping in a final scream and their eyes wide open with fear, because they don't worship Jehovah?

When Abraham was preparing to murder his own son to prove his faithfulness, do you think he was thinking of his son, or was he thinking about how good he would look in the nation's eyes and the blessings he would receive from God? And was Isaac so in fear of God himself by then, and his father, that he didn't dare beg Abraham to stop?

The story of Abraham's readiness to kill his own son was used, repeatedly, to illustrate how far Witness parents should be willing to go to prove their faith in Jehovah – who, we were told, repeatedly, had paid the ultimate price by sacrificing his only son for the redemption of our sins – whether that be surrender of their children to his will by allowing them to die because of not having a blood transfusion, or abandoning them should they prove willingly unfaithful themselves.

How does this make you feel? Are you really okay with it? Don't tell me you don't have doubts; that you don't lie in your bed listening to your child sobbing because you've just thrashed them for fidgeting at the meeting, or saying a 'naughty' word, and you don't have your own ice cubes that tell you, somewhere, that this is not a good way to raise a child?

I remember when porn was discovered on the computer at our local Kingdom Hall. Only three brothers – obviously brothers – had the password to the computer: the presiding overseer[27], the elder who installed it, and the congregation secretary. So we had three suspects, all of whom denied responsibility, of course. The techie elder, by way of fervent defence, said that perhaps he hadn't fully wiped the hard drive on the reconditioned machine he'd supplied and set up, and perhaps the porn searches belonged to the previous owner. (The dates of the searches were never disclosed, of course.) The secretary's defence I don't recall. The presiding overseer was so far up his own high rise of righteousness that he couldn't possibly have considered himself a suspect, and therefore assumed no one else did either. "Brothers and sisters, a 'wolf in sheep's clothing', is amongst us," he spake from the platform during Thursday night's announcements, and eyes flickered and averted as we fidgeted when the words 'porn' and 'discovered' were then uttered, and then we suspected right ahead anyway.

[27] The presiding overseer has a position of relative authority over the regular elders.

I remember seeing Elder A patting Elder B's wife on the bum, Sister C kissing Sister D on a bench in the town park, and Brother E having a cigarette in his car.

I remember one sister who frequently physically battered her husband until, weeping, he reported her to the elders, and brothers who fiddled their taxes, and others who bullied and beat their children into silent, broken little souls, and others who were compulsive liars, who'd tell you they'd had Cornflakes for breakfast when they'd had Weetabix…

Give me a Satanic after-school tennis club any day.

If I told you that I still shudder when I see the name Jehovah, or say it out loud, and that there's a deep fear of even typing it in case I'm 'taking it in vain', would you believe me? Are you like this? But I'm not profaning it, am I, by speaking about how it, and he, shaped and misshaped my whole life? And what about my delving into Hinduism, Buddhism, and other faiths, just to understand how faith is for those who follow other beliefs?

In an article in *The Guardian* (July 2018)[28] Dan Kokotajlo, writer and director of the 2017 film *Apostasy*[29], a film based on his upbringing as a Witness, says of writing the script (and I have his permission to quote):

> 'Every day brought with it the feeling of transgression […] As Witnesses, we were told to avoid literature that was critical of us. We were made to feel it was almost

[28] https://www.theguardian.com/film/2018/jul/15/apostasy-director-daniel-kokotajlo-liberating-to-leave-jehovahs-witnesses-interview

[29] Streamed on YouTube, Amazon Prime, iPlayer, Curzon.

> on the level of being Satanic. When I first got hold of one of these books, not long after I left the religion, I was literally shaking with fear – and when I started working on this project, that fear came right back.'

I cannot speak for Dan with respect to his childhood belief in Jehovah, or how he copes with his fear, but when you've learned to move in fear, from childhood, and when that fear is dressed up as love of Jehovah and the Organisation, there is no simple letting go, just the life or death choice to stand it up against a wall and face it. You can go to therapists, hypnotherapists, psychiatrists, psychologists, counsellors and doctors, but unless they were there, unless they too sat through childhood in fear of dying at the hands of the god they were supposed to love and who was supposed to love them, they are never, ever going to get it. There is no experience but that specific, annihilating experience that will make you an authority on the subject of being a Jehovah's Witness, or an ex-Jehovah's Witness, or a member of any similar singularly controlling cult. But God how we wish it would go away.

Yet I still cry out for Jehovah in my sleep sometimes during dreams about malevolent forces – demons, as I was told they were – or being tortured during the Great Tribulation[30], because somewhere in a deep part of my brain I still store the truth that he will save me from evil. I hear the verse from Romans 10:13: 'Everyone who calls on the name of Jehovah will be saved…' but even as I'm crying his name over and over, there is another part of my brain that knows I don't believe this anymore, that it was Jehovah God who said he would punish me for leaving his protection, and it tries to soothe me. But the demons are

[30] https://www.jw.org/en/bible-teachings/questions/great-tribulation/

everywhere; I can feel them moving around in the room, opening doors, opening me up to them. So I call on the name, knowing no one will come, as I have forsaken my saviour. These dreams are disturbing on a level I have no idea how to explain here.

I don't recall when the whole Great Tribulation thing got added as a pre-Armageddon torture of Witnesses to test their faith – as if we didn't have enough horror to deal with as penned by the Governing Body – so as to make it far simpler for Jehovah to see who had failed him and must die. Articles appeared in the *Watchtower* using the example of the Holocaust to prepare us for this time of being separated from our loved ones, imprisoned, beaten, starved, tortured, even killed as the world's governments turn on us, the only true religion still standing, when the rest of false religion falls. We were forced to read other accounts too of the torture of Witnesses across the world when they wouldn't comply with governments, from Malawi mainly, and the details were graphic. It still makes me feel sick thinking about them now, much as it did when I was a child. And if you're wondering where this came from, it was a very Witness-specific add-on from Matthew 24:21-33 and Revelation 7:14, where a 'great tribulation' is discussed as part of the end-of-world scene, and another lie as grotesque as the accounts themselves of what we must be prepared to face to prove our faith. I recall being told we shouldn't voice our phobias or fears out loud, because the Devil would be listening, and he would use those deepest fears to torture us, to try and break us – much like in Room 101 in George Orwell's *1984*…

'Love is what we were born with; fear is what we learn', from *Finding Joe* was a line that made me pause the film. Was it possible to unlearn what I had learnt, and lose the associated fear, or was it too deep? Cell-deep?

A few years after I left the Witnesses, my head barely above the depression that clung on and clung on, I went to see a wonderful woman with a heart full of compassion for the human condition, and a beautiful acceptance of all of its manifestations. The first thing she said to me was, "You can't come in here with those legs!" Not what you expected? It was not what I expected! But in a second we were laughing as she stood and revealed she was barely taller than her sitting self. I told her I'd leave them outside next time, which she thought was the kind thing to do under the circumstances.

How I cried in her company, for the first time in acceptance of the depression that had taken me to the emptiest, bleakest place and back, and still clawed at my back. I didn't want to be this angry, fearful human who ranted and shook, just a little bit back from the drop. I hated myself, and I hated Jehovah. I wanted him gone. I wanted it all to go.

This brilliant woman never once claimed to understand; instead she told me about other Witnesses she'd had the pleasure (the pleasure?) of meeting, and how her heart ached as she'd observed them collapse inside in much the same way as I had and still was. She promised me she would teach me to manage the fear, and the fear of what fear had made me.

"Manage the fear? Not make it go away?" I'd asked.

"Yes, for fear like this runs too deep for it simply to vanish because you so will it."

"What can I do? I feel so helpless against it, I always did… it's too big. Armageddon, God, the Devil, all the rooms, school rooms, the elders, my stepdad…it's too much…"

"We can go back, to a point where you felt that helplessness, and we can look at the messages that experience programmed into your subconscious. Then we can look at training your conscious mind to manage it."

I knew she meant hypnotherapy, and immediately all the silent screaming began: this is the Devil's tool to get inside your mind; this is how evil gets in; this is how he controls the world; you shouldn't have come here… But I was beyond caring. Hatred of life was threatening to overcome my promise to myself to never go back there again, to where I'd stepped off, so I knew I must do something. And actually, I didn't care if the Devil got inside my head; in truth, I thought he was already in there.

I don't know how long I was under, but when I emerged I was screaming – "*I should have protected him! I was his big sister! I should have been able to protect him!*" – and I told her about the day the postman kicked my brother, and the helplessness of knowing I couldn't say a single word because I'd have been accused of being a rebellious child, and most likely he would have used his hand or foot on me too. And goodness knows what he would have done if Mum had dared to confront him, because he was the head of the family, as Christ was the head of the congregation, and must be respected. So we'd just sat there in terrible, horrible silence as my brother sobbed.

I leapt right out of the chair: "I hated him. I *hate* him! What purpose has this served other than to reaffirm my loathing of him…and elders, and my real dad, and God…all kicking and bullying and controlling, all offering love and protection with one hand and taking it away with the other because I've done or thought something they don't like that much. And especially God, *especially him*, with his all-seeing all-knowing fucking judgmental fucking spying on me crap, waiting for me to sin, waiting for me to displease him. I've tried to be good my whole life, smiling and fetching and carrying and helping, being the one who does the driving, carries the boxes, even when I have *nothing* left to give, even when I know I'm not good really I'm just pretending. I can't be, can I? I can't be good, or I wouldn't be like this, would I? I want to not have to do anything for anyone anymore. I want silence! I want to scream! *It's not the Devil in my mind, it's God! He's the one destroying me! I want the Devil. Give me the Devil, please, because he'll accept me as I am! I'll finally be good enough. All I want is to be good enough."*

She didn't interrupt. She didn't quote scripture, or tell me my faith wasn't strong enough, or that I wasn't praying enough. Instead she looked at me with such love that I was stunned, humbled, calmed. And, in that moment, I knew I could rise above the drowning.

We spoke for a long time, and then she said, "I'll see you and those legs next week?"

"Yes."

It was so exciting when Ballerina Sindy gave birth to twins in the spring of 1976. For nine months she had waddled about with cotton wool balls up her frock, and Deep Sea Diver Action Man had lived up to his Palitoy-appointed name and built them a home in a cardboard box under my brother's desk, and worked hard at the diving school to provide for his wife and babies. (We did decide to marry them, before Sindy started to show.) Our mother too had given birth, to our sister, so life was pretty busy, what with Rachel and Rebecca, the pink bean-baby twins, and a real-life baby in the house.

We loved playing out all the stereotypical gender roles as Action Man actioned and Sindy nurtured. But we had a new game to play: Sherrie and Hunt, our human version of Sindy and Action Man. I fashioned Hunt a sword out of cardboard – a lot of my childhood, aside from Witness stuff, seemed to revolve around building things out of cardboard – and he slayed various beasts in the jungle of our long landing, bringing back food for his wife and child. I had born him a son, Lucas, in the shape of my ancient, button-eyed teddy (who was actually called Simon Ted and was now dressed in one of our sister's white Babygros). For hours upon hours we were lost in this world away from *Watchtower* magazines and rules; here, we made the rules, and there was no Tuesday night book study group, I can tell you.

Our cousins came to stay in the summer, and I so badly wanted to go back with them to *shire. They were so cool, and they had a telly – ours had gone back, because it was 'dividing the family' according to the postman – and I wanted to watch *Multi-coloured Swap Shop* and *Happy Days*, like they did. Phillip, who was born exactly one week before me, looked a bit like the Fonz with his dark hair and angled chin, and he'd taken to wearing white T-shirts and say 'Aaaay!' a lot, which I didn't understand the significance of but was in awe of; Matthew was younger, softer, like my brother, and was content to line toy cars up in a motorway across the long landing. My brother was torn between mimicking Phillip and motorway-building with Matthew. I was with the Fonz. We didn't tell them about Sherrie and Hunt.

Some of my friends from our congregation came over to play – Jayne and Marie – and we wandered down to the brook, the dried-up stream at the bottom of the estate where the school field divided us from the town. We swung on a frayed rope and dared each other to kiss each other as the summer of '76 blanched the land and tanned our skin.

Jayne and Marie were the two eldest of five sisters, Jayne as odd-looking (at the time) as Marie was beautiful. They lived in a large house on the edge of our estate, built by their builder father, who looked like Elvis. I had sleepovers with Jayne and Marie fairly regularly, and we were allowed to sleep in their caravan sometimes and fry cocktail sausages for breakfast on the little stove. For me this was something straight out of Enid Blyton's *Malory Towers*, and I was in heaven.

An odd thing, though. I'll never forget the first time I stayed over and their mum, a large, loving woman who would bear more children, announcing that "only dirty people wear knickers in bed" when we were all brushing our teeth that night. I didn't like this one bit. I always wore knickers in bed. (I still do. In fact, I can't sleep if I haven't got any on, which has always amused various husbands and lovers.) So, anyway, knickerless I got into the double bed we were sharing in the spare bedroom, wishing I'd brought pyjamas instead of a nightdress, and we snuggled down to watch TV. This was also very odd. Jayne and Marie's parents had four TVs – *four!* – one in the kitchen, one in the lounge, one in their bedroom, and one in the spare bedroom. And they were always on. Not on for *Blue Peter* or *Tom and Jerry* as a special treat. Just always on. I don't remember what we watched that night, I just remember their mum saying, "Don't watch anything rude!" as she closed the bedroom door, and thinking about the knickerless-in-bed thing and wondering if they were closer to Jehovah than me because they didn't wear any, even though they only ate deep-fried food, or Daddies sauce on weird white bread called Mother's Pride, watched four tellies and had vinyl sofas. My cousins were slightly mocking of Jayne and Marie – well, Phillip was, because he was the Fonz and very cool; Matthew just copied him – but this didn't prevent them from kissing them in flat-chest-to-flat-chest innocent curiosity.

Later we went back to our house and peeped at each other through our hands whilst their dad thanked Jehovah for our lovely day and the company of family and the delicious food, relieved when the rambling prayer was over so we could devour Mum's epic sausages and mash and beans. And, later still, we whispered in the dark, and they rustled about in their sleeping bags until we all went quiet, and I felt such love for them.

Since leaving the Witnesses nineteen years ago (at the time of writing) my cousins haven't been in contact. Their devotion to Jehovah and the Organisation prevents them from having any kind of friendship, or even basic communication, with their cousin, who still loves them so, so much. I found Phillip's online profile the other day and looked into his face, lined a little now but still so him, and felt such a longing to call him, to ask about the niece and nephew I've never met, and just hear his voice. What is it about someone's voice...?

Mum and I are indulging in our cake and tea ritual, while the early summer of 2019 slams against the windows and regurgitates, bubbling and churning, from stressed drains.

"You children were playing in the garden," she recalls. "I thought it was one of your friends knocking on the door, but Brother Johnson was there, and I immediately wondered if Anne [his wife] was okay, or if he wanted to speak to [the postman]. No, he wanted to speak to me, he said, 'about a serious matter...' Well, I couldn't invite him in, as you know, because we weren't supposed to be alone with a brother, unchaperoned, so I asked him to tell me what the serious matter was, explaining he'd have to stay on the doorstep."

I can imagine Fred Johnson all too clearly, all head inclined and feigned humble stoop, old dust dulling his cheap toupee. We'd heard he made his wife wear frilly red knickers – my brother played with his sons, and they'd seen them on the washing line – and I remember wondering at the time what on earth was wrong with that, but registering the looks of *tch-tch* that passed amongst the womenfolk.

"He explained that my 'forthright attitude' was demeaning for a sister in the Truth, and a disgrace," she continues, "and I was bringing shame on my husband, and that he would never be made an elder if he had a 'contentious wife'. When I asked him what he was referring to, he said I had shocked him after the book study last Tuesday, and in his very own home, by expressing doubt about our creation. But my point wasn't about our creation, as I have always believed we were created by God, or certainly designed in some way by a far superior intelligence; no, the point I made was I had always wondered where it had all started, what it was that had created God – haven't we all wondered that? – and mentioned I had always struggled with this. But he was of the opinion that if I had such strong opinions I should, quite frankly, keep them to myself, and certainly not shame my husband in public by voicing them!"

I watch her as she talks, animated by both the injustice of no freedom of thought, never mind speech, back then, and the freedom now to roam wild with conjecture – and oh, how we do, just for sheer joy.

"Well, I was furious. *How dare he*? And the way he used to speak to Anne, pinching her so she would answer up in the book study and not embarrass him, and how he used to bully those boys – well, the older two, anyway. I'll never forget seeing Daniel cry, so many times; and as for Tom, it's no wonder he rebelled. Vile man."

"It's the oldest question of all time, debated by the Greeks and portrayed in paintings," I reply. "'*Where Do We Come From? What Are We? Where Are We Going?*' by Gauguin, for example. Pity you couldn't have hit him with that; that would have shut him up."

We were not permitted to ponder other philosophies, though, for fear it create in us dreaded apostasy. No, we were only allowed to read publications written by and produced for the Society, and its translation of the Bible, The New World Translation of the Holy Scriptures, with its own footnotes and references. So closed, so closed.

I will never forget finding a really old leather-bound version of the Bible at an auction, and poring over the poetry of the language…and the books still in there that had been removed from the NWT. I discovered some of them had been written by women, and others appeared to cast doubt on the very worth of the so-called 'righteous' and the raising of the dead to life – the whole basis of faith in Jesus's very existence on Earth and his resurrection. No wonder the New World Translation had been so doctored.[31]

I remember my mother back then, a mostly-silenced version of the well-read, open-minded woman she is now. I know she struggled. I know she was pinned to the wall by fear of the postman; of the disgrace of him having a wife with an enquiring mind. I know she was pinned by fear of

[31] Yet how the Governing Body insist the NWT is the closest translation to original scripture, and how other translations have been deliberately reworded by false religion to shore up their lies…

what would happen if she dared to confront him with her doubts and fears; if she dared pack up three small children and leave the arrogant, self-righteous bastard, and the Truth. If she had – and she so longed to do so – a whole network of brothers and sisters and family and friends would have turned its back on her, leaving her adrift in Satan's world, the world she'd willingly chosen over the safety and protection of Jehovah's organisation. She had no job, no money of her own, elderly parents, and nowhere to go. There was literally nowhere to go.

Yet always she was the calm to the confusion of our young lives; the voice of kindness and love amongst the judgment and fear; the sure thing when all else was shifting.

And here she is, eating cake with me and laughing as talk lifts to finer things than vile Brother Johnson, and how she shines.

I would like to tell you that in order to remove yourself from the cage you simply opened the door, because the door is not locked. But as anybody who has left the Witnesses (or would dearly love to) will tell you: it doesn't have to be locked, as what lies beyond is far more fearful than that which traps you within, so you stay within. That's a pretty hefty finger to point at a sect/cult/religion, whichever manmade construct it comes under, and whose whole message is love, yet whose whole by-product is debilitating fear, but point it I will.

Analysing my long on-off relationship with a man whose stick was my inability to be good enough, and whose carrot was the happy-ever-after we would enjoy when I was (and when he finally decided he loved me), I was alarmed one afternoon to see, for the first time, the disturbing similarities between my loyalty to him and my past loyalty to the Truth. For a long time I truly believed his long monologues of promises of love; for too long I put my faith in how he saw our future once we had read this book, studied this method or perfected that model of how a successful relationship should look, and conformed to each and every one of his ideals of what our relationship would look like when it was working. I believed him because I loved him, and because I wanted that future so badly, for us both. We deserved it, he said, because 'we'd suffered enough in this life already', and I agreed.

But as time passed and the future never arrived because there was always, always something wrong in the present, some 'sin' or other I'd committed that meant our happy future had to be postponed, or because his heart still wasn't ready to love me, to choose me, I grew weaker and weaker, whilst my fear of his displeasure grew stronger and uglier. I was frightened to speak in case I said the wrong thing. I was frightened to not speak in case I was labelled a 'poor communicator'. I was frightened to tell him I was frightened, because his reaction to my fear frightened me even more. Yet life without him seemed too impossible to contemplate. When he wasn't annihilating my soul, he was lifting it up, praising it and honouring it, promising it a beautiful life. When he wasn't ordering me to leave because of some misdemeanour I had committed against us, he was telling me his house was my home, that I was safe, that he was a safe man. And I was back in the Kingdom Hall, secure within its walls, protected by the people around me who all believed in the same future as me, praised and honoured as a good Christian girl who deserved that beautiful future for her love and loyalty to Jehovah...yet in fear for my sanity, my soul, my life, and growing quieter and quieter in the place where I had gone to hide to survive.

With the help of a counsellor the final time, I was able to look at what had been happening both on a psychological and a physiological level as my need to believe in the good-time future we would have overruled the reality of the fearful present with him, over and over again. Like a captive who comes to rely on her captor's company, and who defends him in her heart as a poor, damaged boy who became a damaged, turbulent man, but who knows, too, that he is breaking her, piece by piece[32], I would hear myself speaking only of our good days. I would talk about our love, our plans, and our hopes to those who asked, much as I had spoken about Jehovah's love, his plans for his faithful worshipers, and my hope of eternal life in paradise on Earth. So I stayed, and left, and went back for more, and left, in a cycle of loving him so, so much, and aching to believe him, and wanting that future so badly.

I had no idea that just as cult members become psychologically and physiologically addicted to their cult, I was quite literally addicted to this man, which was how (and why) I devoted nearly eight years of my life to him. My brain was swamped with huge amounts of oxytocin, serotonin and dopamine when fed the happy-ever-after stories, and cortisol and adrenaline when those stories were exchanged for judgement and threat of the happy-ever-after being denied, which severely impaired my capacity to break the addiction. I excused the name-calling and despicable comments about my upbringing on a council estate. I hid my bad days from him as, more often than not, if I

[32] Read Lauren Kozlowski's book *Trauma Bonding* on the subject of attachment to abuse, Stockholm syndrome, and breaking the cycle.

revealed them I would be accused of 'bringing bad energy into the house', which was 'damaging our relationship' and him. I lived in a constant state of anxiety, wrapped up in his promises, promises, promises, in love and in fear.

Yet how he would self-flagellate about his failings. Bewailing them and appealing to me to forgive them. I'd never seen such humility in a man, such a longing to be a better man. But then he would see something in me – and it could be anything from putting too much water in the kettle to eating a few M&Ms after lunch, to not flinging my arms around his neck when he walked in the door, to not being able to express myself in the way he preferred – and the doomsday lectures would begin on how we would never survive if I didn't change, how we would never have our happy future if I didn't learn to communicate properly, learn to trust him, believe in him and how happy we were going to be. I don't know how many times I asked why we couldn't just be happy now, in the present. Why did happiness always have to be a future thing, like living forever in paradise, the childhood carrot I had been tormented with, the reality of which never arrived?

It was a bleak January afternoon, wet to saturating, when I sat in my car at a motorway service station and saw all this. I saw my life without him as I had seen my life without the Truth back then, as a thing with something missing. But just as my devotion to the Truth had battered me and emptied me out, my devotion to him was too, and I cried from the desolate place where I was frightened of life with him and without him. I thought about this fear, the hold it had on me, just as it had when I had sat silent and resigned in a Kingdom Hall, an unhappy, unwilling slave to the Governing Body's construct of my future, yet unable to live without it.

My biggest mistake when I left the Witnesses had been thinking the fear would simply go away. It simply doesn't. As the wonderful woman I saw said, from the deepest part of her compassion, fear of this nature can only be managed. The fear back then, and the realisation of this new fear, how horribly similar they were, and how wretched the hurt.

I opened the window and leaned out and gulped at the sodden air, tears and rain on my face. It had taken a long time for me to believe I could manage that old fear, and even longer to actually look at the fear for what it was: an emotion rising from deep within, cellular-deep, noticed by the mind that remembered and fed the fear with its memories; an emotion-mind-memory perpetual cycle of no escape. I couldn't let that happen again. I knew I would never set foot in a Kingdom Hall again, but I wanted to love again, so very, very much, and not be frightened of being annihilated and comforted and annihilated in a never-ending loop of disapproval and promises. The Witnesses had put the fear of God in me; this man had put the fear of love in me.

Eckhart Tolle[33], the modern-day spiritual teacher and author of the astonishing *The Power of Now*, confirms you can never 'get over' fear, but instead learn to accept it, embrace it, surrender to it. He explains, in his sometimes stuttery always staggeringly simple way, that this is hard, but it won't kill you; the fear will kill you, he says, but surrendering to it will not. By surrender he does not mean lying down and giving up, he

[33] 'Eckhart is not aligned with any particular religion or tradition. In his teachings he conveys a simple yet profound message with the timeless and uncomplicated clarity of the ancient spiritual masters: 'there is a way out of suffering and into peace.' From *Stillness Speaks* by Eckhart Tolle.

means giving up the need to do battle with fear. 'Just look at it,' he urges softly. 'Acknowledge it. Let it be. That is true surrender.'

By way of example of how the fear would emerge, when I used to drive into my old town, where the Kingdom Hall sits next to the Catholic Church, long before I'd even clapped eyes on the building I would start shaking and sweating. I might have the radio on, or be deep in thought, but coming off the roundabout and turning up that hill my body would start reacting, and my mind would tune in and make the connection – the Kingdom Hall is at the top of the hill – and then would come the ache of the sadness, the throb of the old fear. It was a protection of sorts; but what purpose other than that was it serving? I knew I was never going to go there again, but how could I stop the involuntary body reaction to being in close proximity to the place? the cells' own memory of a time that had broken me?

I tried Eckhart's surrender, and then I tried again, until it became a practice I never gave up. As the sweating and shaking kicked in, I didn't try to fight it. I started to see it for what it was: trauma stored deep in my body, and something which I could work with now we recognised each other.[34] Could I do the same with this new fear? As well as being an almost unbearable hurt, it had also become anger and shame at allowing myself to stay so long, to keep returning, and to believe for so long. Why had I gone back, when I knew? Why had I been so weak, so *stupid*? There were two answers to that.

---

[34] On the subject of trauma stored in the body's cells, even in the DNA, Dr Peter Levine is a master. Many of his talks are on YouTube, and are invaluable in beginning to understand the effects of deep trauma and how to start healing. So too the incredible, beautiful book *The Body Keeps the Score* by Bessel van der Kolk.

Firstly, I loved him. I had never loved a man like I loved him; I hadn't even known I was capable. And from the depths of that love, where I saw us ever stretching our enquiring minds, and caring for each other's hearts, and celebrating our individual and collective evolution, I really hoped he'd love me back, because he badly wanted to, and spent hours a day trying to, begging me for more time more time as he tried to exorcise his fear of loving me.

Secondly, I was bound by trauma[35] to this man I loved so very much, where the regular rules of what is acceptable, and what we are able and willing to put up with, are horribly distorted.

I can still see his face, furious and pleading, needing me and sending me away as his own childhood traumas impeded his reasoning and unravelled us time after time. I knew I triggered something in him, something dark and unmanageable, just as he triggered the girl, and the woman, in me who wanted to believe love can be real, and now, contentedly imperfect and not the second-rate upshot of successfully obeying endless rules, and thought I'd found it with him. How wrong I'd been, on all fronts. I'd believed too hard, wanting for us both the thing he was unable to be. The awful, awful pain of that.

So I started the car, tried to be comfortable with the hurt, as much as it hurt, and the anger and my shame, and let the awful sadness roll through me and away until my heart slowed and my breathing came to settle as through the rain I made my way home.

Eckhart was right when he said fear can be 'the greatest teacher'.

[35] https://www.harleytherapy.co.uk/counselling/what-is-trauma-bonding.htm

And he was right when he said, 'Acceptance of the seemingly unacceptable is grace, a miracle, your alchemy'. He also called it an 'arduous process', with that brightness of eye that tells you without further words that he knows.

Isn't that what all of us need, to know that someone knows?

I'm laughing as I begin writing this bit because, oh my goodness, I've just remembered some of the other games my brother and I used to invent when we were kids.

Everything we knew was from the pages of the Bible and the *Watchtower*, so I understood a lot of what we played and why, but where did all the other stuff come from? I understood the games where we would sacrifice my naked Tiny Tears baby doll by dropping her down the stairs – symbolic of a mountainside – in a Canaanite ceremony to appease Molech. And I understood why Tiny Tears would sometimes get held by an ankle and be pretend-sliced in two, as per King Solomon's wisdom with the real and fake mothers of the child they were fighting over. And we even built an altar and held a cardboard dagger over her heart, stopping at the last moment when our merciful god Jehovah stayed our murderous Abraham-hands. I understood all that because we'd been raised on crows and human sacrifice and halted stabbings in the name of faith in Jehovah. I do remember Mum peering round the banisters, though – she'd obviously heard the rubbery thump as Tiny Tears met her death against the ottoman at the bottom of the stairs – and asking us if we were okay. Yes, Mum, just playing child sacrifices.

We also loved Doctors and Nurses, the fairly common childhood game that would morph from pretending to take each other's pulses, to the removal of undergarments and having a good old look at each other, to falling in love and broken hearts! Personally, I blame Ross Poldark. One year in his company and, well, the Devil was in residence in my imagination and composing some pretty racy scripts.

Phillip and I, with our bonkers imaginations, wrote plays which we would put on for our horrified parents and grandparents; plays that involved him strutting about in his leather jacket, and me being tied to a chair as the 'men' fought over me, and my brother being shot with the plastic gun we bought from the newsagents on the High Street. (We really got a telling off for that one.) It was great, though, the acting and the naughtiness. All that gorgeous, natural curiosity playing out as trying to put meaning to our world.

But really, aside from sitting outside Mum's bedroom door giggling and imagining what was going on in there, and the mind-boggling talk from kids at school about shagging and boning and sixty-nine-ing (?), the only thing we knew about sex was through the pages of the *Watchtower* and the Bible, which was all 'may your fountain be blessed' and 'rejoice in the wife of your youth' (cue delightful metaphor of loving doe and graceful deer), and 'drink water from your own cistern' (nice) or else you'll die. So when we investigated each other's bits (and our own), did we consider we might be taken outside the city and stoned? I can't speak for my Batman-loving brother or my cousins, but I know I did.

I remember the discussions I had with myself though; the half-hearted *Now, you know this is naughty*, to *Wow, this is so great I actually don't care if I die*. Then would come the fear, though, like the grip of an animal trap you know will kill you slowly. But you don't shout out. You never shout out.

My soul sister, Hannah, this bit is for you. The nights and days we've spent in each other's hearts in your old conservatory or here in my tiny cottage.

When you tell me how it was for you, you fill our space with a hurt and a rage that has me crying too. I've watched you trying to describe a thing neither of us will ever fully forget, and I barely hear the words – although they're registering somewhere, where I'll be able to recall them – I just see you. Your hands point out the boxes in the room you went to if you needed a 'new' school skirt or a pair of knickers, the boxes containing the cast-offs of your fellow brothers and sisters in the faith. You lean forward with the pain of being the kid at school who never had new-new shoes or the proper school sweater, who lived 'in that weird place where they worship Jesus'. Your eyes are bright with the injustice of the enforced poverty of life as a child in the Jesus Army, yet drowning too in the deep, primal fear of ever having to live with poverty and shame like that again.

"She's unbroken, Robert," the elders would say to your father. "You need to break her will. She's not yet broken in the Lord. Your other children, they're broken, but Hannah, she's too wilful. You must break her, or she'll not belong to Jesus."

And you would be forced to watch as the Devil was 'removed' from your brothers and sisters, as they spewed nonsense and ranted, their eyes rolling as they were indeed broken.

We talk about the film *I Am Not Your Guru*, where about half-way through a young girl relates the sickening story of how her parents would hand her over to elders who would rape her, repeatedly, because it was 'God's will' that she show her faith in this way. She was six years old when this started. And then we can't talk about it anymore.

We talk about cases we've both heard of where serious sexual abuse and molestation has gone unreported and unpunished because of the 'two-witness rule'.[36] The Witnesses love the two-witness rule, based on Deuteronomy 19:15 which states: 'No single witness may convict another for any error or any sin that he may commit. On the testimony of two witnesses or on the testimony of three witnesses the matter should be established.' This rule was given to the Israelites to safeguard them against a 'false witness', one who might lie about anything from theft to rape. *But what if the 'false' witness was telling the truth*? There would still be no conviction unless there were two or three witnesses to the theft or the rape, something which still applies to this very day. Barbara Anderson[37], a former member of staff at Brooklyn Bethel whose task it was to deal with letters from Witnesses writing in about their abuse and molestation, calls this rule 'an impossibility', as would anyone with an ounce of intelligence. This is a rule which conveniently protects the robber and the rapist, not the robbed or the raped, because who commits such acts in full view of two or three witnesses? And then we can't talk about this anymore either.

What we don't understand, either of us, is how such things are still permitted to continue.

What we do understand is the grinding fear that keeps you silent, compliant, until that day when, on your hands and

[36] https://aoadvocates.com/jehovahs-witnesses-new https://lawandreligionuk.com/2020/02/14/jehovahs-witnesses-and-the-two-witness-rule-a-comment-on-bxb/
[37] https://www.nbcnews.com/id/wbna21917798

knees, you know you cannot continue living this way for one more second.

You showed me a photograph once, from back then. I recognised your gorgeous hair, the blue of your eyes, even the fold of your arms. But I didn't recognise you.

At sixteen you walked away. Away from the Jesus Army's version of God, of Armageddon, of being told from birth you would be one of the only ones who would be saved, but only if you were a good sister, by those determined to break you so you would become that good sister. Away from your entire biological and spiritual family, and the literal and psychological entrapment of them. Away from your faith and how it had stripped you of the life force I see in you tonight.

No one was ever going to support you in that, were they? You had walked out into the Devil's world, willingly prostituted yourself to his guiles. You had turned your back on the protection of the Lord, and life would be hard for you now, sister.

And then you go quiet.

We understand that for those who have never been subjected to and silenced by this level of indoctrination it might be hard to comprehend this pain, the helplessness and the rage. So, please, be with us for a moment, because this walking away is like losing someone you love and hate equally; someone who protected you but who emptied you of all light; someone who told you daily you were safe, but who showed you the door every time you so much as raised an eyebrow of doubt at what you were being forced to believe was the truth. Nobody just walks away from this.

In the first hours and early days, if you do manage to leave, you feel nothing but relief. And it's funny the things you want to do: swear, not pray, hurl your Bible down the garden.

You test what it's like to walk down the street as a normal person, to listen to the radio without listening out for Satanic lyrics that will corrupt you. You try sexy clothes on, though you're not quite sure what sexy is, just to see how it might change you to wear them.

But that initial relief walks you straight to the precipice. If you thought you were in a dark place within faith, without it is darker than the human heart can bear without truly breaking. There is a part of human psyche that needs to believe, to belong to something and, when it is gone, all the boundaries that bound you collapse, and there is nothing to hold on to. Any relief you may have felt gives way to tumbling; any small joy of normality to falling headlong from the edge of who you thought you were and what you thought life was.

So, no, you do not just walk away. You drop. And your life without collapses inside itself. You drink anything, just to manage to laugh at something, and smoke dope for the same reason. You venture into the big drugs, if that becomes the thing that releases you. And you climb into people's beds, and take many into yours, because it's so lonely, the drop, and the dreadful, empty sex distracts you for as long as it lasts. But it hurts so very much, and somewhere inside you know you can't do it anymore, the rebellion. And so you climb. And climb. Up and over, from the very bottom of the drop, until you can see beyond the relief of leaving, the release, and just across to where it might be okay.

It was inevitable I got pregnant that evening on the settee in the untidy house I didn't like with the man with beautiful hands. I went to look for him, to tell him. He was in the music room with my brother, his hands a dance across his keyboard, his head leant over the sound. They were laying down a track, and I pondered telling him then or later or never. My next thought was for Charles, and as I looked down at the positive pregnancy test in my hand I saw his face feigning joy in the doorway when I'd told him he was going to be a daddy.

I'd really wanted to be a good wife to Charles, all fluffy and cooking and doe- and deer-like so he could be proud of the 'wife of his youth'; but I was this so-young thing who didn't want to live in a house with no central heating and have no TV (still). I wanted night clubs and short skirts and to be, just for once in my life, openly and exactly the opposite of what everybody in the Truth thought I was.

I had walked down the aisle in the Kingdom Hall, a tear in my veil and ice cubes in my blood, a real and proper virgin. I don't recall a single word of our wedding talk, or the scripted Witness vows I said that meant I must honour and respect this honourable and respectable man, I just knew he was a good man…just not the man I should be standing there with. Maybe he knew too. I was a wild creature who'd never had the chance to be wild; a caged wannabe explorer who worked in a café that dripped grease on my head; a nineteen-year-old girl who made everyone laugh but who wouldn't sing out loud.

I enjoyed keeping house and gardening, and decorating and hosting dinner parties, and I was still selling the *Watchtower* and *Awake!* and studying my Bible, but I was already edging towards the edge of the cage.

I remember writing a postcard to Mum from our honeymoon saying, 'Enjoying every indulgence, love C and K xxx.' I meant sex. I'd hoped she'd guess I meant that. I wasn't, though. Sex didn't feel very nice, and actually it hurt.

And honestly, looking back, I know that I simply didn't fancy Charles. There was absolutely no sexual chemistry between us – well, certainly not from this side of the bed. Had we had the freedom to discover this before we got married, we may have been able to discuss it, work out whether it was my innocence on the whole subject – doctors and nurses, O-level human biology and the Bible being my only real education in matters carnal – or something deeper, and either worked it out or shipped out. But Witnesses are not permitted to go on unchaperoned dates, whatever their age, which obviously makes it impossible to explore sexual compatibility never mind the compatibility of your personalities away from prying ears and eyes. So when you marry, almost always a virgin and with no idea really about who you are marrying except that they're 'a strong brother' or 'a good sister', it's a complete lottery whether you're actually going to get on. But divorce is not permitted either unless it's on the grounds of adultery, so you're absolutely screwed unless you decide to commit adultery (with a minimum of two witnesses to verify it took place). Lots of brothers and sisters did, fathering children with other brothers' wives, or being the 'harlot' who lured him with her 'dripping honey and silken skin', or something like that… So, instead, I shut down, and he was in turn kind, desperate, frustrated, confused and kind. I didn't want to have sex at home, on holiday, anywhere. At least not with him. I remember him asking me so sweetly if we could have 'holiday sex' on our summer holiday, the year after we married, and just saying no, I didn't feel like it. He never asked again.

But then, three years later, I asked him if we could have a baby. I was aching in that place where (many) women know they need to hold their own child instead of everybody else's, and in his soft Solihull burr he said, "We'll need to have sex, sweetheart, if you want a baby," his eyes all blue, and always kind, but obviously reluctant about the idea, and I said, "I know," so we did.

I got pregnant that first month, and I remember thinking how unfair that was on Charles, as it would have been lovely for him if it had taken lots of attempts. Perhaps he was thinking that too when I'd told him he was going to be a dad. But then I lost the baby; and then I lost my mind. And all of his imploring about needing to be stronger as a couple before we started a family scrolled like a transcript, and his face in the doorway when I'd told him, and the terrible pain and the bleeding, and the people who didn't know I had miscarried stopping me in the street to congratulate me on my pregnancy, and the piece of glass across my wrist, and *What did I do wrong, Jehovah*?, and the elder I went to who said he loved me, who I loved, and, Charles, I'm so sorry. You were, are, such a good man, and I was too restless to be good right back. So much of my acting up with you was because I knew I'd have to leave you anyway, to get the fearless Witness-less life I needed so badly. Did the universe engineer it happening, the miscarriage, so it could free you up for a better, more Christian wife than me? Because, after I was gone, that's who you found. Those few weeks, though, when I was pregnant with our little half-Brummie, perhaps bendy-thumbed baby, I was so, so happy; and, just for a moment, I really thought I, we, would be okay.

The father of my second chance to be a mother looked up from his majors and minors. "If you want to get married, I'm around the last weekend of August," he said when I raised the positive test, and I lingered in my reply until there wasn't one. I don't think he'd meant it to sound quite like it sounded, but his head was full of chords and riffs and a spliff dangled from his fingers, the smoke drifting in slow motion like his eyes, and I sighed, barely a sound, and turned away.

Why do we need to believe in gods? Why do we need to believe in anything at all? Wouldn't it be easier to be a human without belief, without hope, without faith? The brilliant book, *A Little History of Religion* by Richard Holloway, former bishop of Edinburgh, opens with the lifetime questions of life, the universe and everything – and how I thank you, Douglas Adams[38], for your polar, inspired and bonkers angle on this! – and makes the simple statement that 'what we call religion was our first crack at answering these questions.' But I have a million times wondered how natural human curiosity about how and why we're here, where we're going, and what it's all about in between came to mean a disapproval of further education, a ban on oral sex, and women not being allowed to wear trousers at the meetings or on the ministry, even when the weather was foul or freezing.

If there is a god, or higher spirit, or source of creative energy we'll never fully grasp the concept of, how it must chuckle at the utter stoopidity of the men in suits who still pen this stuff as the true interpretation of its will on Earth, and the way by which to escape its wrath at Armageddon, and that anything else is the Devil's work. Not to mention the darker stuff, the lies layered and layered as passing time required them.

It's difficult to find the words to describe how the futility grips you when you sit before the careers advisor at school, and

[38] From *Hitchhiker's Guide to the Galaxy*, one of the best books by one of the best authors on being human in a huge and largely dark universe.

they tell you your strengths and where they may lead. How *dare* a group of men in Brooklyn write and publish articles targeted at bright, young minds across the world and tell them not to study? How *dare* they associate the joy of books, of learning, of widening your mind to a whole wide world of knowledge of each other with the Devil? How *dare* they tell you that when Jehovah comes looking and sees you at college instead of on the ministry you must fear for your life?

At the time of writing this, in bed with my laptop on a Sunday morning, beautiful young souls will be sitting in Kingdom Halls being told this, turning pages of a *Watchtower* and reading that the only career is a career in Jehovah's service!

Yes, I'm being angry about this, because, yes, you should be paying attention to this. God (or whoever), gifted you with an amazing brain, and what are you filling it with? All those neurons are hanging around asking why they're being ignored, and why you'd rather let them die than put them to use in engineering or mathematics or design or medicine or whatever else you love. What were you good at as a child, before the Truth got its claws into your imagination and creativity? Did you love taking stuff apart to work out how the whole was the result of the amazing sum of its parts? Did you see a car and think, *If the bonnet just dipped a little more there, or the roof just tapered a little less there, then its profile would be so improved*? Did you play the piano from your heart? Paint from a place deep in your soul? So why aren't you doing these things? Do you honestly think your creator wants you to hold your talents in check, in fear of them? In fear of the elders who might take you to one side and tell you you're getting a bit too 'worldly'? In fear of the Governing Body, who from the lofty heights of their own importance tell you the wondrous workings of your immense brain are the works of the

Devil? Just look at that, just for a second, and see it for what it is: fear breeding fear.[39]

There is a beautiful, alternative perspective on creativity, on why we compose and write and paint, which places the creator of life in us, as us, manifesting itself through every minor chord and line of verse and brushstroke, feeling the lift, the ache, the beauty as one. Have you felt that in the piece of music that takes you beyond yourself, a poem that makes your heart beat faster, a masterpiece that stirs an appreciation you cannot fully grasp? Have you read the ancient philosophers, and the new, and sensed a deeper something that resonates and chimes like a coming home? Have you studied the paper of an expert in their field, sensed the hours and months and years they have dedicated to their subject, be it the brain, the heart, the unborn child, and felt the gratitude and the respect for their knowledge? *Do you still believe these are the works of the Devil?*

These men in Brooklyn, they're afraid. They're afraid of being outed as wrong – very, very wrong. They're afraid that the colossal lies they've been telling for *decades* about their being part of the 'Little Flock'[40] of Christ's ruling class – so special, so special – will be exposed, as raw and foul as rotting meat. They're afraid of the colossal lies they've told you about being part of the 'Great Crowd of Witnesses' who'll they'll rule over, *again*, this time from heaven, in order to keep you exactly where they need you.

So, yes, these men just keep banging the Devil drum, sounding the Armageddon horn, dangling the paradise carrot, and telling you you're doing just great as you are (and where

[39] 'Fear keeps you from your mountaintop' – from the movie *Finding Joe.*
[40] Of which there are only 144,000, (Rev 14: after 1-4), otherwise called 'the Little Flock' most of whom have died and can't testify otherwise.

they need you): stifled, frightened, weakened and controlled. They'll keep writing their balderdash in the name of Jehovah, telling you your lack of education is an honour, proof of your unshakable devotion to his will, whilst you struggle from pay day to pay day in menial work, unable to study for the qualifications that would improve your mind and your bank balance. As Paul Menzes said in the graphic and moving *Rainbow Milk*[41]: 'The *Awake!* magazine was wide-ranging in its grasp of science, technology and modern examples of faith under persecution, but it was no substitute for an English degree.'

I remember the odd male friend who broke ranks and went on to become a chartered accountant or quantity surveyor, or whatever fired their neurons (and certainly made them happy). They were frowned upon as 'having their paradise now' and not really being 'for Jehovah'. Why? Because of the one foot they'd obviously placed firmly in the world so they could drive a BMW, take their wife and children to see the beaches and mountains and cities of the world, and live on the safe, respectable side of town. It mattered not that their surplus income paid for the Kingdom Hall to be built, or that they donated generous sums to areas on Earth torn apart by natural disasters, or that they paid for the funeral of a brother who left his wife and children penniless because he had no life insurance. No, what mattered was that they weren't quite for Jehovah enough, and were therefore not to be emulated for their life choices. All I saw were men proud of their ability to provide for their wife and children, and a wife and children blossoming, not shrunken by the austerity paraded by husbands 'strong in the faith'.

[41] Published by Dialogue Books, 2020.

There were men who joined the Witnesses later in life, who hadn't been born into its stifling ridiculousness about what was deemed a proper or improper career. If these men were already successful in secular terms, were intelligent and educated, they were quickly lured into becoming an elder *because* of their intelligence and education, because they bought a certain sophistication to the platform! I have to say they made a refreshing change from many of the regular unsecular elders who could barely construct a sensible sentence or pronounce pronunciation correctly. And as for the pronounciation of hyperbole… It always struck me as interesting that these elders who had come in 'from the world' were humbler, kinder, and far more reasonable in their approach to the Truth – a far cry from the elders whose *only* success in life was becoming an elder, so wielded their achievement like a Nobel Prize in faith…

What I never understood was why faith had become this sackcloth versus Saville Row show of who had the best faith, the faith most likely to be rewarded. Do you?

Talk of imminent Armageddon continued, whilst the eighties got louder with every new tune and movie and was I paying much attention? Yes and no. When surviving the Great Tribulation and God's righteous war is the purpose of your whole existence, it gets a bit monotonous as a theme tune. It was there, but so were the Smiths and The Cure and Depeche Mode, and music I was listening to that I'd never heard before, like Bob Dylan, whose lyrics were beyond anything I'd ever encountered, and I loved my new perm and dungarees. I had this humour, this left-of-fieldness that my school friends seemed to like and, somehow, it became part of me, when I felt confident enough to let it. I drew some exceptional riverbeds in geography lessons and understood grid references; but I sat on our geography teacher's lap on the coach on the way to a field trip and kissed his funny flat face. I wrote comprehensive essays on communist China that were well researched and constructed; but sat with a wastepaper bin on my head in double history declaring, "Only when you make this lesson interesting, will I remove the bin." Miss Wagner, with your blouse-clad bosom and jostling jowls, I know you were laughing inside because your eyes were bright behind the dismissal from your lesson – and besides, you told me twenty years later in the queue in Waitrose that I'd brought 'a light relief of sorts' to your classes!

But the ache of the ice cubes was still there, and the horror of rooms full of people. Walking into classrooms – and the dreaded Tuesday night study group, which was still held in claustrophobic living-rooms – became harder and harder. It had become impossible to separate the fear of the room from the why, but it became this horrendous, monstrous thing that churned inside me, making my stomach churn, which everybody could hear and, oh God, the fear of that too. And if it was my turn to read a scripture, or if I'd marked the study book with an answer I might be brave enough to make, that hot-cold meant I always had my eyes on the door.

That whole answering up thing, who invented that anyway?[42] You may find this hard to believe, but the phrase 'second-class Christians' was actually used from the platform in our local Kingdom Hall in association with those who did not answer up; and I distinctly remember the elder who used it, most Sundays, as his introduction to the review of that week's *Watchtower* study article.

---

[42] The Governing Body in Brooklyn Bethel.

"May I remind you," he would begin, "that it is your God-given responsibility to encourage your fellow brothers and sisters with your comments. Holding back – and those who do, you know who you are – is not the mark of a good Christian, so I want to see all of you who do not answer regularly, and often not at all, raising your hand as is your God-given responsibility and duty to your brothers and sisters…"

He even used to name names, my mother's included – "Do you have a comment, Sister X? No?" (pause) – and I would die with her. Was he afraid the lack of forthcoming answers would reflect badly on him as an elder – and husband of a wife and father of five children, who rarely answered up? I hoped so. But I loved his kids, and two of them were close friends of mine. They were good, kind children, who went mostly in fear of their father. Fear breeding fear.

Yet there was this side of me that so wanted to please Jehovah, and Mum, and the elders. So I would prepare good answers, well thought out and phrased – just like my history essays – and raise my trembling hand, wait for the microphone, wrap my fingers around the cold metal and say my piece to a firm, "Thank you, Sister X." But how I hated the sound of my voice, and hated the words I shaped into those intelligent, elegant points. And then I hated myself. Who the hell was I?

We'd study articles about leading a double life – both in the *Watchtower* and in the *Young People Ask*[43] book – and I knew my cheeky, laughing, masturbating, snogging (there'd been lots of

[43] One of the Society's books written specifically for teenagers which parents were obligated to study with their children, fathers with sons and mothers with daughters. Some parents revelled in discussing deeply personal subjects like masturbation with their children and asking, "Do you?", and then telling them Jehovah was watching and would judge them as unclean for exploring their own bodies. My mother didn't.

snogging by this point) life was the very epitome of 'double'. But just as I played up in double history and still got an A, I thought I might be able to play up outside the Kingdom Hall and still survive the Big A. I was completely split in two. Right versus left brain? Ego versus alter ego? Jehovah versus Satan? How ever you want to couch it, I was screwed as a genuine bona fide Witness from the moment I realised I could screw about in both worlds and thoroughly enjoy the yin and yang of it all.

Out in the world, where I was funny and liked, I could be funny and liked and not judged. But here, in God's organisation, I could be funny and liked but judged to death, literally, if anybody got wind of the other me. We all knew that; we grew up with that. Which was why we'd make the pact: I won't tell if you won't. So we'd snog each other, and sometimes get touchy-feely, and drink alcohol we weren't supposed to drink, and listen to music that would no doubt corrupt us.

I was up a ladder for some reason, in the jeans shop I was now working in (I hadn't lasted very long at the café), and Sam (Charles's friend) came up behind me, slid his hands up my legs and around my waist and lifted me down. I could feel the heat and the hardness of him and, yes please, it was good. (Sam's father, the elder who owned the shop, sent me out to buy 'winter' decorations the first Christmas I worked there…)

And those nights with Jayne and Marie, when we were allowed to sleep in their caravan, we would undress and explore each other, so afraid but unable to stop.

Ben and I, we would listen to Bob Dylan and Santana and Fleetwood Mac, and kiss until we could hardly walk, and he would talk of marrying me and taking me to live in South America – he was always talking about taking me to South America – and then we'd put our suits and frocks on, answer up in the *Watchtower* review, go out on the ministry on Sunday afternoon, put our field service reports[44] in on time…

In all truth, what else were we supposed to do? We were always terrified of being tortured in the Great Tribulation, or dying at Armageddon, but the rules for survival were so many, and the impossibility of being able to keep them all so debilitating, and the weight of it as teenagers just wanting to learn about each other, and ourselves, and life, so overwhelming that of course we led double lives. Did you honestly think we weren't?

But sometimes we were caught, and sometimes a lovely 'friend' would report us to the elders. If we smoked and weren't sorry – out. If we were gay and not sorry – out. If we simply didn't believe the Truth and weren't sorry – out. And that was it. No contact with our family, our friends, or the congregation. They must not communicate with us, as that would make them complicit in our sin and liable to be removed themselves – and who wants that sort of responsibility on top of being gay or a non-believer and out of favour with Jehovah God? – and we certainly must not attempt to communicate with them. I'm not saying I disagree with keeping an organisation respectable – moral codes exist to shape us into respectable human beings

[44] At the end of every month we were obligated to submit a 'field service report' – a record of how many hours we'd spent knocking on doors. It included how many magazines or books we had 'placed' with 'householders'; how many 'home studies' we were conducting with members of the public or 'return visits' we had made on them. We also kept notebooks where we'd record details of every single response we'd had at every single door: DNC (Do Not Call), CA (Call Again), NI (Not Interested) etc, etc. If your personal report was somewhat lacking an elder would corner you for a little chat about your commitment to your baptism, your congregation, the Organisation… roughly translated as 'Do your bit, please, because your very poor numbers are affecting the overall numbers, and the Governing Body don't like that one bit.'

– but to destroy families, to threaten those who remain in the congregation with expulsion if they have anything to do with the expelled…

You'd be correct in thinking that surely no intelligent, free-thinking human being would agree to such cruelty; but people are SO fearful of Jehovah's wrath, never mind that of the elders, and the utter disdain of their fellow Witnesses, that they will cross the street to avoid their own child, or mother, or brother, or childhood friend rather than risk being marked as 'bad association', being disfellowshipped themselves, and ultimately dying at Armageddon. In *Rainbow Milk*, nineteen-year-old Jesse McCarthy is ordered to stay in his room by his Witness mother and step-father, who will not even allow him to come downstairs and eat with his own family.

In the film *Apostasy*, Dan skilfully presents a Witness mother's relationship with her two very different daughters. This is not a screaming bells and whistles movie; it was not written to get shouty about what life as a Witness is like when all doesn't flow as smoothly as the pages of a *Watchtower.* Rather, it is an unobtrusive portrayal of the slow grind of fear, of a mother torn between honouring Jehovah and being seen to be a strong Christian woman within the congregation, and her quiet anguish when her eldest daughter announces she no longer wants to go to meetings and be in the Truth.

For anybody reading this who knows this inexorable pain, how my heart breaks. For those who don't, just try to imagine seeing someone you love in the street, and instead of waving and hurrying to hug them and chat with them, you must cast your eyes to the ground and keep walking. The reason? To demonstrate your love for and loyalty to Jehovah, and to teach your son or daughter, or mother or father, or brother or sister or friend, a valuable lesson with respect to that love and loyalty. Had they not been disfellowshipped, however, and just drifted away, or been a straightforward non-believing family member, then limited contact was permitted in order to 'keep the door open'...the door that will be slammed shut anyway if they do not return or convert.

Like so many others, I find it hard to belief I lived like this, and that being in the Truth, no matter how conflicted, was more important than living an honest life – and by honest I mean living a life that had not been forced on me, but one I had chosen for myself. Some of my friends got caught breaking the rules and either told the truth or lied about their double lives. Some confessed out of fear; some trod water for years, their Truth-spouting heads just above the surface of the sin below. Others simply left when they could no longer sustain both lives; others drowned under the weight, sinking into the depths of dark depression, and were left there when it was decided they weren't worthy of saving. I was one of them.

Do you have any idea what it does to your heart and soul to live that life?

When my brother was discovered stealing to buy cigarettes it was not with kids from the estate, it was with two boys from our congregation. I remember thinking about this a lot. On the estate we were surrounded by graffiti and fried food smells and the occasional burnt out car – ours included – all at the hands of the people with the spray cans and the frying pans and the petrol cans; but the boys he stole with were not from this world – *the* world – no, they were the good Christian boys he'd been told to associate with. The first boy was the eldest son of Brother Johnson, the elder who terrorised my mother on the doorstep for having an opinion about the source of our source of being, the son who he tormented and mocked and bullied in broad daylight in the name of not spoiling him by sparing him. The second boy was the younger son of a sister who I found hard to cope with because of the god-awful smell of her house and armpits. I knew little else about her, except that she listened to the Rutles, the knock-off Beatles. When I asked her who the Rutles were, she put a mixed tape of their songs together for me, recorded from vinyl, which was really sweet…and made me feel bad about holding my breath in her company.

I also thought about my sweet, funny, farting, Hunt-to-my-Sherrie brother and these other two. I imagined the beating the first one got, the squeaky telling off the second one got, and as for the way the postman treated my brother… But I also remember wondering what I would have done if they'd been my sons. Stealing is stealing, isn't it? What would you have done?

The family holiday we had that summer was a torture all of its own. I was sixteen and grieving for my beautiful biology teacher. My brother was quiet. My mother quieter. I got very sunburnt on the only day we were permitted to go to a beach – the postman thought beaches were a waste of intellect, preferring castles and mounds where castles used to be – and had my first Babycham at Cardiff Theatre. Sarah Kennedy was narrating *Peter and the Wolf* in her husky, wonderful voice, and we saw David Essex in the lift. Had anyone told me Sarah would one day become one of my most beloved friends, and that by the time she was I would no longer sit in theatres in the dark space of my hatred of the postman, my fear for my brother, my aching worry for my mother, and instead be filled with life and energy and plans, I don't think I would even have had the energy to lift my eyes and say, *No, I'm here forever. I have nowhere else to go.*

I got very thin, and very tired. And my hot-cold fear of life turned into walking out of my A-levels into that grotty part-time job and a pioneering life I was too exhausted to fight. And I learnt by rote Bible texts instead of studying my adored English literature and sociology and art, and qualified for baptism[45], and Charles held my hand and we courted, mostly respectfully, and I married him, a virgin and not in love. I think I thought baptism might help, that something might change in me after I chose Jehovah and his service. The thing was, it didn't feel like a choice.

The Witnesses parade the truth that all baptised members of a congregation have 'chosen' to dedicate themselves to Jehovah on the basis that, as adults, they have used their freewill to make such a decision, and they criticise the world for baptising their babies, arguing that a baby cannot make a conscious choice about its religion, and has it thrust upon her by her parents. But was that any different to my baptism, just because I was eighteen? I no more had the freedom to choose than the baby crying as she is held over the font. Choosing any life other than that of a dedicated Witness meant death for me. And that is *freewill*? I remember hoping the postman would be proud of me for getting baptised and pioneering, and it wasn't that he wasn't, it was just that he was furious with me for walking out of school. I was so confused. I thought school and further education were the Devil's thing, the very thing that would distract me from my true purpose of being a good Christian sister, a pioneer and wife?

[45] Which required studying a series of baptism questions, over a course of several weeks, associated with loyalty to the Truth and Jehovah, and your motivation for wanting to become one of his faithful servants, and then answering before a panel of elders who approved or declined your application.

I remember thinking I had done what Jehovah had wanted of me, and all would be lions and tigers in paradise from now on – well, whenever that head-fuck of a notion would become reality – and Charles and I would live happily ever after with our row of rosy-cheeked children.

I remember the conversations and the *Watchtower* articles about people in the world 'having their paradise now' – along with the Witnesses who chose to have careers and BMWs – because they lived fulfilled, happy, prosperous lives, unable to delay the Satanic urge for all good things. No, it was Jehovah who, in his due time, would 'open his hand and satisfy the desire of every living thing' (Psalms 145:16), and it was not ours to engineer our own happiness. So why did driving my unbelieving husband's Mercedes and living in a lovely home mean I was being blessed by Jehovah, according to some?

I remember thinking that none of this – *none of this* – made any sense whatsoever.

But as the postman raged at me for abandoning my studies, it made me see him a little clearer as the frustrated man he was. The way he treated my mother and brother and grandparents was disgusting. And the sanctimonious bloody mile-long comments he made at the meetings, full of pontification and quotes from scripture, were infuriating. But I also saw the boy who had been bullied by his own father; the man with a vast intelligence who had longed to go to university, but who had also been pressured into pioneering; the step-father who had taken on two children he had no idea how to love as his own. I still loathed him, have no doubt about that, as his behaviour was at best vaguely tolerable, and at worst truly despicable, but I started to notice the things I was interested in because of his input: history, architecture, literature, theatre, opera, classical music, even castles… He would save, and once a year we would take a trip to see a Gilbert and Sullivan production in London or Stratford – *The Mikado, HMS Pinafore, The Pirates of Penzance, Iolanthe* – and how I adored the genius of those lyrics.

I don't remember quite how it came about, but Mum suggested I write him a letter thanking him for what he'd done for me. Despite the above interests, all he'd ever 'done for me' was make me feel stupid and afraid of him and disgusted by him, but I wrote the letter anyway. I guess she was trying to get me to acknowledge his efforts as a step-father, and there was this sense that my enquires about my real father had somehow diminished those efforts, so I should offer up my written 'thank you, stepdad, for taking care of me' as an attempt to make him feel needed and appreciated, but it felt horribly fake writing it. Perhaps she hoped he and I would bond over my thanks, but why would I want to do that? I couldn't bear to be in the same room as him. Seemed she loathed him, too, most of the time.

In the letter I thanked him for reading me the classics and Shakespeare (to balance my obsession with Enid Blyton, perhaps) when I was a child, because my love of words was born listening to those words, and I still shiver at the sounds and the rhythms they make. I also recall writing something about him doing the best he could to take care of a daughter he had adopted, and how grateful I was for that. Grateful for *what*? He'd kept a roof over my head and food in the cupboards, but the rest was a ceaseless cycle of pretending to be nice to him to keep him happy, which wasn't very often, and dodging his temper when he wasn't, which was most of the time. I don't remember how I ended the letter, and I doubt he kept it. I'm mighty glad I didn't keep a copy. It's making my soul itch even mentioning I wrote such a thing. Anyway, I hear he's a lecturer now, which was something he really wanted to be. But I also hear he's still an arrogant, self-absorbed, judgemental bastard.

We all struggled though, after this time. My brother, when his smoking and stealing had faded from being front and centre of our lives, floundered around on the edge of faith for a while. He and Ben, our Yamaha-riding friend and my secret boyfriend at times, did fly off to South America to 'preach where the need was great'[46] – in other words, preach where they could also be at large with the lax Ecuadorian life, drink beer and get amoebas, and return with suntans and a deal never to tell. Ben, by his own admission, came back to marry me, but by that time I'd gone and married Charles. My brother came back because Ben did. But they were changed, and I knew it was only a question of time before my brother slipped deliberately and permanently through the open door of the cage.

My sister was pubescent and in love with Ben's younger brother, and the postman washed his hands of her when he found out, which broke her heart because she was the only one of the four of us, Mum included, whom he'd seemed remotely interested in.

Mum was still trying hard to be a good Witness wife, and pioneered when she could, starting Bible studies with people on the estate. I remember going with her one afternoon to meet a couple she had recently started studying with, and being absolutely repulsed. The couple had eight-month-old twins and two large dogs, who never left the house. I had never encountered a sight or smell like it, and the memory of two small girls crawling around on the carpet in the lounge is still

[46] It was considered admirable to fly off to far-flung places on Earth where the Truth was less known and make it known.

vivid. My mother rallied some stalwart sisters and together they as good as gutted the house, and showed the young mum how to clean and take care of the dogs. The change was astonishing, and the couple came to the meetings for a time. I don't recall what happened to them, but I remember the conversations about 'the power of the Truth' on people's lives.

As said, I'd been asking about my dad, desperate to understand who he was and where he was. I'd waited long enough, surviving on snippets and glimpses. Who was this thumping drunkard who'd fathered me? Is that why we'd had to move? Is that why I remembered being in a large blue pram, my brother one end and me the other, and Mum running fast, pushing it bumping and bouncing down an alleyway? I was crazy with needing to know, and I think I must have driven her crazy too.

When I woke up in the high dependency unit in hospital I was convinced I had lost my second baby, and didn't think I could live another day if that was true. But I was handed a Polaroid photograph of a baby girl, with her father's piano fingers and black-black hair, and I loved her instantly, like a heat, like a rush of something that filled every cell of my body. Hunched over my caesarean in a wheelchair, I was taken to see Grace on the premature baby unit. I felt her in my arms, soft and warm, and she flexed her fingers and arched her back, and I sensed her strength and all the reasons she had survived. She was a gift, so we could learn about each other and from each other, and I had never known such love.

She was rather reluctant to walk, waiting until she was twenty months old and on holiday in Tunisia; and didn't utter a word until she asked me for a piece of bread and butter please, which was amusing and alarming simultaneously seeing as I had my back to her at the time, and wondered who on earth had asked such a thing in such a polite and grown-up voice. She was a live wire of life. Her love of music and dancing and jumping and singing; her concentration when she glued leaves to coloured paper or had tea parties with her dolls; her unbridled fun with her cousins, and her laugh as they ran around the garden and poured buckets of water over each other's heads. I won't dwell on her outrageous temper, and lying face down on the floor in Waitrose, or wherever she felt like it, whenever she felt life wasn't quite to her liking…!

When Harrison, the baby boy I thought I was having, turned out to be Annie – and so named by her big sister, who took one look at her and simply said "Let's call her Annie" – arrived four and a half years later, I honestly used to think I would implode from the love. I still do. Annie was this smiling, wondering, wandering mischief who put coal in the washing machine, and pasta in the washing machine, and spread Sudocrem, that claggy white nappy rash preventer, all over our beautiful red velvet-finish stair carpet. She climbed the trellis in the garden, right to the top, when she was a year old; she crawled to the back of the wardrobe, and lay still and quiet whilst Grace and I searched and called for her; and clambered into the boot of the car to hide, prompting a search that included all the neighbours; and hid behind a pile of loo seat boxes in B&Q, resulting in a colossal search of the colossal store…

Grace would look up and shrug at my "Have you seen your sister?" in the end, and at this tiny little girl whose shenanigans I simply don't have the room to list. Yet she was the stillness to

Grace's intensity, the hey whatever to her big sister's temper, but most definitely the *My Naughty Little Sister*[47] to Grace's very good big sister.

Some days, what I wouldn't give to have them back either side of me in the big Mummy and Daddy's bed saying, "Read it again! Read it again!" when I was so knackered I just wanted them to go to sleep and let me off the mother hook. But I'd look at them. Their pyjama-ed bodies all warm and next to me. And so I'd read again, and they'd settle.

I did this thing though, which, forgive me, I thought was the right thing to do. For a time I took them to all the meetings, and I taught them about Jehovah and, I'm so sorry, about Armageddon and paradise. Because, after I had been disfellowshipped into the darkness of the world, I set about being reinstated, the reverse process of disfellowshipping, whereby elders gather to assess evidence for your readmittance into the congregation – are you sorry? are you aware of your shortcomings and need for forgiveness? are you willing to accept Jehovah's guidance in your life again? – and send you from the room so they can pray about you and decide whether you are worthy again of God's love, (and theirs).

I guess I wasn't ready to roam free on Earth with no plan, no guidance. I only knew about *Watchtower* articles and governing bodies and elders; I was used to being told what to do, what to believe, what to think. And despite loathing the outrageous claims on my gift of free thought, my heart and my soul, it was safer in there with the rules than out here, where anything goes. The girls' father would despair at me. (I would despair at me.) "You've no drive, no ambition!" he would yell. But was it

[47] https://www.amazon.com/Naughty-Little-Sister-Dorothy-Edwards/dp/1405253347

any wonder? I'd had my drive and ambition removed by fear of it displeasing Jehovah. And yet as I watched him study for his business degree after a long day at work, helped him with his dissertation, and stood by his side when he graduated with honours with such pride, I had such an ache to learn, to grow, to thrive. Would it ever be mine?

The girls would often ask me why their daddy didn't go to the meetings. Truth is, as my 'unbelieving husband' – such a beautiful expression the Witnesses use to describe a spouse who 'isn't in the Truth' – he was under no obligation whatsoever to attend. Had it been the other way around, however, and I had been the unbelieving wife, there would have been plenty of pressure for me to attend, so as to honour my husband.

The anxiety returned the moment I returned. I should have left again, right then, but there grew this thing which all Witnesses are only too aware of: your children's lives are at stake now, not just your own. So I trained them in the Truth, and taught them to answer up and hand out leaflets when we were on the ministry, and wrote letters to their teachers explaining why they must be allowed to leave the room when the rest of the class recited the Lord's Prayer, or sang Happy Birthday, or made Christmas decorations. I answered all their questions about why, quoting scriptures and hoping it would make them strong in their faith. I watched the confusion and their love for me, and their awareness of the Organisation and Jehovah and their early understanding of the Truth create in them the same horrible confusion and fear (well certainly in Grace; Annie seemed largely oblivious) it had created in me, and in my head there were loud, unutterable answers:

Why doesn't Daddy go to the meetings? *Because he doesn't bloody have to.*

Why doesn't he believe in Jehovah and the paradise? *Because he doesn't bloody need to.*

Why don't we celebrate Christmas? *Because some fucking idiots in Brooklyn say we can't.*

Why can't I have a birthday party? *Because some fucking idiots in Brooklyn say you can't.*

Why was I doing this to the two people I loved more than life?

They mostly seemed to accept the whole Christmas and birthdays thing. Not so with their dad. They were terrified he would die if he didn't come to the meetings. But how could I explain he didn't have to? That it was his choice not to? That he didn't have to believe a single word of what I was teaching his beautiful daughters?

Did I?

In the same article that appeared in *The Guardian* in July 2018, Dan Kokotajlo states:

> 'I was eight when she [his mother] converted. She met this very nice old couple who talked to her about paradise and the fact that the end of the world was coming pretty soon, and all our problems would then be fixed. It was very appealing, especially to our family, growing up where we did.'

What about his father?

> 'He was not convertible. There's a pressure, in the Witnesses, for men who convert to bring their wives in, but it doesn't work the other way round; women can come to the church alone.'

Dan is absolutely correct: that is how it is. My nan had also been called on by a very nice couple, who spoke to her about paradise, and the end of the world coming soon, and all of her problems being fixed. I know very little about my nan's background, but understand there were reasons for the appeal of paradise, and so it was that my aunt and my mother were introduced to a god they'd never heard of, and began the sort of life they hadn't known existed. I think my mother would have preferred to have been riding her pony, but my aunt became a devout Witness, later presiding over her family with the near-lethal touch of the utterly converted. For years my grandpa observed the changes in his family, unconvinced, until eventually he too was baptised, even though there was absolutely no pressure for him to do so.

Despite my longing to leave I continued to attend meetings, bizarrely receiving an odd kind of praise for proving my spiritual mettle by attending alone – well, with two daughters in tow. The girls were polite and well-behaved – and I never had to lay a finger on them to make them so – and my heart was so, so sad. As always, I was this smiling, believing, proselytising thing on the outside; but inside I was fighting every single moment I had to sit amongst these people who praised me and raised me on the 'look at how well she does it all, and all on her own (her husband's an unbeliever, you know…)' pedestal. Not so long ago they had crossed the street when they saw me.

But just who was I through their Witness-coloured spectacles? When I'd ridden bare-legged on Dimitri's bike, I was still me. When I walked down the street and you crossed to the other side, I was still me. When I raised my hand to answer in the *Watchtower* review, I was still me. When I gave my worldly husband a forbidden blow job, I was still me. (Or was I a sinner again, at that point? Or was it okay because he was a non-believer, and therefore not complicit in my sin, much like Sindy and Action Man being oblivious because of their being made of plastic?) And when I played with my kids, or spoke to my disfellowshipped brother, or swore a bit, *I was still me.*

But who actually, on God's Earth, was I? And these girls of mine, who were they? Oh God, the preciousness of them. What was I doing to them, bringing them into *this*?

The anxiety inched into another smothering depression, heavy inside my head and heavier in my bones, and the harder I clutched at the Truth, the deeper I sank.

I come home from school one day to a house of angry people. There is an angry mother and a grandmother, and a girl my age who I'd whacked over the head with my hefty plaster of Paris-clad broken arm in the locker room earlier that day.

"She can't just go around hitting people!" screeches the mother.

"Look at our Tina!" the grandmother adds.

My mother looks so tired. My sister is just a few months old and seems to spend most of her time feeding or screaming, night and day. (The postman also looks tired, but not because he's been up at night helping with their daughter, but because he has to get up at 4am every day, and makes sure my mother knows this, rather loudly, so she'll take the screaming child downstairs. Thankfully, he's out at this current moment.)

My brother has been sent to his room so we, the victim and her posse, and the accused and her mother, can discuss why I can't just go around hitting their Tina. But I know he has crept down the stairs and is listening, because that's what we always do when interesting things are happening in the lounge, like elders coming over, or phone calls that prompt the door being shut.

Tina has a fantastic red bump on her forehead which, it is true, is there because I put it there.

"Do you want to tell us why you hit her?" my mum asks.

"She can't do that! Yow obviously don't know how to control yer own child!" screeches the mother.

"No! No! You don't!" adds the grandmother.

It had felt so good, sounded so good, the thunk, when I whacked Tina's skull. And months of hurt moved from me into her as she hunched at the pain, the girl who had gathered and jeered at me with her horrible estate friends: *You're a Jehovanahh! Jehovanahh! Jehovanahh! You murder your kids and don't do Christmas, that's wot my mum sez. Murderer! Murderer! Jehovanahhhhhhhh!*

"Why don't you tell us what happened," Mum says, turning to me.

"Look at 'er! She don't even have the brains to tell uz wot happened!" screeches the mother.

"Cat got yer tongue, love!" adds the grandmother.

The room is hot and I'm hot, and one of the two women has got really stinky perfume on, and my hands are shaking in my lap, and please, no, not the ice cubes in my bones, not again.

I look at Tina and, for the first time, our eyes meet, just her and me, and all the yelling is on the moon. She looks sad, and kind of sorry. Is she sorry? Is she frightened I'll tell her hideous polyester-clad mother and grandmother that she's been mean to me? That she's been hanging out with Paula and Angie, the estate bullies? Will they be horrible to her? I don't want them to be horrible to her. We're only eight and she's kinda pretty with her blonde fringe and blue eyes and Barbie T-shirt. She goes out of focus as my eyes fill with tears.

"What's wrong with 'er? Why ain't she speaking?" screeches the mother.

The grandmother seems to have run out of add-ons.

"All this shouting is achieving nothing," my mother says. "Shall we just let the girls talk?"

I'm so angry with Tina, and I'm angry for being shouted about; and my voice, just like before, won't come out, and why am I like this? I don't want my mum to be ashamed of me; and I don't want Tina to think I'm nasty, or her mum and grandma. I'm not nasty. I'm just sad because of all the teasing, and I wish it was just me and Mum and my brother again, because I can't cope with all the noise my sister makes, and I hate the postman, and my broken arm really aches some days, and all of this just made me lose it. There must be something I can do? What will make this okay?

"I'm sorry I hit you."

And the energy shifts in the room.

I pass my brother on my way to my room, which I now have to share with my sister. She is asleep in her cot. I creep past her and lie on my bed and sob as quietly as I can.

Talking to Mum now, and my brother and sister, it's clear we've never really recovered, not fully.

My brother married this flamboyance of a sister, about a decade older than him, who devoured and then dismantled him in a matter of weeks. My beautiful, soft-hearted brother had a breakdown, and took up with a pretty little thing – the girlfriend of a gay friend of mine (who was desperately trying to be a Witness, and who kissed like an angel) – who was kind to him. The elders showed him no kindness, however, sided with his horrendous wife and disfellowshipped him.

Mum was never going to follow the vehement admonition of the elders who expelled him to shun him. She loved him as she loved each of us: without question. He could hardly make words make sentences; he could barely climb the stairs to his bedroom, where he lay for weeks with no energy to cry. He was twenty years old and all life was gone from him. Shortly after, Mum's parents died, just eighteen months apart. And then the postman had an affair with the breathy-flirty sister who lived across the street, but denied it, of course. And the elders believed him, of course, because after all he was an elder and Mum was his rather outspoken, therefore very much less-than wife who wasn't considered a reliable witness, or Witness. Besides, she couldn't prove the affair because of the two-witness rule, and the letters she'd found, the sexually explicit written exchange of their feelings for each other, disappeared the moment she handed them to an elder as evidence of the affair, and all knowledge of them was denied. She left before they could disfellowship her.

My sister had her troubles too, and had no interest in being dictated to by elders who never listened to the real truth of any matter. So that was the three of them, and me.

You could say that had we followed the rules none of this would have happened – and the Witnesses who stand cheering at their own steadfastness to the Truth will stand by this for all they're worth – and Jehovah would have blessed us, and kept us within the protection of his congregation. I'm not denying there is a vague notion of sense to that argument: you follow the rules and life is an ordered thing, where everyone knows their place and stays there.

But life doesn't follow the rules. And following the rules of the Organisation meant watching elders and overseers close ranks around adultery, tax evasion, child abuse, but paying the price for the crime of free thought, of the choice to carry on seeing and supporting disfellowshipped friends and family because they were still good, loving people, with expulsion. It meant adhering to truths that allowed your child to die rather than displease Jehovah by being given a blood transfusion, comforted by the knowledge he would remember your act of faith and reward you with everlasting life in paradise with your resurrected child. There was no regard for the terror and confusion the child was feeling as they watched their parents walk away, knowing they must die for a truth they have no power to challenge.

This couldn't have been better portrayed in *Apostasy*. In his artful, ordinary, gripping way Dan put onto screen not just what this is, but *how* it is; in other words, how it *feels*. Words can achieve much by way of cognitive understanding of a thing, and prompt a degree of emotion; but to watch actress Siobhan Finneran bring this half-life to life, to so accurately portray a mother's devotion to Jehovah pitched against her love for her daughters…it was painful to watch. As her character Ivanna, she absolutely captures the *feel* of the fear, her obedience to the stern admonition of the elders, the willingness to shun one daughter because she no longer wants to attend meetings, and encouraging the other to refuse a blood transfusion despite knowing it could save her life. Her belief that Armageddon is 'just around the corner', and that Earth will soon be restored to Edenic paradise is so strong...stronger even than her mother-instinct. In the final few frames of the film we see her sitting expressionless and motionless in a Kingdom Hall, and then standing alone at a JW.org stand on a busy street, where people just pass her by, and pass her by.

There are no raised voices in the film, and no overly dramatic scenes. It is just how it is to be a Jehovah's Witness; it is just how it feels.

A friend shared his thoughts after watching the film with me: "There's a part of me that better understands and sympathises with the power this organisation has over every single thought and action, and wants to go up to the Witnesses and say, Hey, I get it, I'll be kinder next time you approach me with a *Watchtower*; but there's also a part of me that wants to shake the living daylights out of them and say, No, I don't get it. Why can't you think your own thoughts, choose your own path? Why can't you just leave?" He turned to me, his face the mix of incredulity and curiosity I'd seen so many times. "K, why didn't you just leave?"

My aunt called Mum after the death of their parents and the postman's affair, her husband standing next to her for protection against her renegade younger sister. Mum had recently moved out of the marital home and I was staying with her. My brother was visiting too, and my sister lived with her. I was at work that day, but I heard how they'd offered to drive up in their large estate car to help her move some boxes and generally be useful, for which Mum was so grateful. There was a long pause, and then they'd asked her if my brother and sister were home.

When Mum said yes, they replied, "Would it be possible for them to stay in their rooms while we're there, because they are still disfellowshipped?" Mum said she could not guarantee they wouldn't come out of their rooms, it being their home… There was another pause while they conferred, and then my aunt said, "Then we're sorry, but we won't be able to come and help you today."

I know my brother and sister, and Mum, have their stories too, and will remember different parts and have a different view at times to the glimpses of our life I have shared here. But when I look into their eyes, and look into the reflection of my own, deep enough to see, I know we will never recover, not fully. And that is the unbreakable bond, the mostly silent witness to that life that all ex-Witnesses share.

The door, in shiny black with a silver eagle doorknocker, opens. It's cold today, and the young sister beside me has her hands in her pockets and her chin tucked into her red scarf. I have a leaflet in my hand – *Look! I am Making all Things New!* – about God's promise to restore Earth to paradise conditions and humans to perfection, and I take a breath.

"Hello, can I help you?"

The householder[48] is a greying, smart man in his fifties; a doctor maybe, or a solicitor. His face dimples as he smiles, a little curiously, but then twitches with that look of recognition I've seen a thousand times before: Jehovah's Witnesses.

"Hello, how are you today?" I say, all smile and eyes.

[48] 'Householder' is the term used by the Organisation to describe the person behind the door.

"I'm well, thank you. Can I help you?"

"I'd love to ask you a question, if I may?"

"Sure. Shoot."

"If you were able to change one thing in the world to make it a better place, what would you choose?"

You, standing on my doorstep, when I have a hundred things to do this afternoon before my client meeting at 9am tomorrow morning.

"Soliciting," he says.

So is he a solicitor?

"And how would you go about effecting this change, if you don't mind me asking?"

His face softens. I'm so polite, you see, and my eyes are warm even if I'm not. And I think he realises I don't know what 'soliciting' means and doesn't wish to embarrass me.

"Can I ask *you* a question?" he says.

"Of course."

"Why do you do this? You must be nineteen, twenty? What motivates you to knock on strangers' doors and talk about changing the world?"

"I'm nineteen. The world is a mess, bad things happen every day – things that were prophesied to happen at this time but it won't always be like this. God has promised that he will step in, and soon, to remove all the evil in the world. He has instructed us to tell people this good news. In Matthew 24:14 it says, 'And this good news of the Kingdom will be preached in all the inhabited Earth, as a witness to all the nations, and then the end will come.'"

"Bad things have always happened, would you not agree?"

"I do. But the Bible prophesied that these things would intensify as we got closer to God's intervention at Armageddon, and his saving of the faithful, and, as it says further on in Matthew 24…" I reach for my New World Translation, tucking the leaflet into the back in case I need it. The young sister beside me closes further into her scarf and pockets. "Could I perhaps show you, so you're not taking my word for it?"

He smiles those dimples at me again, and I read to him about wars and earthquakes and food shortages and pestilences, things which must occur, 'and then the end will come'.

"And you believe this?" he asks.

"I do, yes."

"Have you always believed this?"

"I have, yes."

"May I ask why?"

"The Bible is an ancient book, but it contains so much advice and guidance for modern life. I have studied it, in great depth, and I see the prophecies coming true every day. There is no denying it's the truth for our times, and it shapes our course of action in the world, what we must do and how we must behave. And the Organisation – Jehovah's organisation – is God's tool on Earth for translating these ancient texts through the pages of leaflets like this..." – the leaflet is presented – "and the *Watchtower* into modern language we can understand."

"So you think the Bible is the only guide we need for modern life?"

"Yes, I do. In 2 Timothy 3:16 it says that 'All scripture is inspired of God and beneficial for teaching, reproving and setting things straight.' So yes, I think the Organisation is right when it says the Bible is the only valuable guide for life."

He looks at me, but more than that. "But what do *you* think?" he asks.

There is nothing other than openness in his face. He is not mocking me, or teasing me. He seems interested, genuinely curious. The thump of my heart hurts.

"What do you think about the world?" he continues. "For the short time we've been talking, you've spoken about changing it, about Armageddon, about Bible prophecy and the Bible setting you straight, and how much you believe this. And you've quoted scripture admirably. But what do *you* think?"

In the silence that follows, where my eyes are locked into his as his question registers, and my utter inability to answer him takes the shape of the white elephant he has the good manners to ignore, I realise: *I have no idea what I think.* Me. A nineteen-year-old girl who has a fear of rooms, who can memorise endless scriptures, who stands in front of the philosophy section in the town's library but who picks up a book on cats. Our breath barely moves in the frozen air.

"You seem like a bright girl," he says quietly, like a sigh in a deep wood. "There are some beautiful things happening in the world, despite the unfortunate pockets of war and other troubles, and some beautiful people doing them. Take a look at that, just to see. I think you'll be surprised. And I think it will help you understand the wider, bigger picture. I'm not telling you what to believe, but just take a look."

He holds his hand out. I switch the Bible to my left hand and take it, shake it. And I want to be him, with his soft, relaxed face and his wider, bigger picture.

By the time I get to the end of his gravel drive I have walked a thousand miles.

In close succession, one summer, several things happened to the postman.

During a very serious, deathly quiet moment in a long, long talk about the recompenses of faithful service at one of the yearly assemblies of Jehovah's Witnesses at Twickenham Stadium in London, the canvas seat of the small metal-framed chair he was sitting on split with a terrific sound. I'd never seen Mum laugh like that, or him for that matter, as try as they might they couldn't get him out of the frame. Other brothers and sisters joined in, recompenses drowned out as they eventually tipped him slowly onto his side and pulled the frame off his bottom. He wasn't a big man, but the chair was so small, and he was a slightly bigger man in my eyes, momentarily, for laughing with the rest of us just then.

A day after this, he was volunteering on the catering team – events like assemblies were entirely run by volunteers who cooked and cleaned and administrated – and, lord knows why, but he was carrying a catering-sized can of pineapple chunks in apple juice, as big as you like, down a colossal flight of steps. He slipped. The way he landed was awful, and his smashed-up elbow swelled enormously. In dreadful pain, he carried on regardless, assembling little pots of tinned fruit and jelly for thousands of attendees. The sight of his elbow was repulsive, and he was still repulsive, but I admired his fortitude and commitment to completing the task.

On another day, at home, he immersed his entire head in a huge tin of white gloss whilst bending down to pick his paintbrush up. He had black hair, and it took several bottles of white spirit to remove the paint. After that, he always maintained his grey streaks were paint that had never quite been removed, something I thought about years later when I couldn't get paint out of my own hair.

The final thing had to do with a television. He tripped on his way out of the loft hatch holding the one that had disappeared after the first series of *Poldark*, and had the wherewithal to lob it onto the double bed in their room as he fell so it wouldn't smash. This was a revelation to me – we had a TV in the loft? since when? were we going to be able to watch it? – and I was so pleased he hadn't dropped it!

It was plugged back in, and I remember two things: the kids' BBC drama *Kizzy*, which left me delirious with thoughts of ponies and raggedy clothes and rescue; and, in 1977, the second series of *Poldark*. I had no doubt that Mum had a lot to do with its reappearance and, wow, I was practically in love with her for that.

Kizzy tore me to shreds. It was the story of a gypsy girl mocked and bullied for being different when she tries to integrate into her local school. She grapples with being misunderstood, of not understanding the world she has been forced to join, of feeling a kind of shame for the world she belongs to. I started dressing like her, in long flowery skirts and an old holey cardigan, and dreamt of fresh air and campfires and the soft breath of my own pony on my cheek.

I couldn't share *Kizzy* with my brother because he wouldn't have felt it like I did, and I wouldn't let him join in with the Kizzy games I played out endlessly in my bedroom – the first time I had ever shut him out. This game was all for me, and how I lived every second, every line spoken in my head, every imagined walk with my pony. I was gone. Lost in the story. Creating my own stories. Writing and imagining whilst glued to every scene on the screen and every scene I replayed in my bedroom. There are TV moments from childhood you never forget. This was mine.

The TV vanished again, probably when *Poldark* ended, but I didn't care so much. I had my little gypsy girl and our pony to go to now, when it all got too loud or too sad.

When Jill Bolte Taylor's left brain started to come back 'online', as she so brilliantly describes it, following her stroke, she noticed several things. The first was that the ceaseless 'chatter' returned about this, that and everything: *No, we don't like that; Yes, we know about people like her; Yes, I think you'll remember we always avoid him; No, don't try that food, you don't like it…* Another was that the stories returned. The longer, *endless* stories. Stories about who and what she perceived herself to be before the stroke; stories about why she acted or spoke the way she did; stories about Jill the Daughter, Jill the Neuroscientist, Jill the Woman Who Reacts This Way to That, and That Way to This. She laughs in her podcast when she says at that point she had two choices: keep the file or ditch the file, the simple profundity of which struck quite a chord with me.

But is it really that easy? Listen to anyone telling a story about themselves. How animated are they? How invested are they in the details and the meaning of that story? How committed are they to getting you to understand the story, and subsequently understand them? The story is everything they've come to believe and perceive, whether six years old or ninety, about the world and, most crucially, their world.

And while they're talking, they'll be digging about frenetically in that story's particular file for substantiation, for embellishments to colour in the faded, or non-existent bits. They'll be gauging your reaction. Are you listening, interested, understanding? If it appears you are not, then you will be deemed as uncaring, unsympathetic, a bad listener; if you are, you will rise to heights of being empathetic, kind and attentive. And another story will be added to the file containing the story itself: no one cares, no one's listening, I'm boring; or, that story always makes people laugh, gets me noticed, lets people see the real me. Chatter and more chatter. Stories upon more stories.

The reason for touching on this is this: we each have the choice as the story-keeper to keep a particular story or ditch it, as per Jill's revelation when her left brain started shouting, *Look at me! I'm back! Aren't you glad you have me!* if that story simply doesn't seem like a good fit anymore. I would suggest we even have a third option: the capacity to rewrite it; to take it apart, piece by piece, and put it back together in a way that reshapes it into something we can learn from, something we can grow with.

The story of being a Witness is so huge, so engrained, and so steeped in judgment and attachment to being right that it never stops shouting. Every piece of music, every movie, every encounter with people of the world…it's all being analysed through the lens of the Witness story. So when people said to me, "Actually, I'm really interested in the teachings of the Buddha," or, "I believe in reincarnation, as I feel that's how we are refined to become our higher selves," well, do I really need to go into any depth as to what happens in that moment, and how that person and their viewpoint is shut down? But shutting our ears and mind and heart to another human being's perspective, their story, is a tragedy. And it often takes a tragedy to undo the story of being a Witness, to rip it apart, to look at it and say: No more.

The depression that at times occupied my every heartbeat, every breath, every movement, is not something I discuss very often. I know that's because I don't really like talking about it, and because of wanting to protect my girls. It also frightened me how bad it was in there, where I imagined laying naked in icy fields until I froze to death, of how it would feel to lose all feeling as life left and I was left behind, a body without a soul. Yet I wanted to do it. I planned it. I laughed when I thought about it, and the literal No more. I continued taking the anti-depressants I had been prescribed, and the sleeping tablets and the Valium, but oddly they made me more sure of my decision. Whilst elders spouted and their wives gossiped, and friends, each and every one, side-stepped around me, I knew only one thing: in a few days' time I would never have to hear their cold-hearted voices or see their disapproving faces ever again.

I was no use as a daughter, or a sister, or a sister, or a mother, or a friend. I was a demented fake, pasting smiles and packing lunches and reading bedtime stories. Look at me, pretending to be a nice person to the idiot who gave me the wrong change in the supermarket; nodding amicably at the advice from an aunt as she trickled me tales of my incapable teenage mother and drip-drip-drip convinced me that she would be better for me; studying my *Watchtower* so I could fill people's heads with the informed fucking answers I loathed. I would look in the mirror and punch my own face. Fake! Fake! Better off dead.

I wrote letters. Dear Mum. Dear Grace. Dear Annie. And paused to make wounds in my skin and dress them. I called a non-Witness friend. Any chance you could have the girls overnight? Yeah, sure. So I packed their backpacks with pyjamas and toothbrushes. Not forgetting Grace's sleep bunny and Annie's blanket. I drove them over there. I kissed them goodbye. My beautiful, precious girls. And I drove home.

There were several moments, just before I lost physical consciousness, of absolute bliss, of a beauty and connection to life so profound that the rain on the window was only joy, the carpet I lay on a softness never before experienced, and the people chatting beneath my window so loved and full of love. My gratitude for the sounds and sensations, and my beating heart and my hair across my face, and the way I could curl this way and bring my knees to my forehead, was all so gentle and so light and so life.

And the story of the room, so hot and me so cold, and all the voices with their judgments, and the man in the doorway asking me what I thought, and the elder's wife telling me I was affecting the spirit of the congregation, and the friends who crossed roads to avoid me, and the aunt talking, talking, talking, and it all, it all. It started to gutter and jump about.

But I could hear screaming, and from the carpet I listened. Someone was in trouble. *Why now? Please, just let me have this bliss.* I curled back down to where a dark red puddle was forming, drifting now, ready to leave. But what was the screaming? It sounded urgent. Perhaps someone was hurt, maybe knocked down in the street? *I'll call for help, give my address so they can find whoever that is outside, and then I can go. Please, I just need to go.* Through the gratitude and the drifting, I crawled across the sodden carpet to the phone. *It'll be over soon. Just do this one thing.* I pressed redial. Anyone would do. I screamed into the phone.

And then it all went out.

PART TWO

So, what are we to do with the playground of life, full of ex-best friends and name-calling, new friends and a whole wide world of mind-blowing, fabulous knowledge to explore and discuss? And whether there is agreement or disagreement is irrelevant, as it is the interactions themselves and the sheer bliss of the debate that shapes and reshapes.

One afternoon, during O-level social studies, the class was split into two teams. We'd been discussing the right to refuse medical treatment, or to sign DNRs, (do-not-resuscitate orders), or, at the point of losing consciousness, whether personal choice, for whatever grounds, can be overruled by medical professionals. I was fascinated by this debate, and had raised some valid points – based on the Witnesses' stand on blood transfusions – which had prompted an interesting discussion all of its own.

It was the first time I'd heard my voice out loud on the subject away from the obvious bias within the walls of a Kingdom Hall, or in response to the ridicule of those determined to call me a murderer, and something shifted in my consciousness as I answered intelligent, genuinely curious questions about why the Witnesses felt the way they did. Not a single classmate agreed with the case for no blood that I presented – based on Acts 15:28-29 which states 'abstain from blood', which meant the life blood of an animal slaughtered for sacrifice to pagan idols, but was extended to mean the use of blood in medical intervention – but I witnessed a respect for hearing another person out, for considering what they believed from a place of human interest I was wholly unfamiliar with. I was so used to conversations about what other people believed being shut down that this shift felt like a landslide at first, unstable and unpredictable, and where would it end up? Where would I end up? But then I found my footing and, although my heart was pounding, I looked at the open, listening faces of my classmates and saw the thing that was so absent in my life: the freedom of the debate, and the wonderful, delicious freedom of being able to *choose* what I wanted to believe.

This capacity to acknowledge that although someone had a different view to me, that they were a valid, free-thinking human being with the right to believe whatever they liked without being judged as worthy of apostasy and death, was something I stored away in the file that suspected A didn't always lead to B and culminate in C.

We were split into teams and the subject of the following week's debate was 'Euthanasia: As conscious beings, humans have the right to decide when and how they die.' Jeez. This was big. The Witnesses believe – and I'm not sure whether 'believe' is even the right word here; perhaps 'insist' is more accurate – that taking your own life is murder, from which they add, with something akin to morbid self-satisfaction, there is no resurrection. The final, painful caveat is that a brother or sister who commits suicide will not be permitted a funeral service in a Kingdom Hall, and a service must instead be held in a non-denominational building, the final nail in the coffin of their clear lack of faith in Jehovah and therefore his utter disapproval of them. As with defiling your body by accepting a blood transfusion and making it dirty and unacceptable to Jehovah, so too taking your own life is considered one of the highest forms of unfaithfulness, and your name would be struck from God's 'Book of Life'.

I was put on the pro-euthanasia debate team.

The afternoon of the debate we moved the teacher to tears and, long after, we often returned to the subject, testing it and weighing it: Would we actually go through with euthanasia? Would we be brave enough? Would the will to live any kind of life be preferable to no life at all? Should the criteria for assisted death be limited to physical illness or disability? Would the choice for assisted death be considered valid and honoured if we were mentally ill?

I remember those who were considered 'weak in the truth' or 'lacking in faith' if they manifested any kind of mental illness. I remember them being given a wide berth, and no longer being invited to social events organised by friends they'd had their whole lives. Elders would visit the 'afflicted' and encourage them to pray more, to 'throw [their] burden on Jehovah' in the words of King David in Psalms 55:22 – never once considering that perhaps the burden might be Jehovah himself, or certainly the dictates of men claiming to represent him. Medication was discouraged, as was counselling, because the former would leave the mind open to the Devil, and the latter would fill it with worldy psycho-babble. I remember all this because of becoming one of those 'weak in the truth' depressed souls.

I can still see the despicable look from an elder's wife as she told me in no uncertain terms that I was 'affecting the spirit of the congregation' that Sunday morning as I sat on the floor of the ladies' room in my local Kingdom Hall, my head a fog of depression and Seroxat, my daughters sat either side of my empty chair in the main hall. I can still hear her voice, and feel my horror, like a cold hand around my heart: *I don't want to be responsible for that; I'll have to do it, so the congregation can be clean, because I can't bring the spirit down. I'll have to go.* It was my absolute belief I was doing the right thing when, two days' later,

2 January 2001, I dropped the girls at my friend's house and kissed them goodbye. There are days when I can hardly breathe from the memory of those last few seconds with them. Today is one of those days.

No, there is no room for mental illness in the hearts of Jehovah's Witnesses. And there is no room for freedom of thought. There is only fear, big enough to drown out the cries of a lifelong friend, to cut all contact with a family member who chooses to leave, to dismiss and discredit an alternative viewpoint that might just open their mind. There is only fear of how compassion or acceptance or curiosity might jeopardise their approval by Jehovah God and, more importantly it seems, their reputation in the congregation.

I recall the social studies teacher closing our euthanasia lesson, where each of us had had our personal views challenged and our minds opened, with words from Bertrand Russell's *Unpopular Essays:*

> '[...] those who have never travelled either physically or mentally find it difficult to tolerate the queer ways and outlandish beliefs of other nations and other times, other sects and other political parties. This kind of ignorant intolerance is the antithesis of a civilised outlook, and is one of the gravest dangers to which our overcrowded world is exposed.'

"Would you be shocked if I told you I really want to just pick that up and smash it on the floor?"

This younger daughter of mine is referring to a large glass turquoise head, one of two on a shelf in TK Maxx.

It's just the sort of random thing she would say – just the sort of random thing she has always said – and before I can reply she adds, "I think that was probably the Satan part of me talking."

There's a thing here: she hasn't mentioned Satan for probably close to eighteen years, so why would she suddenly mention him now? But there are other things: most likely she has (I hope) very little recollection of Satan as a devil/evil spirit/ concept of evil; as far as I'm aware she hasn't joined a cult and is exploring her Satanic self; she has the least amount of Satan in her than any other person I know.

She doesn't smash the turquoise head, of course; but she does wander around the store musing my observation that, if we're honest, we all have a bit of Satan in us. I want to get deep into this. Work out where it's come from. Ask her how she thinks the concept of Satan or the Devil manifests in twenty-first century life. But then she goes all fluffy again, drools over the Tupperware, and buys a pretty mint-green sweater for £4.

Standing across the street, not waiting to cross the road to enter, the Kingdom Hall opposite feels like something that happened to someone else, like an incarnation in an incarnation. Aside from the familiar crawl of fear, it certainly doesn't feel like it's me looking over at the bricks and mortar which the long-reaching roots of the conifers from the adjacent Catholic Church attacked[49], and that was the stage set to innumerable acts of posturing and pontification.

[49] They almost pulled the corner of the building down which, sorry, still makes me smile.

"So, brothers and sisters," an elder began, one Thursday evening so long ago, his hands clamps on the sides of the rostrum, "we are a people accused of brainwashing, of conditioning minds to one way of life to the exclusion of all else. Is this a bad thing? This brainwashing? We would say no, for indeed if Jehovah's true ways are a brainwashing, then we embrace that truth, for it is 'washing our brains' of the lies of Satan's world, would you not agree?"

It makes me smile this should come to mind, just then, standing there.

The Cambridge Dictionary defines brainwashing as, 'verb: to make someone believe something by repeatedly telling them that it is true and preventing any other information from reaching them.'

It makes me smile because I've just come from the library, where I have brazenly been browsing the shelves labelled World Religion in my search for lots of 'other information'.

"It is a cleansing of all thought and belief that will dirty our minds to Jehovah's true purpose for his servants: to spread his word to all corners of the Earth until the end comes, when we will no longer need to live in fear of being sullied by this ungodly world…" he continued. "Jesus said, 'The Truth will set you free,' free from the filth of this current system of things, with its lies and hatred. So, yes, let us be brainwashed, brothers and sisters. Let us wash our brains of worldly truth, and live the truth according to our sovereign father, Jehovah God."

It makes me smile because, since leaving, it has been the washing away of this very 'truth' that has been the sole focus of my every waking moment. I'm clambering out of the baptism pool, with my neat little teenage boobs in my black modest swimming costume, and rolling in every filthy book and viewpoint I can find on every subject on God's Earth; I'm properly getting my shoulders in, like a dog in fox shit, when it comes to other beliefs and philosophies; I am the 'washed pig returning to the mud' and I love it.

My aunt and uncle visited me a few weeks after I was discharged from hospital, after my 'little episode' (of trying to take my own life), because they hadn't realised just how deep I already was in the mirey, lovely worldy learning, and they still hoped I'd return to the Truth. They tried to persuade me to go to a meeting with them, asked me if I was praying, if I'd sought the comfort of the elders, if I'd found any consolation in the scriptures – the whole script as put together for errant Witnesses. I don't think my aunt had ever heard live f-words before, as I gave them half an hour to pack their stuff and leave my house.

A couple of days later I had an appointment with my doctor, so he could check how I was doing. He apologised for prescribing Seroxat, an anti-depressant which would later feature on the BBC's *Panorama* programme for its unfortunate side-effects of triggering (and at times worsening) self-harm and suicidal thoughts. He checked my wounds for infection, and administered a cocktail of a jab to counter for blood loss. He listened when I told him I was reading about how to stabilise my highs and lows through diet, so I could control the dreadful thoughts that seemed to accompany low blood sugar levels, and was this a thing? I told him I was having dinner with friends that weekend, because the girls were going to their dad's, and how we were going to go for a long walk as the bluebells were out, and had he seen them? I told him I'd not set foot in the Kingdom Hall, since, and how I never would, ever again. I was quite excitable about that. And I told him how I'd asked my aunt and uncle to please fuck off back to *shire because they'd tried to make me go to a meeting, and how they'd got back into their big estate car and driven home. I wondered if I'd been talking too much, or seemed a little mad, and I asked him so, and then I stopped talking and looked at him.

He'd listened to all of this, his hands folded softly on his desk. Then he leant forward and held his hand out. I took it. He looked at me, with such kindness, and with a huge smile said, "Welcome back."

This 'examined life', this love of knowledge, this debate of who and what and why we are, it's a wondrous thing. I realise it could be argued it's just a lot of conjectural hot air, because what will be will always be, and always has been, but rather that than the big silent freeze of fear.

When we were studying for our O-levels, Steve Wright in the Afternoon the backdrop to our revision as the sun warmed our backs as we sprawled on the school field, we all thought the nuclear button would be pressed by some fool or other hungry for mass destruction to be the defining moment of their political career. We read *Z for Zechariah*[50], the 1974 apocalyptic novel by Robert C. O'Brien which charts the physical and psychological challenges of Ann Burden, a young girl who believes she is the sole survivor of a nuclear war. Ann still sprinkles water on the altar in her childhood church and prays, both an instinctive and conscious thing, and she's doing okay. And then a scientist, John Loomis, protected by a radiation suit, discovers the seclusion

[50] The book is so called because Ann owned a Bible-based alphabet book – 'A' is for Adam to 'Z' is for Zechariah.

and safety of the valley she has been living in, and what unfolds is the eons-old tale of how men must behave it seems.

Heads together, we would weigh this story against the reality that this may well become a reality. Would we be as strong as Ann? we wondered. (I vowed I would keep this book with me at all times, as a guide, just in case.) This fear of nuclear war, it had us rattled. We debated the uselessness of doing our O-levels if we were going to die anyway – I was used to this one, the whole 'there's no point studying' show, the only difference for me being I'd be playing with lions and tigers in paradise not dead from nuclear war – and there was real sadness and fear in my friends' eyes. And for the first time there was a certain simpatico, and I ventured into the territory of my views on the end of the world, based on my Witness story, and they listened. They *really* listened. And they asked questions they needed to know the answers to: Did the Bible mean nuclear war, perhaps, when it talked about wars 'in one place after another'? Did I believe that God would step in and remove the evil men responsible? What did they need to do to be protected? And for the first time I saw what it might be like from the outside, looking into my world, where I had this faith that people needed. I'd never seen faith look like that before. I had been born into my world, I needed to escape it; they saw my world as a place of safety and protection, a haven in a frightening and unstable time in man's history.

We were pretty open about what we'd do if the four-minute warning sounded while we were at school: mainly snog each other. But even here there was that much-needed simpatico, a oneness, as we tried to make the snogging an ordered thing: who we would choose and why; for how long, and would we mind switching if some of us wanted to kiss the same person, or each other; should we draw up a chart, with a specific meeting place if the nuclear siren sounded, to save time. You can see why I liked these people! They weren't from the nasty estate, where breakfast was an unbranded Swiss roll eaten out of the packet on the way to school, lunch was dinner, and dinner was tea: something between two slices of Mother's Pride bread and a mug of tea-flavoured milk with Sweetex, "cos it's 'elfier un sugar". No, they were bussed in every day from villages with beautiful names, with beautiful diction and brains instead of petrol cans and spray cans.

I was allowed to go and stay with one of them once – tall Phoebe – and sat in terror eating dinner at the scrubbed refectory table surrounded by her three brothers (or was it four? there was a long line of them, anyway) and her parents as they squabbled and ate and laughed loudly, and the dogs lay close by for scraps and the cats surveyed from the windowsills. I'd never witnessed such "Pass the cheese, James," and "Chuck me the salt, Pa," and teasing and sharing of jokes at the dinner table. Our mealtimes began with a tummy ache of nerves and a prayer to Jehovah, and ended with a "Thank you for my dinner. Please may I leave the table?" and a prayer for a quick escape. This wasn't Mum's fault. Mum would have given anything for a refectory table. No. The postman's idea of a perfect family meal was a wooden spoon by his side in case we accidently put an elbow on the table or held our knife incorrectly, and an uplifting discussion from the *Yearbook*, a book with daily Bible discussions provided by the Governing Body for mealtimes to avoid conversation straying into something more interesting (and true).

Phoebe had her own room, high up in the house, with an adjoining attic room – all for me – and we listened to her tapes of recorded music, much like my own, and talked and laughed about our brothers and boys in general. Phoebe had recently become a vegetarian after she found her favourite duck – named Meatball, who she'd rescued as a chick from the village pond – in the big freezer in the barn. Her mum had decided he'd be good for a stir-fry.

I'd been grilled by the postman before going – were any boys going to be there? were Phoebe's parents going to be home the entire time? would I be listening to worldy music? – and I'd promised no to the boys, yes to the parents, no to the music.

I'd shown Mum the outfit I'd chosen to wear on Saturday: my Gloria Vanderbilt blouse and smart wool 'meeting skirt' so I'd still be the perfect model of a perfect little Witness girl. And I'd got on the school bus with Phoebe on Friday afternoon absolutely terrified but feeling giddy with the freedom. I couldn't stay Sunday too, as obviously I would never have been allowed to miss the meeting and the ministry, but I had a whole night and day away! And in between the bouts of nausea, in case I was asked anything I didn't know the answer to, I felt something: a world a million miles away from mine yet right here, so real, so different, so alive.

We got the bus into town the next day and went to see *E.T. The Extra-Terrestrial*, and Phoebe said I looked a bit like E.T. with my big eyes, but prettier obviously. (She bought me an E.T. birthday card a few weeks' later. I wish I still had that card.) We ate hot, salty chips and bought records from HMV. I bought Eddy Grant's 'Electric Avenue' on 12", with the 'Walking on Sunshine' remix, and 'Mad World' by Tears for Fears, and we played them and a whole heap of other chart singles when we got back. Phoebe played some Black Sabbath too, from her brothers' vinyl collection, which made me think about the Devil and whether he was talking to me through

Ozzy Osbourne, but I honestly didn't care. I felt happier and more accepted in those few short hours as me, whoever me was, than I'd ever, ever felt before, which is why I needed to put it in here.

Reading an article online recently, I found this meaning of the word simpatico (my italics):[51] '*It results in a feeling of security, of freedom to say what you want, knowing it will fall on understanding ears.*' Isn't that beautiful. That's what this was, our sharing of thoughts about nuclear war and kissing, and the girls around me – curly Janine and tall Phoebe, super-clever Lisa and horse-riding Becky – I loved them so much for their sharing and for their listening.

Edward Wright, the only boy who joined us on occasion, asked questions as deep on the subject of my faith as I'd ever answered. And still he needed more. I remember his blue eyes, the red sweater he was wearing, the colours of his hair, the feel of his mouth when I kissed him, him whispering *See you in September* when we walked hand in hand out of the school gates on the last day of summer term, our O-levels completed despite the fear of dying. He didn't come back in September, and I died a little searching for him up and down the sixth-form corridor and in our common room. Fifteen years later, there he was, in a suit in the doorway of my local Kingdom Hall. He introduced me to his wife and two daughters. He'd wanted to believe. He'd chosen to believe. And I was ready to leave.

"What's your name?"

"Richard."

[51] http://romantictrances.com/simpatico-and-rapport/

"Mine's Annie. How old are you?"

"I'm thirty-three."

"I am currently four. But soon I will be five. Where do you live?"

"At home."

She considers this answer. "Me too. Why are you so tall?"

Only child and fatherer of no children, Richard regards the four-year-old Annie. I know he's been asked this question many times since hitting six feet tall at twelve. He sips wine. "For the same reason you're so small."

She finds this funny, and announces she's going to the bathroom.

Richard has come for dinner and, erm, a 'sleepover'. The girls are curious about this stretched limo of a man at the table, but it is Annie who asks the questions. Grace asks only one: "Are you Mum's boyfriend?"

We've been dating for a couple of months.

"Technically, yes," he says.

I can hear Annie singing upstairs, bathroom door open, and no doubt doing the actions to 'Stop Right Now' as she sits. She gets the role of Baby Spice when Grace and her cousins put on their Spice Girls shows for the family, a role she suits to their Scary, Sporty and Posh. It's the first time Richard has come for dinner – and met the girls officially as my boyfriend – and he's doing well for someone out of his depth.

But there's an ache for their dad. It's so sad what happened with us, and I'm never far away from the guilt that our breakup was due to my breakdown. And just as the girls would ask if Daddy was coming to the meetings, back when they featured in our lives, they now ask if he is coming here, to live with us. I explain they have two houses to enjoy now, this one and Daddy's, and they can stay in each whenever they want to. They accept that, and actually agree it's fun to have two houses. But here is Richard, folded around my dining table and discussing how 'disgusting' mashed potato is according to Grace. His voice is gentle, his eyes soft, and he's a reminder of Charles in a way, without a guitar and strange thumbs. I like him.

We hear the chain flush.

"Don't forget to wash your hands," Richard calls, and I don't think either of us know where that suddenly came from.

"It's okay, I have," Annie calls back. "I washed them in the flush."

Wherever I went, in those early months after leaving, I noticed it seemed to matter not whether this person believed in Allah or Buddha or Brahma or God, or that person swore a bit or smoked a lot, or she liked to kiss her, and he chose to love him. It was all so Sodom and Gomorrah. It all seemed so free of judgment and fear, which was in equal measure liberating and terrifying.

But I was learning. A light inside was brightening. It's a first for a lot of people on the first step of a new perspective, Rhonda Byrne's *The Secret,* and I devoured the idea that our thoughts become our reality. This was big for me, as was the suggestion that a life of happiness didn't involve everything I'd been forced to believe about happiness. No wonder my life had been the thing it had! Most of my thoughts were bred of the fear instilled in childhood I would never be good enough, and the infernal, indefatigable fear of death if I wasn't in a constant state of supplication and holiness. Right here, in the moment, I could change that just by thinking it so? But wasn't the moment all about 'paradise now'? Surely I wasn't supposed to be happy now, as happy now meant a lack of faith in Jehovah's future blessings? I read one bit over and over again: '[…] transforming how we look at things can lead to the road of success and true happiness.' And this bit: 'What we think and feel sends a corresponding frequency to the universe that in turn attracts events and circumstances of the same frequency.' Well, wow.

This book doesn't always get favourable reviews, however, and I agree it's not a simple case of 'think Ferrari; Ferrari manifests'. But this is a misleading representation both of the book and the bigger picture; the thing the man who opened the smart black door on that cold, cold day laid before me like a banquet: a different way of looking at things.

And listen to this (my italics): '*A belief is only a thought you keep thinking.*'[52] This single sentence changed my life. So A = B = C could be what I wanted it to be based on what I thought about it now, not what I had been programmed to think? When I say that I set about changing what I was thinking, right then, and therefore believing about myself, about life…

Here was the chance to rewrite the relentless animal trap of a hold my old life had on me. I still thought I'd be struck by God's smiteful disapproval for even thinking such a thing, and had quite a tussle with the fear the first few times I tried it. The next time Richard and I made love, I did so without Jehovah's eyes on me, and had an orgasm with him for the first time. On the night before Grace's tenth birthday, I didn't drive myself insane imagining John the Baptist's head on a plate and instead crept into her room to install a Happy Birthday balloon and lay a trail of glittery birthday confetti all the way down the stairs to

[52] From *The Law of Attraction* by Esther and Jerry Hicks.

her present. These are ordinary things for most people, but for me they were momentous. They were a glimpse of who I could become without my old fearful thoughts.

I did get a bit evangelical for a while, and bought the book for several people, including Mum! And then I heard about a woman, or I read about her somewhere, who had read *The Secret* in the wide-eyed way we all have. She really wanted a microwave. She told her sister about the book, and how she was going to get a microwave through her thoughts. She thought about this a lot, and talked a lot about the law of attraction and using it to manifest a microwave into her life. Her sister wasn't into the whole law of attraction thing, but listened patiently. But this went on for a while, and she was getting bored with the manifesting a microwave story. One day, at the end of a particularly long monologue about the microwave, she lost her patience. "For goodness' sake," she yelled, "I'm sick of hearing about bloody laws of attraction and bloody microwaves! I'm going to buy you a microwave just to shut you up!" Her younger sister couldn't resist: "How's that for manifestation…" she said triumphantly.

I didn't need a microwave, and didn't want a Ferrari, but I did want the freedom to choose my thoughts. What would you choose?

The girls are standing either side of me at the bottom of Bedruthan Steps in Cornwall, and their dad smiles down at us from the top of the cliff. The thrashing, magnificent Atlantic has taken their breath away, and they have taken mine. I still have the photographs I took of their faraway faces, the moment they witnessed this other-worldly energy and majesty. Grace is trancelike. Annie has gone someplace too. And we three are one, our hearts beating fast.

We visit the Eden Project, and the World in Miniature, take them paddling and for pulls along the shoreline in a small yellow dingy. We build endless forts and moats and mounds in the sand, and walk across to St Michel's Mount. We eat in the Cutty Sark, where they look at the pictures of the famous tea-carrying ship with a curious amount of interest for two small girls. But it is Bedruthan they want to see again.

This feeling. It's a beyond-sensation that removes us from the chatter and clutter of all concepts and constructs. I know they sense it. I know their wide-open minds have opened wider still for the windswept moments stood there, on the edge of something they don't understand. I don't fill the moments with explanation of any kind; I just let them absorb it into themselves, where I hope it will live on.

Later though I show them on a globe where we were; the reach of that loud, frantic sea all the way to America. Ever Annie, she spins the globe and spins her body, and wants to know if that's where Big Bird lives, in Sesame Street. And Grace, my Grace. How was I to know she would one day fly so far across the globe to call the other side of the world home? And yet, thinking back, I knew she would. It was a thing formed in her soul that day at the bottom of Bedruthan Steps.

I have questions: Must we add debilitating fear of Armageddon (or hellfire, or purgatory, or whatever form our version of torture takes) to the good morals we teach our beautiful children as they learn to navigate this world? To teach a child to do a thing because it is good or kind, that ought to be enough to begin shaping a young consciousness into good decisions, shouldn't it? So why attach anything else?

Statements like, "Just you wait till your dad gets home!" or "You know Jehovah will not allow bad people to live in the paradise!" when a child has been naughty, or even very badly behaved, not only shifts the focus of learning to an external source, but brings fear to the lesson. *Fear is no basis for learning anything.* Or it shouldn't be. Because, suddenly, here is a fear of Dad or God, a fear of what Dad or God will do to you when they know you stole the last brownie, which was meant to be for your brother. Suddenly you're shaking at the thought of the shouting or the beating or the exclusion from paradise rather than just learning the simple truth: stealing the brownie that had been saved for your brother is a bit mean. If this is followed up by, "Hey, let's bake some more, but I'd like you to think about how you would feel if that had been your brownie," then reflection on actions and personal accountability for them can be learned without fear.

The Witnesses aren't the only religion guilty as not-yet-charged for filling their children's minds with the horror of death or eternal punishment if they don't live according to sermons from pulpits or *Watchtower* articles. Would you take a five-year-old to a horror movie? Would you read it something by Stephen King as a bedtime story? And yet this is what you do every single time you teach it about hellfire and purgatory and eternal damnation, and every time you read it passages from one of the most violent collections of books ever written and tell them this is what it must believe or else God will hand them over to the Devil for an eternity of pain and torture. Why not get Dante's Inferno out and read that to them too? Show them the images of twisted, writhing women and men being raped and sodomised by serpents, the sinners cowering in fear, forced to drink their own blood and pus and tears, skin ripped and punctured and burned as they are mauled and subjected to despicable, depraved torture?

Unbelievably, the Witnesses consider their version of torturous teachings and events, as rightly deserved for a life of sin or lack of faith, is far superior to this, because they don't believe in hell as depicted in some versions of the Bible and preached by men in robes who, according to them, represent the Devil himself. Because they know, categorically, they are the only true keepers of the only true truth, they have spent over a hundred years vilifying 'false religion' for their lies and gross misrepresentation of the Bible[53], raising themselves above and beyond the manmade fabrications of hellfire...and presenting death at Armageddon instead as the punishment for sin and a lack of acceptable faith in and correct worship of Jehovah. Do you honestly believe any god would end billions of good people's lives – surgeons who have devoted their lives to developing life-saving procedures[54] [55], volunteers who build shelters and feed the hungry in warzones and disaster zones, the wonderful, gentle Macmillan nurses who provide end-of-life care, the busy mum who still finds time to have a cup of tea with her elderly neighbour every week, and the sweet man who hands me freshly-laid eggs and home-grown

---

[53] And this from an organisation who have heavily doctored original Bible texts to suit their truth.

[54] Surgical procedures that the Witnesses have benefited from, I hasten to add, whilst claiming it is they who have been instrumental in the improvements in surgery, forcing surgeons to become 'better at their job' because of their refusal to have a blood transfusion.

[55] I defy anyone to watch the 'Life Before Birth' episode of *The Surgeon's Cut* on Netflix and not doubt the 'truth' that Dr Kypros Nicolaides deserves to die because he isn't a faithful witness of Jehovah.

vegetables over the garden fence – because they don't worship him correctly? I ask you, is what the Witnesses teach really any different? In many ways I would say it is worse, because of the outrageous claim that it is the 'true truth'.

Imagine if your child came home from school one day, and whilst you are preparing dinner you ask them how their day was, and they tell you this: "Well, Mummy, in RE[56] today the teacher asked us what religion we were. I said I was Church of England really, but we didn't really go to church, and we only went when my uncle got married and when grandma died. Some of the kids said they were Church of England too, and Darpan said he was a Hindu, so did Radha, and some of the other kids said they don't really have a religion. Oh, and some of them said they were Catholics. Then the teacher asked us to look around at each other, so we did, which made us laugh, cos we always get the giggles when we look at each other. Sam Taylor, you know him, he lives by the park, was half asleep, like he always is in RE, so we called his name to wake him up, which was sooo funny. It was nice looking at each other, and some of us waved and pulled faces, but when we started to get too loud the teacher told us to ssshhhh. Then she said she was going to tell us something very important, and we must all listen very carefully."

The child then goes quiet, and you turn around. "What did she tell you?" you ask. You're slightly concerned, because your bubbly child is now looking rather worried.

"Well…she said…she said that most of the children in the room were going to die and…and we shouldn't be friends with them."

---

[56] Religious Education, which Witness children have to sit out of.

You desperately try to keep a neutral look on your face as you ask, in a voice you keep level, "Why did she say that? How did you feel?"

Your child looks up at you and says, "I don't know why she said it, and it made me so, so sad. I was frightened to look at anyone, and I think it was my friend Sarah who started crying, but I didn't dare look round. She said it was because they don't believe in God the right way. I really love Sarah. I don't want her to die, Mummy. I don't know what she's done wrong." And then the child goes pale with a sudden realisation and asks one question: "Do we believe in God the right way, Mummy?"

This kind of teaching is only permitted to exist because it comes under the banner of religion, of the freedom to believe and worship as we choose. It's what I was taught, and what my mother was taught, and what Witness children are still being taught. Indeed, I began to teach my own children too.

My plea, please, is to weigh these next words where you can feel them, *really* feel them: Believe what you must as an adult, and worship your god, or not, how you choose, but when it comes to your children, *please do not fill their minds with concepts and beliefs they have absolutely no ability to process let alone separate as fantasy from reality.*

Nicholas Humphrey, emeritus professor of psychology and neuropsychologist, in his 1998 paper (and talk to Oxford Amnesty) states emphatically that children 'have every human right not to have their minds crippled by exposure to other people's bad ideas [...] no matter *who* these other people are.'[57]

---

[57] From 'What Shall We Tell the Children?' You can download the full copy of the talk or listen to it here: https://www.youtube.com/watch?v=yfr6SkaBuq0

Richard Dawkins, British ethologist, evolutionary biologist and author, although not against teaching that religion exists, calls parents' religious indoctrination of their offspring 'tantamount to child abuse'.[58]

Sam Fade (a pseudonym, as the author of the study 'How Jehovah's Witness Teachings Can Cause Brain Damage in Children'[59] still does not wish to be identified) talks about the damage caused to young developing brains, specifically the hippocampus and amygdala, when a child is constantly exposed to 'extremely fearful events' which trigger the fight or flight stress response. He says:

> 'Jehovah's Witness children are under chronic stress at all stages of their childhood. One of the key doctrines of the religion is that of Armageddon. Magazines, books, their door-to-door preaching, online content and talks from the pulpit are all focussed on the impending doom and mass genocide that is coming. Their literature is littered with pictures of this mass genocide.'

He adds:

> 'The sad thing about this is that most parents raising children in this organisation do not realise the damage they are doing to the development of their children.'

In 2014, the appeal to criminalise the religious indoctrination of children was dropped, to the great relief of The Christian

---

[58] From *The God Delusion*, p.406.

[59] https://freedomofmind.com/how-jehovahs-witness-teachings-can-damage-brain-development-in-children/

Institute…[60] Please read the whole article. Note the language of those in defence of indoctrinating children. I don't think you will like it. Or maybe you will.

There are parents who are unaware of the damage they are causing when they insist their children live in a constant state of expectation and fear of Armageddon, or that they will be tortured in hell if they commit any one of a hundred-hundred sins. Are you one of them?

And there are parents in great pain because of what they felt they had no choice but to teach, because of the damage inflicted by their own indoctrination as children and the fear it created in them. Are you one of them?

And then there are the children of those parents, those who managed to leave but are perhaps still angry that they were taught what they were taught. Are you one of them?

And there are children, teenagers, young adults, still trapped in an organisation which, as Sam Fade puts it, 'doesn't allow them to freely express themselves without fear of repercussion,' and 'keeps them trapped in the organization.' Are you one of them?

You *have* to be honest when answering these questions.

After a long and heartfelt exchange with my mother, she urged me to consider whether I am starting a war about belief itself, and whether I wish to cause more hurt where there is already too much by pitching child against parent. I do not wish to do either.

I wish only for parents to consciously consider their commitment to teaching and endorsing truths that cannot be proved, truths that can cause immense and often irreparable damage, and what the long-term consequences of that are, not

60 https://www.christian.org.uk/news/richard-dawkins-children-need-protection-from-religion/

only for the most precious people in their lives – their children – but for themselves too.

I wish for the basic human right of the *freedom to be able to question and doubt,* without being shut down, dismissed, expelled and put into enforced exile by family and friends who still choose to believe. I also wish for the basic human right to be able to say your piece as a child hurt by your parents' beliefs, and then make your peace with them, with the wrongful truths and the impossibility of it all back then, and the possibility of apology and forgiveness now that an honest dialogue has opened between the two of you.

I wish for the end of infant and child baptism, of the systematic coercion of young children to follow without question what they are being force fed to believe or else they will die, and for them to have the freedom to explore their own thoughts and ideas without fear.

I wish for there to be, by law, an automatic process by which a child is permitted to choose to live when they are sick and need a blood transfusion, and for vital psychiatric counselling to be provided free of charge, for as long as they need it, for children terrified of their parents' (and Jehovah's) disapproval. I wish for the parents to understand *it is murder* to allow your child to die because of some trumped-up truth written by men in suits in Bethel – and, like most Witness truths, a severely manipulated version of original scripture[61] – and to respect that your child has a right to choose life. *That is freewill. And freewill is what every child on Earth has a basic human right to.*

We may feel we have no choice but to share only what we know, but this isn't true. We *all* have the choice to go out there

---

[61] The real truth about the sanctity and use of blood can be found here: https://www.youtube.com/watch?v=U94nUZD05zo

and discover what we don't know. To bring that home is a blessing. It is everything. It's the difference between more of the same and great change. Sam Fade puts it beautifully:

> 'As the amazing Maya Angelou, American poet and civil rights activist, said, "Do the best you can until you know better. Then, when you know better, do better."'

I urge you to read the full version of Nicholas Humphrey's talk, 'What Shall We Tell the Children?', or listen to it on YouTube. Following on from his emphatic point that children have a human right not to be 'crippled by exposure to other people's bad ideas', I have his permission to quote further:

> 'Parents, correspondingly, have no god-given licence to enculturate their children in whatever ways they personally choose: no right to limit the horizons of their children's knowledge, to bring them up in an atmosphere of dogma and superstition, or to insist they follow the straight and narrow paths of their own faith […] We as a society have a duty to protect them from it. So we should no more allow parents to teach their children to believe, for example, in the literal truth of the Bible, or that the planets rule their lives, than we should allow parents to knock their children's teeth out or lock them in a dungeon.'

He adds:

> 'If children have a right to be protected from false ideas, they have too a right to be succoured by the truth. And we as a society have a duty to provide it.'

In September 1990 the original Convention on the Rights of the Child became the Declaration of the Rights of the Child, consisting of 54 articles that address the basic human rights all children are entitled to:

> '...the right to survival; development to the fullest; protection from harmful influences, abuse and exploitation; and full participation in family, cultural and social life.'

The four core principles of the convention are:

> '...non-discrimination; devotion to the best interests of the child; the right to life, survival, and development; and respect for the views of the child.'[62]

Children's views are neither acknowledged nor respected within the constraints of indoctrination; and within the more extreme cults, like the Witnesses, they are actively discouraged, severely impairing their emotional and intellectual development and thus disabling their ability to analyse and think critically. Children growing up in the Jehovah's Witnesses are taught from birth that 'critical thinking can cost them their life'.[63] They are taught that Mummy and Daddy, who love them dearly and will protect them from harm, are also allowed to let them die so as not to go against Jehovah's will. Amongst the fearful images of Armageddon, and believing my school friends were going to die, and I was going to be tortured when the Great Tribulation came, and the embarrassment that God was peering at my

[62] https://en.wikipedia.org/wiki/Save_the_Children

[63] https://freedomofmind.com/how-jehovahs-witness-teachings-can-damage-brain-development-in-children/

body, this truth would make me cry in the night as I imagined getting sick and Mum letting me die, and her walking away and leaving me in a hospital bed on my own. I knew she loved me, but *how could she do that to me? How could she not want to save me?* This is what Witness children are taught from birth, and it *has to stop.*

So, no, this is not war, this is an appeal to be a *better* parent than one who thinks they're doing right by their child (and their god) by teaching them about Armageddon (or hellfire) and blood transfusions; it is an appeal to let children grow in mind as well as body, unafraid of the dire repercussions of developing their own personal views; it is an appeal to be *better* than we have ever been before in protecting children from abuse, *specifically the mental abuse of religious indoctrination*, because as far as I can see there is *nothing* in place to protect children from this.

One day when I was out on the ministry I was invited in by a woman with whom I'd had a really interesting conversation – interestingly about all sorts of things – and I asked her why there was a pile of potato peelings and an empty milk bottle on top of the television. As she made us some tea she explained she had three children, one of whom had stuck a piece of chewing gum to the TV. Rather than sit them down, interrogate them, bite her tongue whilst they blamed each other, and then most likely lose her rag when they started fibbing, she simply started putting food rubbish next to the gum – a sweet wrapper at first, then a couple of teabags, then the potato peelings and the dirty milk bottle. That morning, before they'd left for school, the eldest asked her why she was putting so much rubbish on top of the TV instead of in the bin.

"Oh, I found some gum on there," she said, "and I just assumed it was the new bin."

"But it stinks, Mummy, and it looks gross!" the middle child moaned. The little one just stood watching the exchange.

"Then I think whoever put that gum there should move the rubbish to the bin, where it belongs," she concluded, and off they went to school.

I didn't see her for a couple of weeks, but when I returned I asked her what had happened. I was dying to know. From the kitchen she'd heard a quiet debate between the three children when they'd come home from school about what they were going to do about the rubbish. There was a bit of blaming, and one even growled, "Don't make *me* touch the rubbish when you know it was you." She never revealed which child was the culprit, for which I really admired her, but the rubbish was removed and life continued.

There was no shouting, no punishment needed, no fear of getting a telling off (or worse) from Dad or dying at Armageddon or being burned in hell, just a simple lesson learnt by all three children.

I recalled this when faced with two pairs of 'innocent' eyes years later in the shape of Grace and Annie, and missing biscuits and broken jewellery and toothpaste all over the bathroom mirror and felt tip drawings on duvet covers…

Sometimes I despair at human existence, and humans. All the strutting and fretting and game-playing; all the loving and needing and craving. It's made me a terrible girlfriend and a worse wife at times. Why love someone if that love is the thing that might break you? Why can't we love from a distance, where love doesn't cry out because of the sheer hurt of it being so here and so immediate?

I've watched many women marry many men. I've married three of my own. I'm not sure I really loved any of them completely. I loved parts of them: Charles's laugh and his kindness; the piano-man's piano hands and his love for our daughters; Richard's humour and patience. I only fully loved a man once. The man mentioned earlier in this book; the man who couldn't love me back. He was the only one who stepped up as the resounding sounding board for the strange tune of my old Witness life; the only one who held a mirror up to the darkest parts of who I was. I trusted him, and I dared to look. What I saw was hard, and I told him things. But he took those things and lined them up as ammunition when he felt I wasn't good enough. Just like God.

His god had been his despicable mother, who he loved and feared and worshipped and dismissed and excused in a five-decades-long battle with her despicableness. I saw them both. I saw her strutting and fretting and game-playing. I saw his loving and needing and craving. I saw two people who should never have been mother and son. Just what was the universe thinking when it put those two together? What was it thinking when it put the two of us together? A girl who needed to love and a boy who couldn't? And yet, for a time, we were each other's guru of sorts; plunging into deep debates, alive with the immersion and the immergence of innumerable variations of human truth. We would eat in a twenty-minute interlude of something on Netflix, and then plunge again. Our sex was intense, and beautiful, tuned in as we were to the deepest workings of each other's hearts and souls. There was no way it could have been anything else. And yet how he seemed to loathe me.

And now there is the usual ache because I'll always love him (I don't know why)...from where I've not I retreated from love. I'm not sure I'll ever be able to come out again now.

Curly Janine and tall Phoebe, super-clever Lisa and horseriding Becky, I often wonder where they are now. I wonder if they think about the days on the top floor of our ugly school, where we debated nuclear annihilation and cried over boys and permed our hair into vast things. I wonder if they remember Mr Winston, our other very large specimen of a biology teacher, chuffing on his pipe whilst pointing out the construction of a penis; or Miss Sanders, our English and drama teacher, performing her coked-up Lady Macbeth from page or on stage; and what about poor Mr Chesham, our form tutor for four years – apparently, he chose to tutor our class all those years in a row – who we would tease and declare our love for. He saw us go from flat-chested to breasted, and was always discreet and obliging about the need for extra loo trips when our periods arrived; and he never shouted, not once, no matter how hormonal or tearful or unpredictable we were. This kind, ordinary man... we were so lucky to have him.

When I think of the elders, modelling their attitudes towards women and their self-aggrandising opinions of themselves on a book thousands of years old, it is with a sinking heart and a deep sense of helplessness. And the postman, the very horrid model of a very pious Christian, wielding his status as God-appointed head of our family like the thing we were supposed to respect without question... Nothing will ever change while that book is still permitted to be the dictate.

There is a beautiful scene in the 2017 film *I Origins*, where character Ian Gray's mindset is challenged by a woman who knows his only way of finding what he seeks is to change the way he 'sees' it. Ian is a molecular biologist steeped in science, who believes that each generation builds on the theories and concepts of the previous, thus honing and growing these theories to stronger, better proven versions of themselves as understanding increases. There is no denying the logic of that. Yet her challenge to him is to challenge himself: What if, during the development of theory and research, evidence suggests that a previous understanding is not actually the case at all; that everything scientists set out to prove is, in fact, the opposite? Would he change his thinking? She cites the example of Gandhi, who was asked the same question about his religious beliefs – and whether or not the story is strictly true matters not, as the principle is the point being made. Gandhi is quoted to have said that he would change his way of thinking, his beliefs, 'should the evidence be compelling enough'.

Ian considers this. His life work to date has been to prove the evolution of basic light-sensitive cells by genetically modifying a sightless organism to see. He wants to do this for a deep-rooted reason: to disprove the one thing creationists use to prove the existence of God: the human eye. His pursuit has taken him from a dark, broken part of his mind, to a remote farm in a southern state of America, to India, where he is in profound personal debate with exactly the type of evidence this woman is discussing. I won't tell you what happens, but here is the point: Ian comes face to face with a new way of looking at the world; he is forced to examine his old beliefs, beliefs which inexorably shift to a new perspective when he quite literally looks the evidence in the eye.

When will the world do the same with an outdated book, written by men, that is still permitted to be the dictate for how countless millions behave?

For men to take the Bible as a literal thing, to use it to shape (and misshape) everything from the way women are treated, to medical interventions, to foreplay, to just who is worthy of God's love is a crime against the face of God himself. If there is a god at all, this is God in the wrong hands. And for the women on the receiving end of men who insist it is their God-granted right to control and bully us, is it any wonder we raise and raise some more the bar of what we simply will not tolerate?[64] Please, we do not need your harsh words and your rules about what we wear and what we are permitted to question. We are sickened by your ability (and willingness) to abuse us and rape us. Surely you must know these are terrible, unforgivable things to do?

We need you to listen to us, embrace our enquiries, join us in the debate, and love us. Just love us. If you do this you will come face to face with a woman not bowed down, not voiceless, but, eyes shining, awake in her mind and body and spirit. I think you would like her; I think you would be proud of and aroused by her; I think you would take her by the hand and stand by her powerful womanness.

Or would you be afraid of her? Are you?

If you're not with the vital, thriving, warm woman you so wish to come home to every night, then perhaps you might look at why. Why isn't she thriving? Why don't her eyes light up when she sees you? If you were just to lay your Bible (and/or your ego) down for a moment, or forever, and your insistence on her

[64] A most profound book on the subject is Carmen bin Laden's (Osama bin Laden's sister-in-law) *Inside the Kingdom*.

submission and obedience, you'd see why: a woman in submission is not a fully self-expressed, living, breathing embodiment of her potential. She may be wife and mother, and she may be daughter and sister, but she is dying. Her spirit is dormant under layers and years of your tirades and tyranny; her life force has been compromised to such an extent that, like an automaton, she performs without inspiration or feeling. Do you think a woman rendered thus is going to long for your touch? Will she plump pillows and chop onions and pour wine in anticipation of your return? Or will she plump pillows and chop onions and pour wine as part of an endless list of her requirements, her eye on the clock, counting the hours until she can brush her teeth and comb her hair and close her eyes in sleep?

If you'd like your woman to cherish you, worship her. If you'd like your woman to come alive in your company, worship her. You can worship God too, but look at the woman he created for you…*really* look at her. She is wondrous and kind; she is nurturer and protector of your children; she is stronger than you could ever imagine, yet as gentle as her hand on your cheek. She wants to love you, but you have silenced her with your sermons on how she must be, your need to manipulate and control and berate and downgrade her. Set her free.

You don't have to be witty or wise, or handsome or a big earner, you just have to love her from the heart and not from the pages of a Bible or some other rule book or podcast or blog of what you think she should be. If you do, you will be surprised. She may dip in and out of her deeper self, go quiet sometimes and be verbose at others; she may be tearful or tired, or funny and silly, and sometimes make no sense at all. But she will be her. And how you will love her.

He is standing in the doorway of my cottage holding my neighbour's cat (who arrives at 7am and leaves at 10pm), the man I have been getting to know – dating? I don't know – and I mention how ancient the cat seems, like a wise prince or respected noble from faraway times with his angular features and bottomless eyes. "Hmm, I'd say he's only about six," this man says, and my exhale comes slowly.

Later, in between talk of this and that, I use the word reincarnation, deliberately. Am I testing him? I know I am. But I need to know if he can engage on more than this and that, because... Yet for the first time in such a very long time I feel like a warm regular woman in this man's company. He laughs with me, holds my gaze, and I feel playful, and so relaxed.

Maybe it's okay that he lives on the surface. Maybe he doesn't need to know I'm never really here, on Earth, yet try so hard to be; that I look at the images of Earth through a filter where I admire the beauty, and feel it so deeply I weep, but from somewhere else. Maybe it's time for me to try a life in the shallows of life.

I try to stay there, I really do, just like I tried to be a really good Jehovah's Witness, but I still want to know what he thinks about more than this and that. I guess there's a part of me missing that part of...what I had before...but longing to feel connection without fear – and I am so not in fear with this man, who laughs and gazes, so I fearlessly go where I shouldn't, trying to find something that isn't there. But realising what I'm doing, I stop. I don't want to see the look on his face; a mixture of *What the hell is she talking about*? and discomfort at not being able to offer a viewpoint other than a silent *Can we talk about something else*? But now here I am, not really in his room of wild camping in his van, and the ability of Gogglebox to provide an opinion at work on the week's telly, yet liking him so very much.

We went out to dinner, to celebrate the success of six shorts scripts I had written. He told me I was amazing…and called time on our time getting to know each other.

I live an almost abstract cross between wanting to connect and failing. Of thinking I can operate as a human on many levels and failing. I am not happy about this. Isn't this what the sages and gurus are always talking about? The beautiful oneness of connection without separation? Isn't this what I've been trying to achieve this whole time since leaving the confines of the Witnesses? So why do I still feel *so* separate?

All I wanted, I think, with the man who came and went, was to feel safe and fearless. I don't know what he wanted, really, from me. He talked about not being able to talk to his last girlfriend, because she wasn't really into thinking about much at all. But I think I frightened him away, because of thinking too much, and I heard he went back to her. The easiest thing to do in the world, to stay with what we know, to take the path of least resistance.[65] I don't blame him.

After he had gone I analysed what had happened over dinner, and how I'd sensed him retreating as soon as he realised I was not quite the perfect girlfriend he may have hoped I could be. But I don't want to live in fear of the wrath of a god or a man if I am not perfect. I want to examine and rant. I want to be playful and fearless. I want to live my life alive. No spirit soared nor new path was forged through staying with what we know.

---

[65] 'If you limit your choice only to what seems possible or reasonable, you disconnect yourself from what you truly want, and all that is left is compromise […] the human spirit will not invest itself in compromise.' Robert Fritz, from *The Path of Least Resistance.*

But I'm a little down at the moment, if I'm honest.

I'd like to share the lyrics of another Kingdom Song with you. It's song number 168 from *Sing Praises to Jehovah*, based on Psalms 2:12 of the New World Translation. The music is vibrant, stirring.

1. See yonder through the breadth of Earth
The sight my heart entrances
Jehovah's band of warriors
In unity advances.
Their helmets, bright against the sky,
Bid ignorance and error fly.
They shout aloud their battle cry:
"Christ reigns! O Earth, receive him."
(Chorus)

2. The King, Christ Jesus, leads the way;
His leadership they follow.
He speaks the word, and they obey
And thus expect no sorrow.
They wield their sword, the Word of God.
Their feet are with the good news shod.
They walk the way their Master trod.
Clear to the death they follow.
(Chorus)

3. For, see, the time has come at last
For Christ to reign in power.

Soon all his foes shall lick the dust;
Before him they must cower.
His God, Jehovah, bares his arm.
His trumpet sounds a loud alarm.
Be wise, you rulers, do no harm;
You judges, own Christ's power.
(CHORUS)

4. Kiss the Son, lest God be angry
And you perish in the way.
Happy are all they that put
Their trust in him today!

Yes, indeed. The power of indoctrination through music. I will talk about Jesus a little more later on but, for now, those of us who were fed 'righteous anger' as God's excuse for making all his foes 'lick the dust' and 'cower' for not worshiping his son correctly might well ask just how this married with Jesus the healer and preacher of 'peace amongst men'. And it's interesting that most other translations of the Bible read 'Kiss the Son, lest *He* be angry (my italic)…' It's just one of countless examples where the original phrasing of scripture has been tweaked by the Witnesses.

But my point is, whether it is God or he – Jesus Christ himself – who might get angry at not being kissed is utterly irrelevant if you look at the actual point being made: unless you kiss Jesus Christ you're going to incur his wrath and be slaughtered when he comes again, this time to rule directly over planet Earth. These songs, written by the Governing Body and sung loudly at the beginning, middle and end of each meeting, were rousing religious anthems, and they had us heartily by the heart as we imagined marching side by side as Jehovah's 'band of warriors', to the death if required. We truly believed that if we put our trust in him we would be happy, to the death if required.

Is this any different from political anthems or war anthems, designed to incite and unite?

And what are these wondrous Kingdom Songs inciting? The victorious genocide of eight billion souls who don't believe in Jehovah. Eight *billion*. And who are they uniting? The eight-ish million Jehovah's Witnesses who will be rejoicing their deaths.

It wasn't until I left the Witnesses that I saw our incredible world of people doing incredible things through eyes able to cry for the sheer beauty of it all. Of course there were those whose sole purpose appeared to be to put down and hurt and deceive, but there were all these others, teaching and helping and serving and guiding each other; embracing and accepting and empowering and loving each other. Most of all, they seemed to be enjoying life.

A woman I worked with had so much gold from Benidorm hanging around her neck that it quite often got caught in her perma-tanned cleavage. She swore like a trooper, and gurgled when she laughed, and thought God was a big old bit of make-believe. She did not have a bone of judgement in her body. My chain-smoking know-it-all boss gave his caravan to a homeless guy. I had friends who had gay friends who had atheist friends who had Catholic friends who all hung out and discussed and laughed and cared for each other. These people made me ashamed; they made me look at myself; they humbled me.

And yet I was still frightened of them, and steered clear. Why? Because I'd been programmed to believe they were bad, even though I didn't believe that anymore. I'm not sure I knew what they might do to me with their jewellery and caravans and chats. They were only ever lovely to me.

I admit there was a part of me that thought I was better than them, because I was a deep sea diver of life, not content to lay on a squeaky inflatable on the surface, cackling and rattling my gold and relating Jeremy Kyle episodes. How can a kid who shags two of his mate's mums, and his best mate's sister, and then his best mate's girlfriend, and gets two of them pregnant and can't work out exactly what he's done wrong to end up being beaten up by his best mate possibly be good telly? I was incredulous when Grace and Annie admitted they sometimes watched this top-drawer tripe. And to my incredulous *Why*? they simply said, "It makes us feel happy we have our lives."

That put me slam-dunk back on the horrible estate.

My brother and I are sharpening a couple of Mum's six- foot garden canes with knives from the grown-ups' drawer in the kitchen. We're ducked down on the low wall behind the shed. He has decided that the kids on the other side of the bollards at the bottom of our street – where we're not permitted to cross – need attacking. I'm all for this, in a way.

"So, when are we going to do this?" I ask.

"After school tomorrow. We'll hide the spears in the bushes by the school gates. When the bell goes, I'll wait for you, cos you take ages to come out. I always have to wait so I don't get into trouble for walking home on my own. What are you doing?"

"Putting my coat on and making sure I've got everything. You're always forgetting stuff, that's why you get into trouble."

"Not then."

"When?"

"Now."

"Oh. I'm thinking."

"About what?"

"If it's a good idea to do this." I test the point with my finger.

"Yes, it is, dummy. Those boys deserve it. They stink. They suck."

We sharpen in silence. It's not easy. The knife keeps getting stuck in the bamboo and I'm not really enjoying myself. I know if we get caught then the postman will most likely be told, because I've worked out that's what parents do – share the bad stuff about their children so they can discipline them as a team.

"Why do *I* have to help?" I ask.

"Cos you're my sister."

The next day we meet by the school gates and wait for the buses from the secondary school to pass by, and for most of the other kids to pass us too. My brother is lively, for him, and he's talking a lot, but I'm not really listening. I want this done so we can go home and pretend it didn't. Will Mum notice the two canes missing from her green beans?

"You ready?" he says.

There are three boys, one fat, two skinny, standing on the other side of the road by their bollards. We're standing on our side, leaning on ours.

"Whad'yow want? Why yow 'ere over there? Wot yow got them sticks for?" one of the skinny ones asks.

"Cos we hate you," my brother says, nudging me.

"Yes," I say.

"We ain't scared o' yow," the fat one says.

"You should be cos your fat guts are gonna spill everywhere when I stab them," my brother says, looking at me looking at him.

"That yer sister?" the fat one asks.

"Yeah."

"She can't fight."

"She can."

"Show uz."

"I don't want to fight them," I say, although there's a big bit of me that wants to poke my pointed stick into this fat kid's bulging horrible stomach, and a tiny bit of me that doesn't. I know he calls my brother 'weirdo' and 'Jovah' and I don't like that.

"Wot? Wot did her say?" the fat one asks.

"Why?" my brother asks. "We planned this and everything."

"What if *he* finds out?"

He looks up at me. What is worse? Being called schoolboy names by stupid boys, or the postman with his white face, crueller names and thrashing hand? He knows, and so do I. We turn away, to Brummie taunts, and walk back up the street to home. We're pretty late.

"Hurry up," I urge.

"I'm tired!" my brother moans.

So am I. So very tired.

Mum frowns when she opens the door, but I can hear my sister crying: we're saved.

My life now. This quiet, ordered thing with no estate outside the door and no kids and sticks and taunts. And my life then. A life lived second house from the end in a multi-coloured concrete row, where smokers' coughs and chip pan fires and arguments filtered through the hot air heating systems. Maybe I should look at that and feel happy I survived my life amongst the future Jeremy Kyle guests, with a mum who loved us and baked cakes and told us good things about ourselves. I do. But there's a part of me that wants to take a pointed stick and jab it hard into the life I hated, the people and the sounds and the smells I hated, and make them bleed their blood for hating me too. What had I done to be so reviled? But then what had they done? They were just living, just differently. Just as I was in their eyes.

And so I pick out one of the lesser gaudy gold chains and pay it a compliment, and I am told the story of it being a thirtieth anniversary present from her late husband, who she misses every single day; I chat to the *Big Issue* guy outside Waitrose and buy a copy, which is full of articles I never imagined would be in there; I join in on a discussion Gay Frank and Holy Mass Emma are having about same sex marriage.

I have so much to learn, to understand.

There will always be discussions of God, of gods, of energy and higher or darker spirits. Maybe angels walk the earth, and maybe the Devil stalks them. Perhaps we are a mirage, a simulation of our mind's eye; or perhaps we are made of dust, or stardust, because, like an ancient star, we are no longer really here, just another light shining in the pitch-black silent universe, viewed from afar by other worlds. Yes, there will always be discussions.

Is there any truth in any of it? What do you think? Is it all down to perception alone and there is no one, single truth?

I am a child
I am all the things of my past
I am the half of my mother
I am the face of my father
Staring into space
I am all that I see

Girls arguing about nothing
Boys playing football
Thin and healthy
TV ads of programs I won't watch
And probably never will
Never.

Last week (and from twenty years ago) this showed up in a box of school books and diaries in an attic in Grace's father's house. Grace Facetimed me immediately and we sat looking at each other, her face and mine. This child of mine who was visiting from New Zealand, the home so loved by her and she so loved by me, was eight years old when she wrote this poem. We read that line again: 'I am all that I see.'

"Is this the only truth?" Grace whispered from under the eaves. "That we are only what we see and nothing more, nothing less?"

We consider this. That would make truth a moveable multi-faceted feast, an ever-evolving thing that can drown us or lift us, trap us in or save us from our frame-by-frame reference of what life is.

A flower. A daisy in the grass, for instance. What do you see? For some, that little white and yellow flower is a pretty thing, a thing to make daisy chains from. Some marvel at its tenacity, or its bright, small face that opens and closes for day and night. Others see a flower that bees seek, and healers use in medicine, or a flower that formed part of Celtic, Norse and even Roman legend. Others see it as the weed that blemishes their perfect lawn, and dig it out or spray it with weed killer. Which is the truth?

A child on a swing will feel the air in her hair or the chafing of the rope in her hands; a man in traffic will go over his presentation or sound his horn; the woman told she cannot achieve a thing will see opportunity or acceptance of failure.

Religion, or belief, is the ultimate debate of truth versus truth. There are those who imagine resurrection, and others eternal silence. There are those who teach redemption and those who preach condemnation. A robed man will raise one hand to heaven, and point the other to hell. There are some who will not step on a gnat, and others who will slaughter a lamb. One man will insist on taking your money for your sins; another will tell you you've already paid the price. Still others will speak of rebirth of the soul through many lifetimes, or that we do not have a soul at all.

The Witness truth – of being part of the privileged few million marked personally by Jehovah for salvation; of a life safe within his organisation while the world roils around in its false religions; of the hope of eternal, perfect life in paradise free of illness and fear – has people so in awe at the outset they wonder how they lived without it. I've seen newcomers so alive with it that their faces are like those created by artists for the covers of the *Watchtower*; all enraptured with gratitude and gazing up to heaven, the abode of their saviour Jehovah God. It has them studying and handing out leaflets and answering up – to much praise from their study conductor, who receives much praise from fellow brothers and sisters who would also love to bring someone into the Truth. They'll take part in interviews on platforms in Kingdom Halls and assembly halls, where rapturous applause will follow the story of how they went from a life of emptiness and disillusionment to one of faith and fulfilment as one of Jehovah's servants. I've been there; I've felt that power. It's intoxicating. I've turned to the person next to me and said Wow! when I've heard the struggle the person went through to become a Witness, the sacrifices they made, the friends and family they left behind, the career they gave up to pioneer… "This is the truth, no doubt," they say, and away they are carried on waves of it.

But consider this from Krishnamurti, the Indian philosopher, speaker and writer:

> 'Truth, being limitless, unconditioned, unapproachable by any path whatsoever, cannot be organized; nor should any organization be formed to lead or to coerce people along any particular path. If you first understand that, then you will see how impossible it is to organize a belief.'

Could this mean that there is no one truth? that to claim to have the truth is misleading at best, and a blatant lie at worst?

When I think of the Governing Body clinging like limpets to the rock of their real estate in New York, where great truths are miraculously being revealed to them by God himself – truths about beards on the men and trousers on the women; truths about sex; truths about the world ending now, or ending soon, or definitely ending sometime; truths that allow the death of a sick person who could otherwise be saved – I wonder just how much longer it will be before someone takes a screwdriver and prises them off, exposing the fleshy, slimy insides of their lies. But when they are questioned, they cling harder, huddle closer. They turn deaf ears or rise up to judge, constructing convoluted arguments for arguments that no one dare argue with.

I saw my mother weeping because of the ears that were not listening when the postman had his affair; I heard the case constructed in his favour because he was an elder in the congregation by elders guilty as hell of their own infidelities. I read countless articles in countless *Watchtower* magazines urging faith, because 'we know not the day nor the hour' of Armageddon's arrival, and the ludicrous instructions from the Governing Body (my underline):

> 'At that time, the life-saving direction that we receive from Jehovah's organization may not appear practical from a human standpoint [...] All of us must be ready to obey any instructions we receive, whether these appear sound from a strategic or human standpoint or not. Now is the time for any who may be putting their trust in secular education, material things, or human institutions to adjust their thinking. The elders must stand ready to help any who may now be wavering in their faith...'[66]

If I may quote Krishnamurti a second time: 'Faith was the excuse you used if you didn't have a good argument.' I'd say: Faith is the alibi you use *when you do not possess an ounce of proof or validity for your argument*. There is no one truth to claim to know; there is no one path, no organisation nor organising; there is no one belief with which to lead or coerce. How could there be when we are a shifting, dancing, moving thing, gifted with multiple senses and a brain able to debate and decipher and decide and change its mind, and all the while learning and unlearning and learning again.

[66] From a *Watchtower* article Nov 15, 2013, and quoted in https://freedomofmind.com/how-jehovahs-witness-teachings-can-damage-brain-development-in-children/

I am all that I see.

Truth is what we see in any given moment, wholly determined upon our completely unique perspective, and therefore can never be the true truth.

But it is also the thoughts we have had so many times we claim them as truth.

What do you see?

If we choose to believe the world is a dangerous place, and are suspicious of it and the people who inhabit it, we will only see danger and feel the heart-crush of that constant state of suspicion. We will look for evidence that confirms our belief it is a dangerous place, to prove to ourselves we are right, and it will please us when find that evidence. But it will also constrict and restrict us.

Listen to someone who is convinced the world is out to get them, or that everyone they meet is waiting to screw them over. Listen to the language they use, the tone of their voice. How do you feel after any length of time spent in their company?

It's difficult, I know, when we have been hurt or betrayed, when trust has been abused and even broken. It's doubly difficult to separate that hurt or betrayal from our general world view and stop it from colouring the way we see everything and everyone.

Politicians lie, and the media manipulates and divides, and religion presents as truth that which is far from, but, generally speaking, people are good and want good. If we choose to see them that way, everything changes.

The Witness obsession with a prowling Devil looking to trip them up is not healthy, (and is also used to justify all manner of horrendous acts, which we won't discuss here). I vividly recall the despair of those who would declare, "Satan's really having a go today. He's really out to get me. He made me hit that wheelie bin when I reversed the car so I'd nearly miss the meeting..." Two things here: needing evidence of a Satanic force to shore up the 'truth' that he's out there trying to get them (because that's how the mind works; constantly looking for proof that what we believe is right), and needing validation of their super-strong faith by having thwarted his attempts and making it to the meeting. This is all very odd, and a highly twisted way of seeing the world. It is also a case for the universal law of like attracts like. In other words, if you firmly believe the Devil exists and is out to get you through a series of unfortunate events, you might just be attracting those events. But whether you believe in a devil or not, and that it is he or just your 'bad luck' engineering your life, is this really a productive, positive way to live?

A thing that shifts about uncomfortably in my consciousness at times is that of Bible prophecy. Is it coincidence that Earth is being ravaged by floods and earthquakes and pestilences and fire, as per the ancient prophets' prophesies? Was this bound to happen? or has it become a self-fulfilling prophecy, borne of innumerable minds over millennia spent focussing on these end-of-the-world notions penned thousands of years ago? And why were they written anyway? Would we have been okay without the Bible's doom and gloom? Did we actually *need* Jesus Christ?

It is my feeling, and has been for a while, that Jesus Christ was probably some sort of sage, or more spiritually minded man than the men of his time, but not the literal son of God, and certainly not mankind's saviour and only route to God.

It is also my feeling that, aside from the more inclusive of his messages, he appeared to divide not unite, although this might not have been his objective.

No other spiritual leader has left in his wake such utter worldwide division, devastation and hatred. But from the moment Jesus (according to the Gospels) started referring to humans as sheep or goats, Jews or Gentiles, worthy of salvation or annihilation on judgement day, and talking about 'loving your enemies', there was an immediate separation: *Who is a goat and who is a sheep? Who decides? And who is my enemy, so that I might decide to love him or continue to hate him?* If there wasn't a huge human divide already in existence at this time, there's a chance that statements like these would have created an instant, exaggerated notion of you over there and me over here, and therefore 'enemy', coupled with a curious sanctimonious smugness that loving him put you above him, made you better than him, because he was still grovelling around in his heathen hating of *his* enemy – you. Perhaps it was all in the phrasing. Had Jesus used the word 'humankind' rather than enemy, and avoided the sheep and goats parable altogether, we might be having a different discussion…

And for whole centuries of time we've had the Second Coming to cogitate on; that Jesus will come again and put right what man has created: a massive, violent (or passively violent) pious divide of human beings into clans and countries that will torture and slaughter anyone considered a religious enemy, or not 'one of them'. And how does he propose to do this? By annihilating all those *he* deems enemies (despite the admonition to love them) because they don't worship him and his father how they've decided they want to be worshiped; in short, because they're not 'one of them'. But he will permit a faithful few, his 'sheep', to inhabit paradise Earth as perfect human beings for all eternity – the very sheep who have preached and judged and coerced and made miserable in his name – and an even fewer few to sit by his side in the kingdom of heaven.

I don't need to remind you that many, many religions and cults have a version of this very same event; that they each await their interpretation of what their 'righteous' wars and persecution will reap in terms of salvation, and how rewards for their righteousness in the face of adversity – adversity they've created in his name – will manifest in terms of eternal blessings, amen.

When we consider other spiritual teachings through time, like those of the Buddha or, more recently, the philosopher and speaker Alan Watts, or Eckhart Tolle – and many of their teachings acknowledge the existence of Jesus and quote him[67] – do we see worldwide hatred instigated in their name? Do we read in their teachings, amongst the beautiful truths about love and acceptance, that we will only benefit from the teachings (or the teacher) if we shun all those who don't believe them, consider them worthy of death, and place ourselves very much as separate from them for being privy to such superior knowledge? The Buddha did not teach Buddhism, or place himself in a position of mediator to understanding what it was to be a Buddhist, as there was no such thing (until the label was created by those wishing to identify with his teachings and become 'a Buddhist'). He taught those who listened the

---

67 'Sutras are powerful pointers to the truth in the form of aphorisms or short sayings, with little conceptual elaboration [...] The sayings and parables of Jesus, too, when taken out of their narrative context, could be regarded as sutras, as well as the profound teachings contained in the *Tao Te Ching*, the ancient Chinese book of wisdom.' From *Stillness Speaks* by Eckhart Tolle.

Dhamma, the truth that the cessation of suffering comes about through an understanding of the human condition, and a *letting go of all opinion and judgement.* It was the teachings, not the teacher, he said we should focus on to achieve the state of nirvana, the bliss state of truly being, where suffering and separation cannot exist. There is no mention of sheep or goats or enemies or righteous warfare in the sutras.

So why have so many placed their eggs solely in Christ's basket of loaves and fishes? in a man who preached love in one breath and utter division in the next? As suggested, if Jesus had used the word humankind it is my belief that the notion of enemy would not have become, certainly in the Christian sense, what it has – and Alan Watts has much to say on the concept of enemy and the resultant separation. When I prayed as a child 'through Jesus's name, amen', it emphasised every single time I prayed that I was not good enough to speak to God directly, and made me feel separate from God, and, in my limited understanding, I did not understand what I had done wrong. But then I was told repeatedly I was a sinner, because that's what it said in the Bible, and must constantly ask Jehovah for forgiveness, so I must have done something wrong…?

The Bible is not a reliable, unbiased guide for life. It glorifies and glamorises 'righteous' war – or war fought to defend your faith and separateness. It honours sacrificing your life for a righteous reason – or defending your faith and separateness. It approves persecution as proof of righteousness – or standing firm in your faith. And all through there are elaborate, emotive stories of trumpets blowing and walls tumbling, or sneaking into camps whilst men are sleeping and annihilating each one 'without mercy', in faith's name, and men being thrown into prisons or lions' dens or being beheaded, in faith's name. In the

Witnesses' translation of the Bible, this violence is carried out in Jehovah's name specifically; in most other translations, in the name of God generally.

But then there are the snippets of wisdom, written so long ago and far beyond basic human consciousness or knowledge at the time, that are staggering. Statements about Earth 'hanging on nothing' (Job 26:7), when it was commonly believed until a relatively short time ago that planet Earth was flat. There are instructions about quarantining the sick (Leviticus 13:1-13), and digging a hole and burying excrement 'outside the camp' (Deuteronomy 23:13) to keep the camp clean, not slinging it out of the bedroom window into the street below. And what about the irrefutable logic to some of the proverbs: 'When pride comes, then comes disgrace, but with the humble is wisdom' (Proverbs 11:2 ESV), and 'Wine is a mocker, strong drink is a brawler, and whoever is led astray by it is not wise' (Proverbs 20:1 ESV).

So, yes, there is an uncomfortable ache as I watch Australia burn (at the time of writing), and the rains come and come, and earthquakes break Earth open. Is planet Earth fighting back after years of abuse, like a woman bullied who knows she must rise against her oppressor to survive? Or is it prophecy, self-fulfilling or really from another ancient source who was perhaps attempting to warn us? Either way or both, it feels we might be entering a huge transition of how things work, or don't work, on Earth. So the Witness tribe beat their Armageddon-coming drum, just as the Catholics call their masses to Mass and the Hindus bless a million gods. We need to believe, it seems. But when will we see each other aside from our beliefs? When will we believe in each other instead of innumerable interpretations of seeing? When will we lay down our sword, drop the cursed notion of 'enemy' and become humankind, united as the whole?[68]

If we were just to see that there is no such thing as a Buddhist or a Christian or a Hindu, that these are merely labels we give ourselves to set ourselves apart, and see that the Bible contains occasional wise advice for living, but is generally a harbinger of both personal and world-scale crisis, maybe we could begin to shift our thinking away from the doom and towards what each of us can do for each other…the power of positive collective thought. There are those who believe this is possible. There are those who know it is possible.

No amount of coming or going and coming again is ever going to solve the mass separation of humankind whilst mindsets such as you over there and me over here are the dictate for life. And whilst human consciousness operates on such a base and violent level, we will continue to judge and hurt each other in ceaseless, futile efforts to prove our separateness and our rightness. The word 'mindset' says it all really, because it is only in the mind where these opinions and beliefs and concepts about each other are set. It is where they are formed and accepted as real. But they are not real. They're just a bundle of insecurities and unanswered questions that distort our view of each other. In short, it is all in the mind. Eckhart put it like this in *Stillness Speaks*:

> 'Prejudice of any kind implies that you are identified with the thinking mind. It means you don't see the

[68] 'If you collect 100 black ants and 100 fire ants and put them in a glass jar, nothing will happen. But if you take the jar, shake it violently and leave it on the table, the ants will start killing each other. Red believes that black is the enemy, while black believes that red is the enemy, when the real enemy is the person who shook the jar.' – **David Attenborough**.

> other human being anymore, but only your concept of that human being. To reduce the aliveness of another human being to a concept is already a form of violence.'

Relate this to the wide-held belief of salvation for just the righteous few. Is this what Jesus was doing when he separated us, sheep from goats, blessed from cursed, worthy of his protection or worthy of death based on his personal concept of humanity? If not Jesus specifically, as there's a strong possibility he isn't represented accurately in the Bible, much like God, then certainly the Bible's teachings as a whole. Perhaps he really was a deeply spiritual man, a loving healer and great empathiser, and was killed simply because he was unwilling to follow the dogmatic Pharisaic rules of the time, and the men who invented Christianity reinvented Jesus, son of God, to suit. There is plenty out there on this.

Maybe I shouldn't give Jesus such a hard time, but certainly we need to be careful when relying on a book written by men, and a rigid belief system which preaches this book, and one solitary man, as the only solution to all the world's unpleasantness when it itself is riddled with unpleasantness, as are they.

If such a colossal collective mindset can create such separation, could we not set our minds to better things? Could we try to live without concept and come alive in that, and in each other?

"Honestly, you're like a stuck record," I say, knowing I sound just like Mum.

My brother looks at me like he might like to kill me, except he's too small and I'm too far away. He's wearing red shorts and a stripy red and blue T-shirt that is too short, his chubby legs all brown. I'm sat cross-legged on top of the coal bunker that joins onto next-door's coal bunker, where the boy who lives there sits sometimes, the heat from the west-facing tiles under our bums and the rich smell of the coal a reminder of fires in the grates. I don't know his name, but he taught me to whistle last week, something I felt quite proud of, not realising of course how utterly tuneless whistling is to anyone but yourself.

"I want to go!" he insists, in his annoying little brother way.

"Go in the house!"

"It's too far!"

"Wet your pants, then. See if I care."

I know I'm being mean, but he is SO annoying. But then I look at his little face, all puckered with needing to pee. To be honest, I don't think he'll make it all the way up the stairs to the bathroom in time. I uncross my legs, and slowly start to stand up.

"Hurry up!" he screeches.

"You're such a baby!" I jump down and yank him by the arm, right to the end of the long garden where the tufty grass is unmown. "Go here."

He's already peeing, and I'm laughing now at his little winky showering all that yellow. "*Pull down your pants and smother all the ants in an English country garden…*" I sing, and he's giggling with relief.

"What d'ya do when ya wanna do a plop–" he adds.

"It's 'go the loo' not 'plop'."

"Shuddup."

"You shut up."

He tucks his winky in and turns to face me, his face all scrunched up and cross. "I'm telling Mum on you, you're so bossy!"

"We're not supposed to sing that song anyway, so what are you going to tell her!"

"Shut ya face!"

"Ants in your pants! Ants in your pants!"

"You've got ants, so shuddup!" he screeches.

"You're such a cry baby!"

"I'm not!"

"Cry baby! Cry baby!"

"Not! Not!"

"Stop crying, then!"

I don't see the old chair leg coming. My nose instantly starts bleeding and now in a duet of crying we each try to justify our position with Mum, who sends me to our bedroom and my brother to hers. This isn't fair. I like her room more. So I sulk hugely, my protruding bottom lip a demonstration of my feelings.

"You'll trip on that one day," Mum says when it's still there half an hour later, when she calls us down for dinner.

I don't know why, but this always makes me laugh.

On another hot summer afternoon, I'm exploring the end of the garden, and climb to the top of a mound to survey the backs of all the houses, noting the dirty windows on that one, the fancy-cut bushes further along, and the line of baby clothes even further along than that. All these lives. Side by side. Garden walls between us. I reach down and scratch my leg. The boy next-door waves from his open bedroom window, and I'm instantly self-conscious and start biting on my ponytail, which I've pulled round to the side, and straightening my skirt. My front bottom starts itching, but I can't scratch it with him watching. He says something, but I can't hear him. I jump down off the mound, which is a colossal ant hill, and I am covered to the front bottom in ants.

Ants in your pants. Ants in your pants.

Nearly five decades later I think about this discussing karma with Grace, and I smile about it now, remembering.

Hannah and I often laugh about our stray atomness. Here we are, surrounded by people. Yet there we are, unable to join them. This separateness, borne of being told since childhood we were set apart, makes it difficult to make friends, easier to break friends, because of not feeling comfortable with what should be the natural enjoyment of the connection.

I would watch, and so would she, from the sidelines of the skipping and clapping games, even the bickering and falling out days, and wonder why it all seemed so simple out there. Jane would slap Anne for choosing Sue instead of her as a best friend, and Anne would cry, and so would Jane, and Sue would look piggy-in-the-middle awkward; but soon they'd be all out of fighting and crying and be giggling again. But we couldn't do this; we were too closed off and quick to retreat to a corner, where we could wish ourselves unnoticed and tell ourselves it was better that way, because we had better friends, friends who loved Jehovah (or Jesus) and who knew cleverer things than Double Dutch or Miss Polly had a Dolly.

Hannah owned the deli next to my old-fashioned sweet shop in a quadrangle of converted Victorian barns. We were at home in a moment in the subliminal acknowledgment of each other; immediately conjoined by the feeling of residing on the self-inflicted sidelines from the ladies who owned the other shops. We were so irreverent. Hannah made me get on all fours one afternoon and put a green tablecloth over me, where she piled dozens of boxes of eggs. We constructed a bed made of bubble wrap on another day, stapled ourselves in and drank gin until it was time to cash up. We assumed naughty poses on the staircase on charity night, and sang loudly in the bandstand. The Janes and the Annes and the Sues, they were not happy; but we were, together in our separateness.

It takes commitment to become a chameleon, to get into character to run businesses and attend staff meetings. But we did it, with silent glances of *We can do this* when we wanted to retreat to the corner.

This place, Satan's world, now our world, and we had no idea how to deal with the paradox of wanting to belong, thinking we were far too good to belong, and being frightened to belong.

Jesus Christ, do you see what you did with us all, setting a group of people apart by telling them they were better than, could do better without, and would be blessed for their separateness? You set in motion a divide, whether you were aware of it or not, that clings even when we realise we are not in any way special at all, and that actually we're better together as sheep and goats, just muddling along.

You spoke of your father's abhorrence of idols, symbols of faith carved from wood or stone, these being the crux of the spiritually weak nations, echoing the first and second of the Ten Commandments: 'You shall not have other gods before me' and 'You shall not make yourself a carved image, or any likeness of anything that is in heaven above, or that is in the earth beneath, or that is in the water under the earth. You shall not bow down to them or serve them, for I the Lord your God are only worthy of worship.' *Yet is not the demand that we bow down only to you making yourself an idol?*

Harmless carvings of wood are merely outward expressions of faith that can one day be a Hindu god or a Buddha and the next be fuel for the fire. If you are so mighty, why do you feel so threatened by them? Are they really a challenge to your great omnipotence with their many arms or their blissed-out smiles?

What lives on when the fire burns low are the inward, manmade constructs of faith, of God, built from opinion and created to manipulate and control the weak, which are by far more sinister and dangerous.

This clinging to opinion, to commandments, is a desperation to make sense out of not knowing the answers, which terrifies humans. But not knowing is bliss; it's the smile on a baby's (or Buddha's) face; it's seeing the complicated, complex tangle of ideas we've all created because we don't understand how we got here, or whether it even matters, and saying *it doesn't matter.* Men have made it matter because they don't have anything else. Not clinging to a faith, even if it's a mile-high stockpile of unforgivable lies, is far scarier than letting go and learning to swim without it.

When Hannah and I learnt to let go, not afraid of the drowning, not afraid of how deep we might sink or how far we might have to swim, we lost all resistance to our separateness. If you fight the literal water when you're learning to swim, you will sink; if you relax, surrender to its ability to hold you, you will float, you will become one with the water. You don't know how it holds you, and you don't mind not knowing, because the simple truth is, it is. That is bliss. That is the faith that will sustain you.[69]

[69] The masterful Alan Watts on the subject of faith: https://youtu.be/sfS6jZgjMBI

Sundays were always difficult after leaving the Witnesses. The structure of the day – the morning meeting; the afternoon ministry – was shot to bits, and there was only so much of *The Sunday Times* I could read. It was very often the day when the darkest moods would have me either crying or yelling or both at the life I'd had. I wanted my childhood back. I wanted my mind clear of the script that mocked who I had become without the Truth. *You should be at the meeting, you know. Reading the Sunday papers is not going to save your life at Armageddon.*

I'd more often than not cook a roast, marvelling in the normality of that. I'd walk the dogs and help the girls with their homework. I'd go out of my way to de-structure our day to the extent that it was a baggy thing without elastic to hold it up; a thing that often fell about my ankles when the floundering about got too much. I could become a monster then.

Christmas was worse. The first year we 'did' Christmas I walked a tightrope of jolliness and lunacy, decorating the first tree we'd ever had but wanting to set fire to it. One of the dogs cocked his leg and peed on it, and the pagan presents. The fire I lit in the same room to make it look like a magazine Christmas filled the house with smoke and then went out because the chimney had been capped. I ripped my tights on a splinter in the old chair on the landing, and the cat crapped on the bed, and I knew Jehovah was punishing me for the tree and the presents and the Christmas crackers hidden in the pantry for later.

I started thinking about post-apocalyptic paradise Earth, with some kind of rage. The men in Bethel, they hadn't thought it through. There are eight billion people on the planet. That's a lot of corpses. How many bodies could one crow eat in a week? And what about the trauma of seeing billions of fellow humans slain and laying about? Would Jehovah disable the part of the brain that found such sights horrific, or would the rampant self-satisfaction at having survived make it all rather jolly? And when the inevitable rotting occurred because the crows couldn't keep up with 'the great supper of God', the stench would be unbearable, and the diseases uncontrollable.

And what about when the frozen food started rotting in the supermarkets because the power stations were down – or would Jehovah miraculously keep them open and running? but by whom? none of the Witnesses were qualified? Who would work in the mobile communications facilities, or man BT? What about the sewage plants?

As my friend Daniella had stated so very long ago, we wouldn't become perfect overnight, so we would still get sick – particularly with all the bodies of the wicked dead lying around – but there would be no one qualified to diagnose and treat these sick people, as all the brothers were window cleaners or van drivers or factory workers.

And without power or communication, how would the Governing Body get the 'food at the proper time' from Jehovah onto computers, to printing presses, get the *Watchtower* and *Awake!* shipped or flown? I'd only known one brother who could fly a plane – the one who was repeatedly battered by his balmy (also rather fabulous) wife – but he was barely able to park his car straight in the Kingdom Hall car park. I also knew a brother who worked for P&O ferries, but he was a manager of some kind and I doubt he could navigate a cruise liner across the Atlantic to get the magazines from the USA to the UK. And what articles would appear in *Awake!*, if at all? How to Bury Our Billions of Dead Neighbours; How to Remove a Rotten Tooth Without Anaesthetic; How to Deliver a Baby/Fly a Plane/Run a Power Station…

And what about the promised resurrection of the millions of dead who would get their second chance to learn Jehovah's will if they hadn't heard about it the first time around? Where would they all live and how would they be fed? What if they rebelled and made life hell in the lovely new paradise, with the billions of corpses, no electricity and communication, and no food? The *Watchtower* often showed images of gravestones tumbling as brothers and sisters welcomed their lost husbands and wives – were they still married, since death had them parted? – and parents and children, all beautifully dressed and running towards the reader with wide smiles and open arms. I thought about my nan and grandpa, who had loved us all so much. I imagined them searching for Mum and me, and my brother and sister, asking "Have you seen them? Do you know where they are?" and my aunt saying, "I'm afraid they all died at Armageddon. They just couldn't stay faithful to Jehovah," and I saw their faces pale with grief.

And then there was a really ludicrous thought: *Animals like lions and tigers are not exactly human-friendly, so when would the tumbling around by waterfalls with lion cubs have occurred?*

The rage became feral when I heard the voices of elders declaring, "Jehovah will reveal all in due time"; "It's not ours to know the details"; "We must have faith, brothers and sisters, and not concern ourselves with the minutiae of Jehovah's will."

Richard was always so good at talking me down from the edge, but I was nuclear, ballistic. He poured me a glass of wine, lit the fire (in the front room), and listened whilst I paced in my ripped tights. But then he got it too. How could he *ever* understand? How could anybody *ever* understand what it felt like to actually believe this *bullshit*? To have to learn to live without it? To not know what to do on a Sunday morning because all I'd ever known was inside the walls of a Kingdom Hall? To think I was being punished by Jehovah because I'd bought a Christmas tree and a box of crackers?

When the tears came he covered me with a blanket and let me cry it out. I wept for my childhood. For the little girl who wanted a daddy who loved her, who wanted to live in paradise, who was frightened all the time of dying, who wanted her own bedroom again; for all the fear and lost innocence when she should have been skipping with her little friends without imagining them with their eyes pecked out. I cried for Charles, like I always did, aching with the regret of hurting him. I sobbed for my cousins, who I missed so much, and with rage for my aunt who fed me utter bilge about my mother, offered me her love and support, and then shunned me the moment I didn't buy in anymore, to her or the Truth[70], and at the lowest possible moment of my entire life. Who in God's name, no matter what they believe is the truth, does that to someone they claim to love, someone so obviously in deep, deep distress! The Truth. Even the audacity to name it such! To name a whole book on this utter, utter rubbish *The Truth Book!*[71]

When I finally slept I dreamt I was standing on the platform of my childhood Kingdom Hall. I began quietly, asking the audience if they ever had moments of doubt about what they were being told; if they ever heard the whisper that said *All is not*

---

[70] I heard my aunt mellowed in her latter years, enough to allow her sister back into her life, which was lovely for Mum who had never uttered a single word against her sister despite disagreeing with her deeply hurtful shunning of us all. She even mellowed sufficiently to ask about the nieces and nephew she had cut out of her life, and my girls, who she had loved and made so welcome in their home. She never contacted any of us directly though, not once.

[71] Full title: *The Truth That Leads to Eternal Life* published in 1968 by The Watch Tower Bible and Tract Society.

what it seems. It grew into a monumental display, railing at their inability to see – *really see* – that they were being hoodwinked, lied to, conned out of a fulfilling, happy life now to keep the fabrication of paradise-ever-after alive… *What is wrong with you all?* I implored, as elders moved towards me. *Are you blind?* They took hold of me. *Open your eyes!* I was dragged, punching and kicking, from the hall.

The girls were flushed and full of ackee and saltfish when they returned, and saw a mother in a new pair of tights, with her eye liner on, relaxing by the fire with a book. We pulled the crackers and played with the dogs, and their eyes shining with our first Christmas was the soft closing of a door somehow and the opening of another.

I happened upon a *Watchtower* cover the other day on Facebook, all the regular lions and tigers and children in *Sound of Music* frocks frolicking in a paradise backdrop. I thought about all the children still being taught this as the absolute truth, and how they too might know, somewhere deep inside, that it isn't real, and I nearly posted something utterly defamatory.

When we were young we were often asked to draw pictures of paradise, and how neatly I would shape the trees and flowers and fluffy clouds, colouring in with colours as bright as a summer's day. I wonder what happened to them all? I know what happened when the voice whispered from the depths of where I knew it wasn't quite as I had been forced to believe. It ached at first, like tummy ache when you've eaten too much cake. It then became the all-consuming thump of a broken heart, the sense of betrayal beyond anything I thought I could ever learn to survive.

I remember Grace asking me one day if I would be happy if she was gay. She must have been about six or seven years old. Annie was holding conference in her own tongue with a row of coloured-in baby dolls and Barbies. I looked at them both, Grace with her father's long hands and love of music, Annie with her socks on back to front and her white tutu over her lilac sweater, and my love for them sent the usual rush to my head and heart. What I should have said…about Jehovah not allowing gay people into paradise…wouldn't come.

"Of course I would," I said. "I would absolutely be happy if you were happy," I added, knowing I believed that and absolutely not what the A = B = C voice screamed at me: gay = not acceptable to Jehovah = death. "And if you realised you were gay and weren't happy, we could talk about it, okay?"

Many times I was asked, as part of my work with the Human Library[72], what the catalyst was for leaving the Witnesses. There were so, so many things.

The Human Library is a worldwide platform for open discussion on things prone to misunderstanding, prejudice, judgement, and even hatred, where the 'books' are courageous humans willing to share the story of who they are, or were, with 'readers' open to listening. The Human Library's motto, 'Un-judge someone', is the worldwide call to enquiry and understanding, and is creating a colossal shift in how people choose to 'see' each other.

I was invited to speak as an ex-Jehovah's Witness, an invite which I accepted despite the nagging, gnawing fear of talking about this, of mentioning *his* name out loud in an 'ex' kind of way, of curses and inevitable death if I did. The first

[72]www.humanlibrary.org/

event I went to was a gay, lesbian, bi pride weekend, and I couldn't stop shaking. My hands were shaking. My legs were shaking. My voice was shaking. I knew he could hear me – Jehovah. I knew he was watching me answer questions about Christmas and birthdays and blood transfusions, and why I once believed Jehovah knew best when it came to all of these and more. I was surrounded by men in makeup and heels, and women hugging and holding hands, and girls who looked like boys and boys dressed like girls, and boys and girls for whom gender was merely a label and who had fully embraced their androgyny. It was a boiling hot day, and they were all smiling and chatting and being them, and I was utterly in awe of the staggering beauty of it all…yet rather glad I wasn't one of them, if I'm honest. How must it be to try and live in the midst of the sly glancers and the overt starers and the abject ridiculers?

That day I spoke to a teacher who had Witness children in her class, a CEO who worked with Witnesses, people who had Witnesses in their families, or had members of their families convert, and none of them – *none of them* – knew what on earth was going on, or how to navigate around these mostly friendly, always polite, but rather odd individuals who seemed glued to a script that made no sense to anyone but themselves. They spoke with such conviction, they told me, even the children, and would not be swayed, citing book, chapter and verse at every opportunity to prove their point. What they needed to know from me was why. Could I explain? Could I help them understand?

How do you explain the crux, the prop, the everything that defines life as a Witness in just twenty minutes? The words either tumbled out, or struggled to come at all. And then always, "So what made you leave?"

How could I explain about the crows, about the postman who married my mother and taunted and bullied our family, about beautiful Poldark, about the elder who wrote me poetry and kissed me, about the baby I lost and thinking Jehovah must be punishing me for something, about a man on a doorstep asking me "What do *you* think?", about porn on a computer and an elder's wife telling me to leave because my depression was affecting the congregation, and a six-year-old asking if I would be happy if she was gay in just twenty minutes?

"I had this feeling, since childhood, that something wasn't quite right, but I didn't have the maturity to understand what it was. I just knew I was at odds with what I was being told to believe. But we were not permitted to voice our doubts[73], to ask questions. I had no idea who I was aside from being a Witness, but didn't dare question anything. I was told that doubt was a sign of a lack of faith, and I would be punished for that."

"But you wanted to ask those questions?"

"A million times."

"What would have happened if you had?"

"I would have been accused of allowing Satan to fill my mind with doubt, of a lack of faith in Jehovah's organisation, and Jehovah God himself, and of apostasy."

---

[73] 'If, in early childhood, certain fundamental views and doctrines are paraded with unusual solemnity, and an air of the greatest earnestness never before visible in anything else; if, at the same time, the possibility of a doubt about them be completely passed over, or touched upon only to indicate that doubt is the first step to eternal perdition, the resulting impression will be so deep that, as a rule, that is, in almost every case, doubt about them will be almost as impossible as doubt about one's own existence.' Arthur Schopenhauer, from *Religion, a Dialogue, Etc.*

“Apostasy?”

“Of bringing shame on Jehovah’s name by disagreeing with the Organisation – the men he’d supposedly appointed to be his voice on Earth.”

“And what would have happened then?”

“I would have been marked as bad association, been shunned by my friends and the congregation, and then been disfellowshipped, resulting in death at Armageddon if I didn’t repent and ask for forgiveness. And I would have suffered the second death, from which there is no resurrection into the New System – the new earth talked about in the Bible book of Revelation. I think I’ve got that right, about the second death…I…”

“What…wait…what? What’s the second death, and disfellowshipped – is that being excommunicated? – and the New System? Or new earth? What’s that? And what about Armageddon? Why would you be shunned for asking questions? Surely if you had doubts you could have just left? And who is Jehovah? Is that just the Witness god?”

So much to explain. And I’m using language only Witnesses are familiar with. And suddenly I remember the whole story about the thousand-year reign of Christ over Earth, and the second chance people would get to learn about Jehovah and obey him if they’d died before Armageddon without knowledge of him, but how, if they still didn’t believe, they would be killed – the second death, the final death, the same death as apostates – at the end of the thousand years.

You see, in order for the New System to work it would have to be made up entirely of perfect worshippers of Jehovah, no one else, with no Satan and his demons disguising themselves as truth to mislead us. We were told Satan and his demons would be bound and silenced for that thousand-year period, but that they would be let loose for a short time at the end, to test our faith one last time, and then be destroyed forever. I remember thinking this all sounded a bit far-fetched, and cruel, seeing as we'd stayed faithful in the old system, and in the new, but still might be killed, but being told 'we mustn't rely on our own reasoning', so believed it anyway, and my mind is rambling, galloping, and…

I did the best I could, but I'm not sure the people I spoke to were any the wiser. I encouraged them all to watch Dan's film, *Apostasy*. I said it would explain a little better what it's like on the inside of a Kingdom Hall looking out, and from the outside looking in. I said it might help them find answers to What the hell goes on in there? and Why can't you just leave? And I leave the event a little bit busted up for all the talking about it all.

But as the road curves this way and that on the drive home, and the feel of the tarmac moves into my hands on the wheel and the wheels turn, I can see the faces. The earnest teacher wanting to know how she can help her young Witness students feel part of her class; the CEO eager to make his employee feel part of his team; the friends whose friend had recently married a Witness and no longer hung out with them; the androgynous pair, full of self-conscious teenage twitches and a genuine need to know why their Witness friend's mum had banned them from their house. And I realise that perhaps I can serve as some kind of conduit between the world within the Kingdom Halls' walls, and the world outside; help one to understand the other. And then the realisation: the only people seeking to understand were those outside; those inside will never, ever try to understand those on the outside, their fellowman. They will never sit opposite a beautiful polyamorous redhead and ask about her lovers and her life; they will never reach out and take the hand of a young girl who desperately wants to be a young boy because her body just doesn't feel right as a girl; they will never hear all the funny, tragic, wonderful stories these people have to tell. They won't because they're afraid. They won't because, unlike the brave, humbling, inspiring people who organise and attend these events, they do not want to. And if they do listen, even for a short time, it will only be with a view to telling them that Jehovah's way of life – their way of life – is better.

And once more I cried with the lesson I'd learnt, because I may not be a six-foot-six man in an M&S sundress, or a young girl disgusted by her breasts and her periods, or want to live a life of many simultaneous lovers, but I have felt that pain of separateness, of being teased and even openly mocked because of being different. I knew then that perhaps I could allow my Witness world to open just enough to let people see what it's like in there, so they could understand, and develop a sort of empathy. Would that help? But then another realisation: it wouldn't make one iota of difference, because the Witnesses would not even meet that empathy halfway; they would not step out of their self-constructed cage of rules to greet their fellowman on their fellowman's terms. I was wasting my time. All these amazing people seeking to understand each other, to embrace each other's differences in the name of welcoming diversity, and they wouldn't stand a chance against the stonewall of Witness resistance that would keep them at arm's length.

All I can say, just at this moment, is thank goodness the Witnesses are a minority. Perhaps we can live without them. They seem quite happy to live without us.

"So what about all your other husbands, apart from Dad?" Grace asks me, for some reason.

All my other husbands? I've only had two!

"I've only had two!"

"Who?"

"Charles and Richard."

"They sound like kings," Annie chips in from wherever she's been dreaming.

"You sound like a king," Grace says.

"They are kings! Tell her they're kings, Mummy!"

"I know they're kings, Annie-fer, *thank you*." Grace rolls her eyes.

"Well, they're not queens, are they? Queens are called Mary and Elizabeth and Victoria."

"You're called Victoria."

"You smell of horse poo."

"You are a poo."

Are all sibling conversations like this?

"I'm going to make a cup of tea while you two sort your kings and queens and smells out," I say.

"Who's Charles?" Grace calls as I leave them head to head as an eleven and seven-year-old can only be. Bill Dog charges past me down the long hall, Meow-Meow, the cat, in his wake.

Who is Charles now? I wonder, and wonder too how much is too much to tell a curious daughter. After we split, he met and married a sister who looked so like me that, from a distance, apparently, people assumed we had got back together. Funny how I can still hear his voice, the Brummie-ness that I used to tease him about, especially when he went for a bAth not a barth, or weeded the pAth not the parth.

That life feels like another incarnation in this incarnation, and how can it be that every literal cell in my body has been replaced since then, yet I feel and hear it in every cell now as the kettle boils and my daughters debate the proper names for kings and queens and different types of poo? I can feel Charles kissing me (we kissed a lot when we were courting) and my brother, fed up with the kissing, pretending to hang himself with his scarf from a tree in Glen Nevis; I can see the three of us up mountains in all sorts of insane weather, and I'm laughing (now) at the white-out that nearly thwarted us on Tryfan; and I can hear the guitars and harmonies…always that.

It's different with the girls' father. There's a sense of immediacy to our relationship, because it is. All the toings and froings of their weekends with him, and him outside this house in his car and me outside his in mine, and us always checking in about them, with them, to check they're okay.

He was glad I left 'that religion'. I was glad too. But there was a sadness too, even shame, as I knew I could have been a better wife without it. All the times he would vent his frustration at my lack of ambition; and all the times I would plead with him to understand I'd had it programmed out of me, that I didn't know how to plan a future that didn't involve lions and tigers and paradise. God, if I hadn't had that, what we could have been. All the times I would watch him writing music and think *What's the point?* instead of joining in, of putting lyrics to his chords, of encouraging him. And all the times he would talk to me about his plans to move there, or study this, or build that, and I would think *What's the point?* instead of considering how we could make that happen, so we could grow. And all because I'd been told it was futile. I look at you now and I am beside myself with pride for what you have achieved, and how you have inspired our girls…the soft-spoken young man with ten Jamaican dollars in his pocket, to the soft-hearted man with a wealth of world experience and a wealth you deserve every penny of.

The swing in the garden moves childless in time with the wind, its shadow shortening and lengthening and shortening. I'm not sure how I cope with my love of the two girls who climb on it, and argue over it, and put the dogs on it, and I return to the room where Annie has resumed dreaming and Grace needs an answer about Charles.

The thing about being a bit Satan seems to have caught on, with Annie often dropping her Satanic urges into conversations – wanting to bash people who cut her up on roundabouts, wishing she could tell the woman who starts every sentence with 'So I' at work to go do one – over Chinese food and episodes of *Sex Education*. And then I meet a Satanist at a Human Library event and I'm obviously in fear of him, but also fidgety with the questions I want to ask him.

I watch as he fields the usual jibes about sacrificing a goat before getting on the train to be here today with an effortless grace; but then I realise these people teasing him, they all know him, and I feel once more like I'm looking in from where they'll see me looking in, not sure what to do with me. Even as I'm typing this, I wonder when/if it'll ever end, this outside-of-the-inner-circleness. I'm tired of feeling it; tired of thinking it. He seems to sense it, and soon we are in easy, gentle conversation, and he is funny and quiet, which calms me. And then others arrive and the conversation launches into all manner of things and it's okay. But I can't help thinking I still have the biggest defences up, like great sandbag constructs, where I hide and watch the tide, knowing it's safer than playing on their shores. So why do I come out and play, only to run up the beach when I'm invited to join in? The noise of all the laughing is deafening, and I'm going back inside now. But how I am inspired and humbled by these people, with their unbridled sharing of stories and insecurities. I love them. All the gory, glorious pain of their lives splurged about, safe and without shame. Beauty is this; this openness.

I'm seventeen, maybe eighteen, and sitting cross-legged on my bed, my back to the door. I'm aware of the door opening, but don't turn around to see who it is as I'm engrossed in what I'm doing.

"What are you doing in here? Have you studied your *Watchtower* for Sunday? I told you to study it two days' ago!" It's the postman. Who never knocks. I roll my eyes.

"Have you studied your *Watchtower*? Turn around when I'm talking to you!"

I suppose I should answer him. "I–"

I am pitched forward, and my neck cracks as my chin juts up and I have no idea what just happened. I try to turn around but my head has locked, my hands feel numb and I feel sick.

"I asked you a question!" he roars, and how I fucking fucking hate him.

I manage to get onto all fours and turn to face him. I wave the *Watchtower* at him I have been studying, and there he his, his face clenched with rage, a Bible in his hand, one of the large reference Bibles we use. And somewhere behind the blurring and the sickness I realise he has hit me on the back of the neck with it.

I rise up, wild now, and he starts to step away from me. I lunge for him, but he is out of the room in a moment, fast. But I am fast too, and as he crosses the hall into the dining room I am right behind him, and beyond the anger and the odd, deep pain in the back of my neck and the scream-howl that erupts from my mouth is the heavy mahogany dining chair hurled the length of the room and into his cowering body.

When Mum appears at the top of the stairs she wants to know what on earth is going on, as anyone would. I can't speak. I'm shaking and my head doesn't feel right.

Why do I bother speaking to this man? Why did he hit me when I was doing what I was supposed to be doing? I want to maim him, silence his vile mouth and slash his nasty face. I actually don't care if I've killed him. But then he appears behind the dining table and I honestly think I might either collapse or smash him to a pulp. I collapse.

Later I tell Charles what happened, and we kiss ferociously in his car, which we're not supposed to be sitting in on our own, unchaperoned. But he starts talking about taking a break from each other, just for a while, and I wonder what I've done wrong, and I'm frantic, begging him to stay. I'm on the verge of panic. Why does Charles want to break up? I can't think straight, but I'm trawling through the last few months thinking about when I was moody because I had PMT, and when I moaned about his Mum always leaving the milk on the side in the kitchen in the sun so it stank, and my neck still hurts, and I'm pretty sure I must have done something wrong and ask him to tell me, please, so I can stop doing it. And Charles sighs and puts his arms around me.

Charles. His kindness was never far away, and I still sense it now. He was the first person to welcome me back to the congregation when I was reinstated. Despite all that I'd done… my demented behaviour when I'd lost our baby, me going to Greece, and then marrying out of the Truth and having another man's baby, not our little Brummie baby…he still came up to me as I stood shyly in a corner of the Kingdom Hall, with Grace in my arms, and smiled that sweet smile and welcomed me back. He even peeped at Grace's sleeping face and said, "She's beautiful. You must be so happy."

And in those long seconds before someone else came over to congratulate me, I felt the grace of him, and I loved him.

> 'Thoreau, like Descartes in *Meditations*, begins his argument by accounting for how he has come to believe that questions need to be addressed…and his method is predicated on the belief that it is philosophically worthwhile to clarify the basis of your own perplexity and unrest…'[74]

My brother went to a Witness fancy dress party as a fried egg. I went as a Sun (the newspaper) reader. This shocked a few people. I wore white plastic high heels and a really short denim skirt. My Kate Bush hair was yanked into a facelift

[74] Reid (2012, pg. 46) on Thoreau, www.plato.stanford.edu/

ponytail, and I wore blue eye liner, blue eye shadow and blue mascara. I enjoyed being in character all night, minus the bad language and Marlboro Lights – although I had purchased a fake fag from a joke shop, which shocked a few more people – and found it rather emptying of anxiety to pretend to thrive on a diet of satellite TV and toast and brown sauce. Gone the clarification of perplexity and unrest; enter the bliss of vacuousness and a kind of peace. I'd grown up around these sorts of people, on the stinky estate, and they seemed pretty content to me, when they weren't setting fire to their chip pans and fighting outside the chippie.

I still observe sometimes, when put right before me on a train, for instance, the four- to five-mile debate of whether to buy the purple or the pink, cos you have the pink, babe, so should I get the purple, or do you mind me having the pink too, cos we don't need to wear them at the same time, do we, or we could, if we wanted, cos that might be fun, to both go out in the pink, so what do you think, babe, shall I get the purple or the pink? And I want to swap seats when we stop at Town X and try it for size until we stop at Town Y, but why? Because I've been drowning in the deep, rocking with the da-dum da-dum of the carriage but unable to sleep or rest in the motion, my mind hopping, and I'm exhausted. Why does it seem so much more fun over there? Not even fun as such, just lighter and dancier. Yet here, always, is the need for the diving, the finding out. And when I arrive at my meeting, at the fabulous Royal Horseguards Hotel, and we are suddenly alive in *Jonathan Livingstone Seagull*[75] and our will to learn to fly, I am flying high, my soul alight and my eyes wide with the

[75] One of the most beautiful books on experience ever penned.

questions firing in my mind that just a short while ago wanted to decide about the purple or the pink. Can I be both? Can I have both?

I nearly dislocated my shoulder once ranting at the universe, pointing my finger at it in outrage that I didn't understand, begging for a signpost. But look at this life, this mountain top and dark ravine. It's all a signpost. It's all the same thing: experience, or life, happening in every single second. And we are all the same thing: the experiencer experiencing every single second. There are as many paths as there are experiences and experiencers, all jostling to be noticed and understood. Have you noticed? Have you seen something? Is he handsome, or is she pretty? Is the job description tempting you to apply? Does the book cover make you ask questions, or the song make you sing or cry? Are you prone to standing still at the window when the robin turns his head, just to see his face a little longer?

It is all perception; it is all experience.

I am all that I see.

Which is beautiful until it forms the stories that separate us from our fellow experiencers.

The cottage has fleas, for goodness' sake. The reincarnated prince cat left them in his wake.

"She's so good at being a human."

I look at my eldest daughter talking about my younger daughter, the Annie who loves cushions and candles and curly girl hair videos on YouTube, and who we love to utter bits.

"Oh my goodness." It's the only thing I can think of to say.

"She's got it all sussed, hasn't she?"

"Oh my goodness." Again.

"We spend our days thinking and debating and analysing and suffering, and she lives in an Annie world of…"

"She's the one who's fully present, isn't she? When you're with her, she's not thinking about what incarnation she's in, what she's supposed to be learning, whether she's doing it all wrong, she's just…"

"Here."

"Yes."

"Just being a lovely human." Grace looks at me.

"Yes."

"What's wrong with us? Why are we like this?"

"Like us? All deep and meaningful and exhausting?"

"There has to be an easier way to live."

We contemplate this, standing side by side as frenetic Christmas shoppers part around us.

"When you read *Jonathan Seagull* you'll see why we're not content just flying backwards and forwards, why we can't live with our eyes shut to the joy of real flying. I bought it for you, for Christmas."

"I can't wait. I am a seagull."

"You're a seagull?"

"People have always said I'm a seagull."

"I didn't know that."

"I can't wait to read it."

"It's something of a spiritual classic, but everybody seems to get something different from it, much like everything." We start walking again. "It talks about the three reasons people choose not to fly, to remain a regular seagull who won't challenge the norm."

"Which are?"

"Fear, boredom and anger."

"It's so weird being back in this place after three years," Grace says, looking around the town she left for the southern hemisphere, and then, "Nothing good ever comes from fear."

"Except maybe escape from a tiger in a jungle, and the joy of survival after the fear."

"Yep, that's the truth."

"And boredom is lethal. And anger is wasted unless it is understood," I add.

"So what does Jonathan learn?"

"That there is more to experience than the 'squawks and grockles of everyday life'."

"And?"

"I'm not telling you anymore."

She must read the book for herself; really feel herself in its stunning story. For those with wings who long to fly beyond the existence of a mere grockle of life it is a most precious piece of writing.

We purchase a blonde wig from a charity shop, and wrestle through the wretched racket of Christmas to the car park.

"Sometimes, don't you just want to eat bacon sarnies and watch crap TV and talk utter bollocks all day?" I ask.

"Like Jeremy Kyle types."

"I can't believe you used to watch that."

"You know why."

"I know why. But maybe we're the ones talking bollocks."

"Yeah, maybe we should just shut up now."

"Yep."

Imagine a world of humans with no identity other than that of being human; imagine eliminating all rank or file, title or label, colour or creed. This is not to discredit or refuse to acknowledge any of those things, but to remove them for the purposes of this discussion. It would be like going to a library or a book shop of blank book covers filed under no categories; it would mean having to physically take a book down to gain even a glimpse of what it was about, and without any prejudgement or immediate opinion over the choice. We would be open, curious, in a childlike state of no preconceived idea of what we might find inside. Where did it come from, this need to identify and categorise? And then to separate and organise into you are this and I am that?

Over lunch, Ronni, the founder of the Human Library, and I had a similar conversation with respect to the whole concept of human books. I completely understand the titling of the human books, and the brilliance of readers choosing a title at public events in order to examine what is behind the cover, to expand, initially, their immediate mind and, ultimately, their world view, and how this works. Conversely, at private events, when a book sits before a group of readers who do not know the title this works too, in a different way, because there they are, with no idea of the genre or subject, ready to learn about something they may never have otherwise chosen to learn about. But it could be debated that this 'labelling' creates two things: an immediate sense of you over there and me over here, and over-identification on the part of the books with their book titles. Both are somewhat apparent at the outset of an event. But, by the end, something quite magical is happening.

Some books wear their titles quite literally as their choice of clothing or presentation. The 'picture book', for instance, is a remarkable book covered head to toe in tattoos, piercings and body enhancements, and once readers recover from the initial surprise of the book's cover they discover a quiet, supremely intelligent and sensitive read. Other books are a complete mystery until opened.

By all accounts, for example, I "do not look like a Jehovah's Witness" – and I have to smile at this and, where appropriate, ask what a Jehovah's Witness actually looks like, which prompts all manner of observations about frumpy skirts and heavy bags full of *Watchtower* magazines! – and there it is: the unstripping of preconceived ideas based on appearance alone. And then the flicking through the pages begins, and, before long, there emerges the beautiful truth: the book before the reader is the reader before the book; each a human being with insecurities and worries and beliefs and stories; each as in need of being heard and understood and accepted.

But not everyone is willing to enter into this uncomfortable (at times) territory, and the dynamic at the table at private events is very revealing as to just who is open, who is not, who sits silenced by the 'talker' at the table, and who flaunts their 'I'm so beyond all this rubbish' in the shape of negative statements or body language, or scrolling through their phones or looking over your shoulder. Learning to read your table is often as challenging as being your title, particularly when fielding the egos and navigating the undercurrent. But then the aforementioned magic happens. You are looking not at each other, but into each other, and perhaps seeing for the first time that beyond Gucci this or Primark that, or colour or religion or sexual leaning, or accent or limp or size, or diagnosis or piercing or accent, we are all each other, just in a different form. And when we see this, and lift ourselves above judgement, and the place setting of you over there and me over here, there is no rank or file, title or label, colour or creed. There is only painful, beautiful humanness.

Look into someone's eyes. Really look. You'll see them just as you want to be seen: someone worthy of being heard, accepted and loved for precisely who they are and not what we have been conditioned to think they are. For what we are is only a story we have created, and something we must ponder later, because like the realisation that it is our thoughts that create our beliefs, it is our beliefs that shape our stories, which is a huge and fascinating subject.

I asked Ronni what the catalyst was for creating the Human Library, what he had seen in himself that he found so uncomfortable he set about challenging it – and, as a result, all of us who wish to live without judgement or an inflated sense of our own rightness. His answer was immediate and honest.

The Human Library is active in over eighty countries of the world. The fraction of a taste I've had of its power to get people taking the hands of their book – ex-drug dealers or prostitutes, alcoholics, immigrants, manic depressives, Satanists, those who identify as transgender, gay, bi, polyamorous, those diagnosed with brain damage, bi-polar, erectile dysfunction, cancer, Jews and Muslims, women who have been subject to domestic abuse, or have had abortions, or been raped – and thanking them, with tears in their eyes, for helping them to understand has changed my world. At Human Library events, prejudice and judgement – why would you want to believe that? look like that? love like that? – becomes please tell me about that, so I can understand. The energy in the room is very different at the end than at the beginning.

Are we beginning to want this now? A better way of living with each other no matter what we believe or wear or how we love? Is it possible to believe this could become a reality one day? That we will no longer see you and me, but us?

Just as we harbour the judgement and misunderstanding that creates separation and hatred, I know we are capable of cultivating the understanding and acceptance that creates trust and an 'us' way of living.

But in order to do so, *we must want to do so.* It reveals phenomenal arrogance to live a life of self-enforced segregation and exclusion; to think that the harder we dig the heels of rightness in, the higher we fly in any god's eyes. What we're teaching the next generation, they will teach the next, and the next. And if what we're demonstrating is raised eyebrows and smirks, or rolled eyes and mockery, to outright loathing and rejection of all that is not 'right' in our eyes, is that right?

If what you are teaching your children, neat in rows in Kingdom Halls (or in any building or home dedicated to validating whatever your choice of truth is), is elevating them above their 'worldly' peers, giving them a false sense of rightness, of me but definitely not you, yet keeping them in intellectual and emotional and developmental poverty, then stop. STOP. What you are forging is yet another misshapen generation, shaping up for more arrogance, more separation… in short, more of what so many of us have finally had the courage to walk away from.

You might think I'm wrong, and I might think I'm right; and that man over there, he might think we're both wrong, or right, or he might not care at all. So, just for the record, I'm not writing this to be right, I'm writing it to say:

'Beyond ideas of rightness and wrongness, there is a field.
I will meet you there.'

– Rumi

Because only in this field will we find what we need to live without judgement or hatred or fear.

"I don't want to go in there."

"It's okay, we can do some gluing and sticking and stuff. Mum gave me the money, and we can get a drink and a snack." I peer through the window. I don't want to go in there either.

The weather is so hot, not slumped in a mood like most British summers, and has been for weeks, and I think we've been sent to the community centre's Kidz Day thing so Mum can get some peace from two of her children.

We loiter, and I toy with the coins in my pocket, not wanting to give them to the oversized woman sat sweating into the admission list. She's fanning dramatically with a pamphlet, flapping the hot air about, and generally flapping about. The woman sitting next to her, in red and white skin that matches the outline of her sundress, looks at me. "You coming in, Bab?"

I can hear too many kids inside, smell the sweat and the sun cream and the warm orange squash. "It's okay, we're just thinking about it."

"Well, move over then, Bab, there's a queue behind you."

We've been in there before, my brother and me, and I didn't like it. I'm already two years into hating living in this place, with the name-calling and staring and 'Yow right posh, yow are', and I wish I knew where the station was that we walked to so I could get on a coach to my nan's. My grandpa can't come and get me in his beloved Ford Granada anymore because he had a stroke and his right side doesn't work, so I can't lay out on the back seat and watch the trees and the bridges sideways from the window as he drives all the lovely way back to *shire. I'm already a year into planning how I'll escape, any which way, away from the rows of coloured concrete houses on streets dotted in dog shit and a collage of fag packets and chip wrappers. I'm not sure if my brother will come with me. But then I haven't told him I'm going.

We peer through the lid of the freezer in the newsagents, just across the way from the community centre, and then sit on the swings, fidgeting them about with our feet, sideways and backwards and forwards a bit, as we contemplate my executive decision of double rebellion – no to the community centre, and yes to cola lollies. We were never really allowed to have the cola lollies because cola was bad for us, we were told, so we always chose the raspberry or orange, pretending we agreed they were healthier because they were made of fruit, when all we actually wanted was the cola ones, like everyone else. Why did we have to do everything differently to everyone else?

"We won't have any models to show Mum, cos last time we took models home," my brother says.

"We'll say we didn't make any," I reply, which would work, as you don't have to make models. You can opt to join the miming class, or sit cross-legged to watch a man intersperse magic tricks with coughing fits, both of which might involve being picked out to either mime baking a cake or pick a card, both of which fill me with more horror than being told I must answer up in the *Watchtower* study this Sunday.

"When will we go home?" he then asks.

"At finishing time," I reply, and we spend the next hour scuffing about in the big fat heat that has made big fat lumps rise up in the tarmac of the playground. We jump from bump to bump, and try and squidge them; and then we're shrieking at the heat of the slide, gripping the sides to raise our bums up as we paddle down with our feet. But soon we're fed up of the playground and I'm looking across the road at the steep hill that rises to the communications station at the top. The postman told me the station was used in the war, and that it was too expensive to take the huge pylons down when the place was eventually closed. They stand as a landmark now for directions to where we live (unless it's really foggy): 'You'll see the pylons on the hill, you'll have reached us then, we're third right after the shops."

"Let's go up the hill."

Why does he look at me like that? Why am I so much braver than him?

Grumbling, he lets me hold his hand across the road, and follows me as I start to dodge through the blackberry bushes like the nine-year-old adventurer I am. The berries have turned from green to red to black, and some of them drop and splat, too ripe, and leave purple tell-tales on my pumps and legs, and the brambles snag and scratch. But I don't turn back. We're at the treeline now, and I scan for a path, in my stride and smiling. But my brother's whining behind me. He has a point: we can't do this without being found out, cos we don't have a model to take home, and we're gonna be late home now cos we can't see from here if the kid's thing has finished yet, and we've got blackberries on us…and suddenly I'm defeated and angry, and all my sense of adventure and freedom has been replaced by the thought of the postman's punishment.

I sit down, my legs a little shaky from the striding, wrap my arms around my shins and place my forehead on my knees, which smell of knee skin and summer and sun cream, and tears sting the scratches.

I don't want to go home. I don't want to read my *Watchtower* for Sunday. I don't want to share my bedroom with my sister anymore. I want my grandpa to come and get me so I can climb in the fruit trees in his garden, and sit on the roof of the shed with a bird's eye view of the lives either side.

I want to sit on this hill forever.

"Sister X?"

"It says in paragraph eight, from Revelation 21:4, that 'God will wipe out every tear from their eyes, and death and pain will be no more, neither will sickness and mourning', and I'm looking forward to this because my grandpa has been really ill and it will be great to see him in paradise and not ill anymore."

Mum has tears in her eyes, my sister on her lap; and the postman nods his approval; and my brother sticks his tongue out at me from the other side of Mum, and, on the face of it, all is what it is.

The world is a fabulous medley of types, with their clothing choices and mannerisms and accents. They all exist as a parody of themselves, postulating and defending, and justifying and explaining. But, boy, some of the characters who inhabit a Kingdom Hall – and I know, I was one of them. They (not all of them, of course) occupy a strange construct of themselves, steeped in piousness versus lapses into debauchery, and seemingly at home with the hypocrisy.

But when you live an honest truth, one that acknowledges we all possess a goodness that can be upstaged by being a tad Satan at times, there's no need to be a hypocrite, you can relax in that honesty. But once you attach fear of death to intervals of naughtiness, you have to work extra hard to maintain the piousness rather than just be comfortable with the fact we are all a bit bad. The lengths I've seen Witnesses go to to counter their conflicted life: the hours and hours of kingdom service; the making sure everybody sees their 'let not your right hand know what your left hand is doing' acts of goodness; the endless, endless answers during the *Watchtower* review; the sad head-shaking and chest-clutching at the news of another brother or sister's sad lapse into sin.

And yet I knew some truly beautiful, genuine souls – as there are in any organisation or religion – and their unadulterated love of the Truth and Jehovah was so whole that to even so much as utter a word of derision in their company about one of the Society's latest rules would quite likely have broken their hearts. My sister's grandmother, a wide-hipped, enormous-earinged woman, powdered and perfumed to perfection, was the embodiment of the Truth in every corner of her being. Her kindness and generosity was profound and humbling. I doubt she doubted a solitary sentence of a single *Watchtower*, and died as faithful as the day she was baptised, but as we left, one by one, her beloved granddaughter included, I know it made her weep. I don't think she understood we couldn't breathe in there, or maybe she did, I don't know, but I don't recall her ever judging any of us, which made her, in my view, a very special woman. For her, living the Truth was her truth, but she managed to live it without doubt or fear or condemnation. I don't know how she did.

When I left, I felt I was at last being an honest me. I felt freed from my personal conflicted life, which did involve colossal doubts about the truth of the Truth rather than lying, stealing and fornicating – although I was frequently accused of the latter. I couldn't walk into a room without some sister or other leaning to another and whispering that I'd been seen getting into so-and-so's car, or going into such-and-such's house, alone and obviously to commit adultery. It didn't help that my husband was a non-believer and I was therefore considered something of a loose cannon (and woman) as I was not duty-bound to a Witness husband, whose name and honour in the congregation I must bow to as a dutiful wife. It was assumed I was on the prowl for a Witness husband because of the 'uneven yoke' of being shackled to a non-believer, and the unfortunate worldy association associated with that, which, in their view, was obviously corroding my faith and making me rampant for a believer.

One spectacularly nasty sister – nicknamed 'the poisoned dwarf' – single-handedly ran a highly successful crusade against me, waddling from house to house with her gossip and converting anyone happy to listen. This was a sister I had confided in, foolishly, when I'd been at a very low point, and how it hurt when I learnt of her chattering.

The truth was, I was beginning to prefer the company of unbelievers. Through my husband I'd been introduced to all sorts of interesting people, one of whom had a vast personal library of books that made me delirious with excitement – from philosophers and poets, and artists to musicians – and he was happy to discuss anything from Freud and Jung, Burns and Homer, Picasso and Monet, to Dylan and Cohen, and I was in heaven in his company. Dinner with him and his beautiful family was a great, big, wonderful exploration of everything. It mattered not one jot to them I was a Witness. There was no talk of me being unevenly yoked, and how that was for me, and how it was having to mix with the likes of them. They treated me as an equal, just as they treated my husband and our daughters, and I felt the magic of that 'wider, bigger picture'.

Like my beloved biology teacher, these people saw me as an actual human being, not just Sister K X. I was somebody they were interested in beyond are you a pioneer? have you ever pioneered? are you planning on pioneering? We talked about a hundred things, not just how many hours I'd done in the field service that month, whether I was studying with anyone at the moment, and if I'd ever brought anyone into the Truth. And it was perfectly okay to enjoy a glass of wine in their company, or even several, and compare single malts and sip a fine brandy after dinner, without the glances from those who loved to keep an account of these things. These good people, they were everything I craved, everything that had been missing in my life.

Yet it was at this time that I'd begun to slide around in the dark again, and my body had become a criss-cross of the relief of a razor blade. It was also the time my aunt had put in that bid for my attention, plying me with love and the spiritual support she clearly believed I was lacking, convinced, I have no doubt, that this was what I needed.

She also, of course, had plenty to say about my marriage to an unbeliever and how difficult that must make life for me, so too having an entire family out of the Truth – and I am suddenly trembling with old rage as I type this. Her vehement advice was that I must distance myself from Mum for the sake of the girls, because if they got too close to their nan, only to be told she was going to die at Armageddon, it would be very upsetting for them.

Mum and I were barely speaking at this time, but how I loathed what my aunt was trying to do and what I was becoming as I succumbed to her, too ill to fight, too tired to even try. I was this horrible, sneering, rubbish human being who took pills and saw the world through their filter; who sliced her skin open and bad-mouthed her family and craved them; who ranted and planned to do an awful thing to herself, but who smiled and died a little more every time she did so. I had no idea who to trust, who I could talk to who wouldn't judge me or gossip about me or manipulate me. A wonderful elderly sister, one of the kindest souls I have ever met, would look up into my face and implore me to get help. But where, and with whom? I needed professional help, but still believed a therapist would harm me in some way. And there was no way I was going to talk to a single one of the elders, one of whom was heard to have said I should 'just get on with it' if I was suicidal. The temptation to name him at this moment is very, very strong…

A close friend of mine, one of the only ones who hadn't turned their back on my deep distress, now turned her back. The message she left on my answer machine was clear: 'I love you, hun, and care about you, but you're really hard work… because of your depression…and so needy. I'm sorry, hun, but I need to concentrate on my relationship with Jehovah… and…well… being friends with you might be affecting that, so I'm really sorry but I think I'm going to have to stop seeing you…'

Annie came into the room as the message ended, and knelt on the floor beside me and whispered, "Are you broken, Mummy?" when she saw what had become of me in that moment.

No three-year-old should have to ask a thing like that.

I felt the dark closing around the effort to breathe – the dark that would very soon bring me to that violent moment of blessed relief on my bedroom floor – and my heart in pain. I saw the threads on the rug and Annie's curls. I heard the silence I longed for and held this daughter as she patted my back, as I had patted hers a hundred times to soothe her over little bumps and grazes, or through snuffly colds and teething. I gathered what little of my spirit I had left and we walked up the hill to collect Grace from school.

Clarissa Pinkola Estés, in her astounding book *Women Who Run with the Wolves*, speaks of the dark psyche of a woman's mind, of the predator there who can show up in many forms as a warning that she must take action to protect herself. These dreams, or visions, whether awake or asleep, must not be ignored. They are the eons-old messages of our current and former selves, and those of our foremothers and foresisters, to 'pay attention'. The predator here is not a bad thing, and may even show up in dreams in the shape of a dominant male – and we have all had dreams that involve those – who provides a subconscious warning of 'danger'.

She relates the story of 'The Doll in her Pocket: Vasalisa the Wise', a tale told in various forms throughout the Baltic countries which predates even classical Greek culture. It is a story of realisation that 'most things are not as they seem', and a mother's dying gift to her daughter of a small doll which will always guide her, should she choose to listen. The daughter does not understand her mother's words, but keeps the doll with her, secreted in a pocket, and tells no one of her existence, as instructed.

Time passes, and she naturally grieves for her mother; but then the day comes when, tested beyond the knowledge of her tender years, she seeks the doll's wisdom. She instinctively knows she must trust this wisdom, despite not understanding how the doll knows what it knows, or how it is managing to share it with her.

To trust this wisdom is to recognise it exists as both a subconscious warning and a call to action about danger which, on a conscious level, we may not be brave enough to acknowledge let alone face alone. And the danger itself can be as specific or as broad-reaching as we dare to investigate. To quote Clarissa:

> 'Sometimes it is a message about the threatening aspects of the culture one lives in, whether it be a small but brutal culture at the office, one within their own family, the lands of their neighbourhood, or as wide as their own religious or national culture.'

When the predator appears, in whichever form, we must pay attention, she urges, and we 'must not be afraid'.

As a little girl deeply disturbed about what I was being told to believe, yet too frightened to say so, I didn't have the consciousness required to reason why, and I didn't have a magic, talking 'doll'. And if I had, would I have been brave enough to listen to her? I doubt it. What would I have done anyway? I had nowhere to go. Even as an adult, I didn't have the courage to listen to my metaphorical doll, that deep, dark voice that kept whispering: 'most things are not as they seem'. I kept ignoring her. I kept thinking that if I just kept going a bit longer it would all be okay, that Jehovah was just testing my faith when I felt wretched, and soon he would bless me again. Hadn't I had it drummed into me that persecution was part of being one of God's chosen ones? So I went back for more, again and again, whilst the metaphorical doll writhed and my psyche whispered and then kicked to be heard.

I didn't know then that by its very nature extreme indoctrination (or religious fundamentalism) inhibits the developing brain's ability to think critically, or to rationalise and compare other viewpoints, thus removing the possibility that it even wants to, and making it almost impossible to escape its control as a result.[76]

I didn't make the connection that the persecution was coming from within, not until I left. I didn't make the connection that my writhing doll wasn't the Devil trying to break my resolve to be a good Christian girl, but was in fact my psyche screaming that I *was* a good girl, Christian or not, and that I should get the hell away from anyone who told me otherwise. But it didn't matter what I did. If I was bad, I was judged; but if I was good I was judged, because I was obviously being good to cover my bad.

We are born as instinctive human beings who respond to heat and cold and hunger and safety and fear not as conscious reactions but as unconscious sensations. If it feels okay, we are okay. If it doesn't feel okay, we cry. But then we learn language

[76] https://www.salon.com/2019/01/08/a-link-between-brain-damage-and-religious-fundamentalism-has-now-been-established-by-scientists_partner/

and everything is given a label – good or bad; yes or no – until life becomes a series of labels, of rules, of boundaries that silence our dolls.

I wish I'd known about *Women Who Run with the Wolves*, and Krishnamurti, and Watts and Tolle. I wish I'd known even the first thing about what was happening to my spirit, my mind, my soul. In the dark places, where I thought it was Satan talking, I realise now it was my personal doll, my psyche, fighting for its life from within as I was abandoning all interest in living.

And then that day.

People discuss suicide as if it's a selfish choice, a rather dramatic and final 'look what you made me do' statement of exit. Suicide is many things. It is a moment of taking control back when a person or an organisation or a situation seems to have you fully and completely in its control. It is a desperate, spontaneous act, or a quietly planned pact to yourself that your pain, and that which you cause everyone else because they have to witness it, will end soon. It is a release from captivity. It is a lonely, exhilarating, dangerous, curious moment.

It is waking up on life support having failed, for some of us, and thinking, as I did, *I'm so, so sorry, God…whoever you are…for taking the life you gave me…*and then the awful *What am I supposed to do now?* And then there is all the talking about what led to it, and the why didn't you tell us how you were feeling? and were you ashamed of your depression? and the distinct possibility of being sectioned and, God no, please not that.

I realise now it was an awakening, the desperation to die, triggered by a spiritual crisis so profound, a threat to my soul's freedom so absolute, that it had no choice but to take me to the very edge to prove its existence. There was something sacred about it, something I could not ignore, and which would speak louder and louder in the days to come: We can do this; we can get through this.[77]

And then there was the face of the friend again, now I was back, who had bathed and fed my daughters that day and put them to bed in her house when it should have been me doing it, but I couldn't, because I was so very, very tired. But how I loved them, and how I didn't want them to see me like this. But here they were, a little confused but so pleased to see me, and my mother too, pale and full of love. And sitting over there was the aunt who'd tried so hard to keep me away from Mum, because it was she who wanted to be there for me now, because she could take me back home with her if I liked, with the girls, and feed me spiritually…

The friend made pasta for the children, hers and mine, and later for us, but I couldn't eat, and a headache struck, beyond pain, and all the opinions of what I supposedly needed mingled with the children's chatter, and the tug of my stitches, and the hospital psychiatrist asking and asking if I was going to do it again so he could decide what to do with me.

Q. Are you aware of the severity of what has just happened? *Yes.*
Q. Are you still feeling suicidal? *No.*
Q. Are you planning on trying again? *No.*
Q. Did you plan to commit suicide? *No.*
Q. So it was a sudden decision with no prior planning? *Yes.*

[77] *The Spiritual Awakening Process* by Aletheia Luna and Mateo Sol is simply the most beautiful piece of writing on the subject of spiritual crisis and awakening after extreme trauma, whether mental, physical, psychological, cultural, religious, or any or all experiences our body and mind registers as life changing. Please, please read it.

Q. You understand I need to conduct a psychiatric assessment and must know how you are really feeling… before I can let you go home… *Yes.*
Q. How are you really feeling? *Okay. I feel okay.*
Q. You lost a lot of blood, vomited painkillers, anti-depressants and alcohol, and tried to electrocute yourself. *Yes.*
Q. And you feel okay? *Yes.*

I'd realised I was in trouble, but this man was not going to see in me a single reason to section me. I had to get home to Grace and Annie. I convinced him I was sad and sorry about what had happened, fully understood his difficult position because of the seriousness of what I had done, and would begin the course of therapy he recommended. My priority, I assured him, was getting well after a short spell of depression following my marriage breakup from the girls' father. That and wanting to take care of my daughters, who needed a well and happy mum. I didn't utter a solitary word about anything else at all. He finally discharged me.

I needed to sleep, and lay down on my friend's bed. She sat with me for a while, quiet in the gravity of what had happened, and then she whispered, "It'll be okay. It's all going to be okay," and I loved her and hoped she was right.

When I awoke my mother had gone, yet here was the aunt. The doll stirred again. I heard words spoken in earnest in a phone call from a strong sister in my congregation: "You need to make sacrifices to stay in the Truth, love." And the aunt was talking and talking, telling me what vitamins to take, and to pray, and to drink more water because she'd heard me weeing and it wasn't nearly enough so I must be dehydrated. I heard the children playing hide and seek in the kitchen, giggling as they tried to squeeze inside the cupboards. I saw Mum's face in my mind, pale and full of love, and the pain of having hurt her made it hard to breathe. Out of earshot of the aunt, my friend told me Grace had thrown her arms around her nan just before she left, and held on and held on, and how Mum had been the first person to go to my house, had scrubbed the blood from the walls, changed my bedding, and paid to have a new carpet fitted. Oh, Mum. I used my friend's phone to call her: *Please, Mum, come and get me.*

From cave art to the masters, from the early formations of single letters to Shakespeare, from tales around campfires to podcasts, humans have always communicated via stories in one form or another. But what are we doing when we share a story through art, literature or telling? Why do we need them, and why do we become both the listener and the teller?

From the moment we are born we are told stories, often beginning with the story of our mother's pregnancy and our birth – was our conception planned or unplanned? our birth easy or difficult? – and she tells us of her cravings, her aches, our kicking her in the night. We may also be told that she was excited, nervous, indifferent or heartbroken to learn she was pregnant, and we may get the story of our father being X, Y or Z – ecstatic, unimpressed or blatantly horrified – or out of the picture either because he ran a mile or was kept out of the picture.

We hear fairy stories, moralistic stories, life-saving stories from books, through parable, from other children – our siblings or cousins or little pals – all of which result in one thing: we, too, become storytellers in some form, testing our own against the ones we have already been told or read, comparing them, embellishing them.

A cave artist used the pigments of earth – limonite and hematite, red and yellow ochre, charcoal from the fire and lime from the rock face – to shape the story of his horse, the battle, his sacrifices. A man in flickering candlelight used a quill or graphite to shape the iambic pentameter of plays set in places he had never visited, about characters he had never met, and they strutted and fretted their stories upon his pages. A girl steps up onto a stage, the TEDx logo bold above her head and her beating heart fast in her chest, and takes a breath, preparing herself to tell, in eighteen minutes, the story of her life. Why?

In basic terms, to perhaps impart a lesson.

In a more far-reaching way, even to leave a legacy.

But what is the sharing and receiving of a story achieving in a deeper, psychological sense?

When a child tells a story, in the language she has grasped to date, what is she seeking? When the parent listens, busy and impatient perhaps, what are they hearing? And when a story is told, at which point do the teller and the listener, despite both coming to the story from their personal perspectives, look at each other and feel the connection, the *something* that binds them to each other?

'It's better to have a story to look through at life than an explanation: the story is richer.' I love this quote from the movie *Finding Joe.*

You could say I'm merely telling a story here, the story of being a Witness, and that is all. But those who read early versions of this book, from all age groups and cultures, saw so much more. One said, "Like a really good film that has moved you, and stays with you, this book has changed me. It's the sort of book you never forget"; another, "Knowing you as I do, I don't know how you survived living that life, it was so cruel"; and another, "There is so much here about how we should and should not be with each other, about what we're teaching our children"; yet another, "I was captivated, shaken, changed. I did not expect that." Each responded to the story differently, but ultimately were united in that they all had a response of some kind, from where they were in their lives and thinking at the time, and went on to discuss that with me, and other people, and thus we were bonded by the yet deeper, more expansive discussions.

Did I set out to do this? Initially, no. The very first version of this book, written nearly twenty years ago and in the months after my utter collapse, was a ninety thousand-word unpublishable rant. It seemed I had no other objective than to scream my story, and that was that.

But time passed – sixteen years, in fact – and the pain frayed a little, like the silk ribbon edging on a blanket that has been carried here and there for eons. When I wrote the first 1,600 words as part of a life writing assignment for my English literature degree, I did not expect the response I got. My tutor urged me to write the full story, but the story itself, like the blanket, had softened and softened, and I wasn't sure I wanted to unfold it. But it was still my blanket, and I came to appreciate how it didn't need to stay as it had been when it had first been told, and I loved how, when I shared it, it bought a little comfort to those who, like me, had been so angry, so hurt once upon a time. There is something in this that goes beyond the telling. It is the eyes looking into eyes that know; the heart beating side by side with another who has most likely been broken too. It is your story and theirs, different but the same.

Just before the publication of this book I ran into a couple of old Witness friends in a car park. She seemed rather happy to see me, strangely, and urged me to chat to her husband while she ran into a shop. We talked about this and that – his grandchildren, his work, my work – and I told him I was about to publish a book. The smile vanished. "Is it apostate?" he asked, without a moment's hesitation.

With those three words this man had instantly rendered my story as irrelevant and, worse, dangerous. But more worrying than that, he had revealed his appalling attitude to anything that might possibly present a different viewpoint to that which he had been brainwashed into believing was the only viewpoint. The arrogance that accompanies that attitude, not to mention the fear of being judged as complicit in the apostasy and thus likely to be disfellowshipped if he so much as even read one paragraph of this book, was palpable.

"No," I replied, without a moment's hesitation, "it's not apostate, it's honest," and felt the familiar flicker of rage at the way these intelligent men and women are simply incapable of deciding for themselves what they want to read. The conversation ended when his wife came out of the shop and informed me that all the meetings were on Zoom now, and did I know?, with that tilt of head and little voice that purrs *You know it's the truth really… and Armageddon's closer than ever now…and we'd really like you to be saved.*

I haven't set foot in a Kingdom Hall for two decades. Did that not tell her *anything* about how I feel about the Truth and what happened inside the walls of that building? Unwilling to ruin their day and mine with the tirade on the tip of my tongue, and because they are truly lovely people, I said how great it had been to chat, informed her as politely as I could muster that I had no wish to discuss the meetings, and left.

I am able to accept that these people choose to believe what they believe, despite it being what it is, but can they not have a *single* conversation without using it as an opportunity to remind you, albeit dressed up in smiles and round-the-houses language: *We're right, you know, and you're wrong, and you know you're going to die if you don't come back to meetings…* Like the pedlars of pyramid schemes that'll make you rich beyond your dreams, every encounter with every person is a chance to sell, sell, sell, with no interest in or acknowledgment of the fact that the answer is always going to be a polite or an impolite no, no, no. Watch *On Becoming a God in Central Florida* on Netflix. It's about the up-sell down-sell of such a scheme, set in the eighties and brilliant. Some of the scenes reminded me so much of the big Witness sell – and made me cringe loudly!

Initially, after leaving, my biggest rage was at God himself, and the men who used our need to believe in him – or something like him – as a lure and a trap, and that lasted, if I'm honest, for a long, long time. But to realise that the Witness faith, like most others, is simply God in limited, inhibited hands, and that even the men who represent him so incorrectly do so only because of their own need to believe (and unfortunately the need to control through belief) was such a release that I wept. It was when I realised the profound truth of that, that this book lost its fury – though it still lingers in places where things needed to be said – and became the bigger story of manmade belief, how it shapes our life story, and how it can damage young minds unable to separate truth from non-truth.

It may not surprise you to hear that I do not believe in God, at least not the god of the Bible, and definitely not in the made-up god Jehovah. God became everything to do with everything I was angry about, and where he was there was no peace to be found. But recently there arose in me a sorrow. By denying his existence in the shape of the manmade lie he has become, I was denying the trueness of who he or she might actually be: the architect of life itself, whole, wondrous, a miracle of energy we will never, ever understand. Perhaps writing this would help to clear God's name a little? Restore faith in the concept of a god in the form we crave – a magnificent, loving father and mother who rejoices in us, feels our aches and broken hearts, helps us find the beauty in the grass that grows in the cracks of a concrete slab, the touch that says *It's okay, I've got you.* The peace of that story works for me. How does it make you feel?

But why? Why the stories we create and tell?

In basic terms, they create a space for the exchange of information, the opportunity for learning, the chance for understanding.

On a more far-reaching level, they encourage the forming of bonds, trust and connection.

But on a deeper, psychological level they are the stuff from which the experience of being human is built.

Take away an artist's brush and you take away the expression of his experience, his story. Take away a man's story and you take away his voice, diminishing him and reducing him to being unworthy of being heard. Stories contain code for living. They say, 'I was here and I experienced.' They say, 'I listened and I examined and I learned.'

All stories have behind them a reason for the telling. And there are stories which carry a deeper motive – and this can be a two-edged thing, a foot-stamping tirade, but equally a petition. Perhaps the foot-stamper is crying out from the fear they will one day die with a story that may change minds and lives. Or perhaps they are simply saying I need to tell you this, so you understand. To deny the storyteller is to destroy her, is to say, 'You don't matter', and break her heart.

Not all stories are told from a velvet cushion; some are screamed from the edge. Not all stories have a beginning, a middle and an end; some are a discordant and disjointed outcry. But they all have a reason.

To listen to each other's stories is to say I see you, I hear you, I feel you.[78] It is to express gratitude for the telling, whether through a child's babbling, a lover's rant, or a man's tears. It is to acknowledge the early sketches through to the masterpieces of the eons-old parables, the sages, the philosophers. It is to say thank you to the ultimate storyteller, our universe, for allowing its mysteries and beauty and dark places to play out through us, in us, for us.

But what about the stories that get stuck, that go wrong, that become so big and so ugly and so compelling a tale for the storyteller to tell that lies become truth, truth becomes the way, and the way causes damage, division, hatred and prejudice?

Dictators insist on their story being right: the only story.

Politicians invent stories they think the people want to hear: to continue their story.

Liars add layers and embellishments to convince: this story is the truth.

Storytelling, without a doubt, has a dark side.

---

[78] Michelle Obama in her Netflix documentary 'Becoming', and in her book of the same name, describes human stories and the importance of acknowledging the teller, and the connections they help us to make with each other, in language that is as beautiful as she is.

It comes right back to this: if the story you tell, and the belief you have in that story, brings another soul to their knees, has a child crying in fear, and sees hurt inflicted and judgements fired as though from a gun, do you still wish that story to be the dictate of your life? Or are you willing to go out and find new learning? to rewrite what you thought was the only truth? to stop crippling a child's mind and psychological development?

Some days, as I'm typing, I wonder why I am. But there's this irrepressible urge, fired in part by immense gratitude for those who wrote their stories, who put the darkest and lightest thoughts they possess together for us to read to do the same. It is also fired by the voice inside that sometimes speaks from a velvet cushion and sometimes screams from the edge: *Be careful with your stories, with your truths, because some of them are causing great damage, both to yourself and those you inflict them on.* There is also the thought this book could be an arm around a shoulder, or the required prompt someone needs to look at their own story and say, I'm glad you told it how it was for you, because it's both similar and different to how it was for me, is for me, and I feel brave enough now to start the rewriting.

Why brave? Because it's the bravest thing on Earth to challenge your own story, to pick it apart and discard the bits you no longer need or believe, or even the whole damn show if it needs to go. The nakedness is almost unbearable, and the urge to dive back inside the clothes you have always worn is overwhelming.

Some are brave enough to make their escape from the Witnesses, and they change their clothes, wear their new story with a lightness of step and a voice they never knew they were capable of…only to return. I had friends who packed up their New World Translation of the Holy Scriptures, and boxed up a thousand back issues of the *Watchtower*, along with the guilt and the fear and the crutch of it all, and limped or strode away, depending on their state of mind at the time…only to return.

"She's come back to the Truth," a sister once said to me in the street in my old town about an old friend of mine, and I wanted to scream from the edge: *No! It is not the truth! Open your eyes*! But her eyes were old and faded-blue now, and she only knew the truth she knew, so I said nothing at all because of a whisper – 'There is a time to rend, and a time to sew; there is a time for silence, and a time to speak…' – and I smiled instead. I'd loved this sister (I still do), and wondered at her speaking to me at all as, technically, I was still highly unclean from all the disfellowshipped wallowing in the world I've done in the last two decades. She asked after the girls and I told her Grace had spent two years in Australia after her degree and was now working and living in New Zealand, and Annie was studying graphic design and making her little house and garden beautiful, the thing she loves most of all, and both were happy and well and thank you. She spoke about her children too, and her grandchildren now, and we laughed at the passing of time and time. And then there was the pause, because we both knew she shouldn't be speaking to me… But we parted with a smile.

There are those who will always be the story they know, and there are those who, like a pop-up book, lift up and out of the page to take on a new shape for a time, but who are eventually folded back inside. The sister who returned to the Truth…sadly my old friend's look of *Ah, well, we knew she would* was right. She was hyper-sensitive and intelligent, but mentally busted up by life. To be busted up in there, inside the congregation, is a busted up that can only move around in very, very defined boundaries, so the constraints of the cage can actually be a safe place to be

– provided you're able to accept the restrictions and have no wish to challenge them. Out here, with no doors or windows or walls around you, you're flying one minute and falling the next. There is no point of reference, no centre of gravity, and you have to create your own boundaries. Not everyone is up to the task.

But if you are, or want to be, no matter what the cage or the story you wish to flee, then flee, and don't fold back inside. It's okay, there are many of us out here, and know this: we'll recognise you, and you'll recognise us, and we're here if you need us.

> 'Sometimes educated guesses can be made about the wounds of childhood by closely inspecting what matters adults irrationally lose their tempers over.'

From *Women Who Run With the Wolves*, this sentence danced like light on a vast ocean, and it's no coincidence I read it at the very time I felt cornered by old rage and had done my fist-shaking at the universe, wanting to know what it was, this painful, exhilarating, infuriating life. It was a release, the rage; it was a tutor, my guru, my signpost.

Rage is insight into old wounds, and should not be repressed, for it points to why the wound still hurts, and accesses the energy to go to the little girl who thought her silence would mean Jehovah would love her, and keep her safe.

One day, enraged at being told to shut up by a man who should have known better, and indeed did, I thought I might break in two, because I'd found my voice now, and it felt like it was under threat when all I'd ever wanted was the freedom to say how I really felt.

"You tell me you care about how I feel," I'd cried, "so *why can't I speak*? Must I be quiet in order to be accepted by you? Must I always live in silence, because silence equals love and safety, and speaking equals rejection?"

I then took that rage and hurled it heavenward: *What do I need to learn? What are you showing me?*

The learning was to acknowledge the little girl who was afraid to speak back then, and go to the man who told her to shut up and tell him about her, again, because she needed him to know. She needed to ask him to not tell her to shut up, please, just because he didn't want to hear what she had to say, because she really needed to be heard without fear of rejection. He rejected her anyway, as was his way, and instructed her on how to communicate effectively before closing the door to his study. Staring at the closed door, she had the first of the revelations that would eventually free her from such abuse. The teacher had spoken.

> 'Attention to the matter of rage begins the process of transformation [...] untransformed rage can become a constant mantra about how oppressed, hurt, and tortured we were.'

That's not to say we have licence to go around raging carte blanche. But to grab hold of it when it does emerge and go to where the hurt is, turn it into understanding ourselves, and convert it into learning, that is transformative.

This book might be making you angry. I promise you, it triggered huge swathes of anger writing it. But do you know why it is making you angry? And are you willing to listen?

Unless we have the courage to examine why our rage was triggered, we will continue to live angry lives; lives where anger is the enemy sabotaging our relationships and reality rather than opening us up to great learning. Go to it, lay it all out with a loving person who will listen, so you can make sense of it. It's enlightening, even funny sometimes, when the connections between this and that are made. But it is also healing when things are seen as the simple and complicated and tangled this and that of it all, and the wounds get an airing through the rage before safely fading a little more from the learning.

I don't know why we're sitting on the front row. It's hot, and I'm bored. The blue sky is like a taunting oil painting in each of the square windows of the hall on three sides; the double doors at the back are open to allow air into where we sit listening to an elder tell us about the joy of being part of the Great Crowd of faithful worshippers of Jehovah who will inherit planet Earth when he annihilates the billions of unbelievers. I've heard this so many times, and for a moment I tune back in. Imagine having the swings completely to yourself, without having to share them with worldly people? But then the sky and the heat stick me in a sort of trance again.

In my pocket I have a little yellow plastic alien. I saw it on the bookshelf last Tuesday in Brother Johnson's house, during the prayer at the end of the book study meeting when everyone's eyes were closed. One of his sons must have left it there. I love its tiny antennae, and how it can freestand on its miniscule feet. I built it a home in a shoe box, with a single sheet of loo paper for a rug, and another folded up as a blanket. It occurred to me at the time I'd probably be killed for taking it home and playing with it for a while. I roll the alien around in my fingers, feeling its round tummy and pointy face.

My brother is bored too and keeps swinging his brown legs. Mum puts her hand on them occasionally, to still them, but he starts up again a moment later. The postman's sweaty face turns to her in a scowl, and she whispers something in my brother's ear. He folds his arms across his blue-checked shirt and his eyes fill with tears. I guess he's been told he'll get taken out for a telling off if he continues, or worse.

I don't know what makes me do it, but I take the alien out of my pocket and make it do a little dance on my knee, to cheer him up. He starts giggling.

Mum immediately turns to us both, spots the alien, looks at me fiercely and raises an eyebrow of warning.

Too late. The postman has seen and heard. He places his Bible and *Watchtower* calmly to the side of him on the empty chair, and reaches over Mum and grabs my brother's arm. And then the tustling and squirming begins as he fights the inevitable hauling from the hall. They return. It's obvious from the utter defeat in my brother's eyes what has happened out there in the foyer.

Before I go on I'd like to share something with you from Sam Fade's discussion[79] on the emotional and physical abuse of Jehovah's Witness children, and based on how high Witness adults and children, and even ex-Witnesses, score in 'exposure to adverse childhood experiences' (ACE) assessments:

> 'Emotional abuse comes in the form of severe indoctrination, restrictions of freedoms, constantly being in the flight or fight mode due to dooms-day

[79] https://freedomofmind.com/how-jehovahs-witness-teachings-can-damage-brain-development-in-children/

> teachings, restrictions on freedom of identity and pressure to conform. Again some of these deprivations of liberty go against the United Nations Charter on the rights of a child. These all add up to an emotionally abusive atmosphere.
>
> Emotional neglect is the other ACE score Witness children will always have. This is again due to severe adherence to doctrine to the detriment of a child's identity. Parents are focussed on witnessing, meeting attendance, control and compliance of their child to do exactly what the rules of the organisation state. This blind adherence fails children's emotional needs; it doesn't allow them to freely express themselves without fear of repercussion.
>
> I hesitate to put in physical abuse even though it's rampant. It should be noted that parents are encouraged to be physical with their children and this is a culture within most congregations. It is not unusual to see a minor child being dragged out to a back room for a flogging due to failure to sit through a meeting. This culture is encouraged through the patriarchal structure and adherence to the doctrine that you spoil the child if you do not administer the rod.'

Raise your hand, if you dare, if you think it is okay to treat children like this.

When we get home, it's my turn. I am ordered to take my knickers down and bend over the settee so he can punish me for causing a disturbance during the meeting. My stomach is churning and I think I might be sick, and I'm pleading, but he tells me I am not permitted to leave the room until I've done as I've been told. I can hardly breathe in between the sobs. I tell him I'm sorry, over and over again, and that I won't disturb the meeting or distract my brother ever again. He just stands there, impassive.

My legs are shaking when I finally stand up and turn, one hand on the settee. With the other I reach around and pull at my knickers, but my hands are shaking too and I'm struggling. He grunts something about getting on with it.

In bed I sob like my heart is broken beyond repair.

Winston Churchill is reported to have said that 'if one doesn't change one's mind, nothing changes.' We each of us have the option to change, but do we, when the need is great? Or are we so invested in our story, even when it's obvious it's pretty pointless or damaging, that nothing either interests or compels us to alter the way we think and act?

Have you ever encountered someone so glued to their story that even consideration of a deviation results in a shaking head and a waved hand, even if their health or sanity is at stake?

An enormous man I know of, with Type II diabetes, chronic digestive issues and ulcerated legs, lives by his particular story of "I only drink one two-litre bottle of sport pop a day now, you know, cos it's 'ealthfier, cos it's got added vitamins in," and "I always eat sugar-free cake and no-fat stuff," and "No, you'll not get me on that rubbish" when asked if he might consider a slightly different diet, just as a test to see if it makes him feel better.

In a hospital bed opposite a dear friend a while ago, a woman with bronchitis, gasping for air in between sucking oxygen through a mask, was heard to say, "Naaaa, not fer me; always bin a smoker me, like me mam, and always will be" when a free service for helping people give up smoking was offered to her.

A man driven half mad with back pain looked at his daughter like she was the one who was half mad, and muttered "Mumbo-jumbo" when she wondered if a few gentle stretches might help him, or a short walk every day, and so it goes on with the stories we tell ourselves about ourselves, and life.

But then we get to the really serious stories, the ones we discussed before that become so big and so ugly and so compelling a tale for the storyteller to tell that lies become truth, truth becomes the way, and the way causes damage, division, hatred and prejudice: a family split apart by a religion that dictates disfellowshipping as the only way to treat a 'sinner'; a child losing their sparkle and then their very soul at the hands of a parent determined not to spare the rod; the wife driven to silence by a husband who wishes her to 'know her place' so he can move up the ranks in the congregation; an entire organisation so attached to the story of their preposterous beliefs that they consider every other human being on Earth as condemned to death.

The advocates of the story of what a religion requires (and not just the Witnesses), do they consciously know what they're doing? Or has it become so deeply engrained they no longer consider their actions? Are they so fearful of admission the story might be flawed that they cling to it despite knowing, without a doubt, they are causing unfathomable damage? Jesus said, 'Forgive them, for they know not what they do', when referring to his persecutors. These modern persecutors do what they do *in his name*. Have you ever considered that?

Have you ever wanted to snatch the bottle of pop or the packet of cigarettes and implore the living daylights out of the guzzler or the smoker? Or would you love to rant at the stubborn fool who won't get out of his recliner and take a short walk or do some stretching to ease his pain? Or grab the parent who diminishes a child, piece by piece until their eyes no longer shine, and punish them like for like? Or stand on a raised dais and rail at the row of men in suits steeped to the accusation in their eyes in hypocrisy and lies?

What is so frightening about change? Without change we are as good as evolution in reverse, because as others learn and change and move around us, we are left behind in the stench of our own stubbornness, growing weaker and weaker, yet thinking our resolve to stick to what we know – our story – is strength of character. It is not. If we only ever think one way about a thing, that thing will always be one way, and will never become a thing of learning, of change.

Enquiring minds willing to stretch their boundaries can turn around and see where they've come from, and then stretch a little more. They come alive with the stretching. The dullness fades, to be replaced with eyes and a mind brighter for the new thinking. And then there are the shuttered minds.

The shuttered often begin their sentences with "Ah, but" or simply "No". The enquirers, on the other hand, ask questions and may try, for a time, to draw the shuttered out. But it seems whatever the subject they will not be tempted to engage, let alone allow themselves to be challenged outside of their own world, their own personal story… M. Scott Peck in the brilliant *The Road Less Travelled* likens this to being unable and unwilling the alter our outdated map of reality. To quote:

> 'The only way that we can be certain that our map of reality is valid is to expose it to the criticism and challenge of other map-makers. Otherwise we lived in a closed system – within a bell jar, to use Sylvia Plath's analogy, rebreathing only our own fetid air, more and more subject to delusion.'[80]

At the dinner parties of Witnesses there is only one story told by all: The Witness Story. All present are unwilling (and unable) to stretch, all trading lines from the flawed story, all the shuttered. Like the brother who immediately asked if this book is apostate, these shuttered men and women are unable to get past the A = B = C of: K is an ex-JW = K is most likely an apostate = the book will be apostate. How damaged must a human being's thinking be to instantaneously label an alternative viewpoint as apostasy – or in opposition to 'true worship' – just because a group of men in New York have told them so? Men who preach, 'Do not put your trust in princes, in mortal men, who cannot save...' (Psalms 146:3 NIV), and yet expect absolute obedience and trust despite being mere mortal men – unless, of course, you believe their claim to a heavenly calling and immortality, which still doesn't alter the fact they are currently very mortal...

These good people may have an ache like no other in a heart so constricted they think they might die. They may know the story is flawed, but they know to rewrite even two words, three words, might mean being cast out.

[80] American poet and novelist (1932-63) and author of the semi-autobiographical *The Bell Jar* published in the UK in 1967.

Do you think this immeasurable universe, with its innumerable galaxies and incalculable stars, and staggering beauty and diversity, came into existence because nothing changed.? *Everything* changed. And everything continues to change.

Like Jonathan, we'll never learn to truly fly if we don't first lift our wings. And with the lifting comes the first chance to soar, and the second, and in a moment we're above where we thought we might have to stay forever, because it was all that we knew, and then here is something new, and thank you…just thank you.

Right at the very beginning, did we believe? And if we didn't, when did we start? And why? Was it not enough that the rain rained and the sun shone, and we connected to it all from a place of innocence and instinct?

Of course not. Because we are curious, inventive creators; because we want to know why, and how, and why all over again. How many times have you heard a child ask why? Once or twice? If you're a parent or someone frequently in the company of children you will know it is *thousands* of times. And it's a sobering thought, but up until a certain age children absolutely believe what they are told as absolute truth. Think about the responsibility of that. And think about this: Did we create a higher power, an infinite source of wisdom – a god? – to defer to because we didn't know the answers to why and how?

Why did the crop fail this season? *God was displeased.*

Why do we have to build more storehouses as the crop is so plentiful? *God has blessed us.*

Is just a short step to: Why did my child have to die? *God giveth and God taketh away.*

But what else is happening here? Blame, do you think, as well as a comfort of sorts?

The reliance on a higher power, an infinite source of wisdom, or a god who will answer all is the most perfect solution, really, because beyond basic powers of reasoning we simply do not know a thing, so we must defer to the invention of something or someone who might, whether or not it or they exist.

Therefore, does it – or I should say *should it* – really matter what any of us believe, because it's all the same thing, put in place for exactly the same reason? And there is absolutely nothing wrong with that. What is wrong is saying my beliefs are *the* beliefs and yours are not, so I am going to persecute you and possibly even kill you. Or saying my truth is *the* truth and yours is not, so I am going to dismiss and shun and judge you. Just because the Witnesses do not take up arms does not mean they live a passive life. Conversely, their defiant adherence to their truth is a form of passive attack: an insidious assault against everything and everyone they consider to be false. When will they – no, when will *we all* realise – it does not matter what we each believe, because it is all a version of the same thing. And it all has the power to destroy lives if we so allow it.

Eckhart Tolle in the wondrous *A New Earth* (a 'new earth' that actually makes sense) says this of religion – and it comes back to the point made earlier that a belief is only a thought we keep thinking, whether personal, political, cultural or religious, and something we attach to as true:

> 'The History of Christianity is, of course, a prime example of how belief that you are in sole possession of the truth, that is to say, right, can corrupt your actions and behaviour to the point of insanity.'

And how does he define truth?

> 'A story you had to believe in; which means, a bundle of thoughts.'

And absolute truth?

> '[…] you won't find absolute truth if you look for it where it cannot be found: in doctrines, ideologies, sets of rules, or stories […] If you believe your religion is the Truth, you are using it in service of the ego.[81] Used in such a way, religion becomes an ideology and creates an illusory sense of superiority as well as a division and conflict between people.'

I do not mind that one person's Brahma is another's Allah, or his Dao is her Way. Should you? We all need, it seems, something to believe in when we don't know the answers. Perhaps we should be comparing answers instead of starting wars or creating separation in the name of the questions we all have, and in the gods we seek in an attempt to answer them. Perhaps we should stop relying on an external source of wisdom at all, and realise all the wisdom we need is right here, inside the heart and humanness of each of us, which some would say is 'the god within' or 'the only true truth'.

But we cannot trust men to do this. And I use 'men' deliberately, for it is generally they who make the rules, start the wars, and seek to control or divide. When will you stop? When will the bully or the elder or the warrior or the politician

---

[81] Or who we think we are based on the stories we create and believe about ourselves.

or the leader of a divisive movement STOP? Do you think you are somehow playing God when you shake your fists or write your sermons or assemble your guns? Do you think you are providing answers to the questions we all have about why we're here with your preaching and your fighting?

When will we realise there are so many questions, but there is no one definitive answer, certainly not one in doctrines, ideologies, rules or stories? There never will be.

So stop looking. And stop telling your child or neighbour or congregation that you've found it. You haven't. And stop trying to coerce and persuade and convince that your way is *the* way. It isn't. Because there is no one answer, and there is no one way. Except this: Look and see that we are all each other, we are all the same, just in different shapes and guises, and accept and project *that* beautiful truth.

The small plane bumps about high over the Irish Sea, the three of us in various degrees of deep thought about what might happen when we land in the Isle of Man. When we do, the drunk man at the wheel talks nonstop as he drives full tilt towards the Grand Hotel. It's the first time I've been to the island, the first time I've seen palm trees. It's the first time I've seen my real dad since I was a little girl. He's the drunk man at the wheel.

He's still talking when we check in, and again when we meet up for sundowners on the terrace. He thinks he's really funny, and interesting. He's making my stomach ache and my hands shake. Charles is quiet and polite; my brother, with a beer in his hand, looks out across the sea; I make sounds that accompany my father's monologue. He raises his pint glass in a toast I don't remember. Am I laughing? If I am, it's a sound that doesn't fit.

Later we go to a Chinese restaurant and eat from the multiple dishes he insists are the best, and he drinks more beer. His eyes are heavy with the drink, and heavier later, after the Scotch.

I'd written a letter to him via his sister, shortly after I'd written the one to the postman. Mum had managed to find out where she was living: in the same house, two doors down from where we had been living, where I'd learnt to whistle whilst sitting on the coal bunker and learnt a lesson about karma standing on an anthill. We'd moved precisely because she still lived in the same house, because Mum was terrified our father would break the conditions of his restraining order and come and find us.

I look at my brother now, across the room, playing snooker with Charles. He's lining the blue up, and Charles is chalking up whilst watching. Our father isn't watching; he's at the bar, talking. And drinking.

My baby brother. Funny how he was as blonde as I was dark, and as chubby as I was skinny; yet here we are, both long and slim, with the same mid-brown hair and our grandfather's cheekbones and dimples. Yes, we look like brother and sister now, despite his blue-grey and my green eyes. I sense in him a further hurt: our father. Why did I do this to us?

He'd been a baby when Mum had fled this man's drunkenness and violence, and he didn't have any memories other than those recorded in his cells. I had both. So why was he the most broken? I have a photograph of us, taken around the time of the ants in my pants. We're standing side by side at the top of the garden, where I'd taken him to pee that day, in shorts and T-shirts and holding hands. I am smiling, posturing, one hand on my hip; my brother is looking away, his face half-closed, like his eyes. The camera never lies.

I'd wanted the hero father of my daydreams; the one who had ponies and would rescue me from Armageddon, not this braggart. I think my brother wanted that man too, or something like him; someone who would scoop him up and point him anywhere but down the road we were trapped on: the 'cramped and narrow road to salvation'. Oh, but how it delighted him to introduce us – *Meet my firstborn daughter and my son!* – but then flounder, because he had nothing to add. He didn't know us. He didn't want to know us. He just wanted to show off and show us off, like some kind of achievement.

This trip, it closed something down I'd hoped it would open. All I'd wanted was to see the other half of where I'd come from, to see my dad, to see if he loved me. I wanted to be his little girl, his best girl, and have his big, long Daddy arm around my life. I needed to know he was grown up now, and not the bastard who roared and kicked and punched, who rolled my grandfather's MG in a drunken display on the newly opened M1, who barely acknowledged his sixteen-year-old pregnant girlfriend – my mum, and it was me she was pregnant with – screaming to make sure she was still alive as the car lay bent and punctured and haemorrhaging fuel. And I'd done this, brought us all together, all because I'd wanted to know, because I wanted a dad. I hadn't thought about how it might be for my brother.

We walked miles on the beach, swam in the sea and in the pool, and played lots of snooker. The three of us were always good together, me, Charles and my brother. But this man we came to meet, our dad, who flew us out here so we could get to know each other, he was either at work or in the bar, and when he wasn't talking about himself specifically he was talking about himself generally. My brother seemed to fold more with each day, and then the day came to fly home.

What had I done?

All the stories I had created about him in my stupid head. And my biology teacher asking me if I thought I'd ever meet my real dad. And my heart hurting when I glanced at my brother as we landed at Luton.

Charles whispered, "It's okay…it'll be okay," and held my hand, like he always did, but another bit of me had broken off and I withdrew to where my fucking crap father couldn't reach me and cried so, so hard.

I'm listening to 50 Cent in the car, after dropping the girls off with their dad. The man is a bit rude. And I'm back in my bedroom the day the postman discovered my small stash of seven-inch singles, some bought, some borrowed. He snapped my Gary Numan seven-inch single in half because he was 'Satanic' – he was wearing eye-liner and a red leather jumpsuit on the cover. Ditto Lou Reed, because whoever it was in his Satanic lyrics 'plucked her eyebrows on the way, shaved her legs and then he was a she…' I had no idea what that meant in real terms, I just liked the song.

The thing about not listening to 'worldy' music, it was stifling, so I took to recording my favourite bits of the Top 40 show on Radio 1 on a tape machine because, I swear, if I'd had to listen to *The Best of the Shadows* or The *Hits of the Carpenters* one more time…

I loved that tape machine; the double-clunk of the Record and Play buttons as Tony Blackburn finally stopped talking and the Police or The Smiths or The Cure left messages in bottles or reeled around the fountain or fell in love on a Friday. I'd always got an ear on the bedroom door, though, in case I needed to hit Stop, shove the thing under the bed and grab a *Watchtower.*

I started saving my pocket money and buying the better quality TDK tapes, or Sony, because the ones off the market were rubbish and ended up spewing the brown ribbons of precious music out.

Danni, my closest Witness friend at the time, was allowed to buy whole albums of Pop music, and had a turntable *in her bedroom.* We learnt every word to every Depeche Mode song, Duran Duran too, and debated who was handsomer, Dave Gahan or Simon le Bon. I had a massive crush on Adam Ant – Adam Ant! – which I didn't tell anyone. What was it about him, Stuart Goddard, in all his gear and posturing? But then I also had a crush on Kim Wilde, and Debbie Harry.

Finally I was able to join in the conversations about music, and even the odd film I'd been allowed to see – *E.T.*, *Chariots of Fire,* and Star Trek and Star Wars films – and although it was tempered with feeling like an idiot in the company of the new older friends, I was finding my feet, and voice.

And here I am, singing 'Clothes off, face down, ass up, come on' to 50 Cent and laughing, and it's hard to explain the significance of this sort of freedom to someone who has never known the sort of restrictions we endured as JWs. I know Hannah understands, because we've laughed our heads off about it; and it may sound silly, or even like a fib, but I think about it almost every time I listen to music. It releases whole chunks of relief but, underneath, the residual fear still lurks, like a faint shadow of the monster it once was. I know it can't touch me anymore, but it'll always be there, the dread that made sure I said my prayers – Dear Jehovah, Dear Jehovah, amen – and tried to find a different way of saying 'forgive me, don't kill me' each time so as not to be guilty of the repetitive prayers of the world, which insincere and by rote held no clout with a god who apparently demanded originality along with my very soul.

The girls think it's funny, me having a 50 Cent CD, and the three of us debate which is the best song. Just to hear them laughing, and singing, and making their own minds up about what music they want to listen to… Are they mortally damaged from listening to 50 Cent? And, they tell me, much, much ruder music? (I think I'm still a little bit naive in that respect.) What do you think?

It tortured me for years that they might have been hurt and confused by the Truth, and I asked them often in the early years after escaping if they were okay. Annie barely remembered a thing, and said all she recalled was being bored and sitting on the floor colouring in or playing with the small toys I had brought with me to keep her quiet (which I wasn't supposed to have done, because letting her play on the floor was not training her to sit still on a chair for two hours and listen to Jehovah's wisdom). She also had little recollection of my terrible depression, although she remembered me 'being sad sometimes'.

Grace had been much older, and remembered being so scared her dad might die, and hating sitting in the school corridor while the rest of the class made anything from Mother's Day to Valentine's Day cards to Christmas decorations or Easter bunnies…all of which were things we were not allowed to celebrate as Witnesses.

Sadly, Grace and I did need to talk about what happened when I was so ill, as she remembered the cuts, and me crying uncontrollably, and the brothers and sisters visiting the house and shouting, and it broke my heart that she remembered. But

I was relieved, too, that I was able to tell her I was sorry I had felt it was the right thing to do to make her sit out in the corridor, and that she had been scared her dad might die, and we talked a little about my depression, and that it had nothing to do with her amazing dad and, no, it wasn't him who had cut me. I assured her we would never go back there, and that it was perfectly fine to ask me anything she needed to about that time.

Looking at the girls now, and seeing the hard-working, independent, gorgeous women they are, both a little mad and very kind and loved by absolutely everyone who meets them, I feel the same love that always threatens to overwhelm me. They have followed their hearts, explored the world and grown, confident in their ability to navigate and make choices.

I think having an unbelieving father helped, as he balanced my temporary return to religiousness with normality. And I was never, *ever* against them getting the most out of their education as they possibly could, letting them join every Satanic after-school club that they wished, from gymnastics to flute to violin to athletics, and encouraging them with my whole heart and soul to love the learning. I did not restrict them to Witness friends only, and allowed them to have school friends over, and the neighbours' friends, where they learnt about other people's lives and learnt a few swear words too, which they used.

I remember Annie being in the car with me on the way to the ministry one day. She'd just started reception class, so she was four or five. She was strapped into her car seat in the back, with a sister next to her, and I had an elderly brother in the front next to me. As we came up to the big roundabout by the park, someone in a black Audi pulled out in front of us and then swung off into the town without so much as braking, never mind looking or signalling. I tutted. But Alice shouted "Hey! Use your bloody indicators!"

How I loved them, love them. And how they love life.

There is an interview on YouTube with John Cedars and Dan Kokotajlo where they're discussing the writing, making and response to *Apostasy*. The interview is revealing; the online comments too:

'I was an elder and was sicken [sic] by my first and only judicial committee[82] I was assigned to [...]. I am currently struggling to save my family from this cult.'

'Some things are so bizarre, painful, and dreadful, all one can do is to laugh to maintain one's sanity.'

Others posted about the 'barbaric rules', or that 'rules are more important than love within the JW organisation'.

When Dan was going over the script with the actors in the week before filming commenced, he knew he needed to get them to 'sense' the Witness life. He spoke to them, showed them articles in the *Watchtower*, and their response: "Why would anyone do this? Why would anyone say things like this?"

There is a short answer: fear. And there is the answer here that has taken over two years to compose into the thing that isn't what it once was – a screaming roar that broke its banks and ran, ranting through the new life it had longed for yet did not know how to navigate. I dragged people along with me, to test their mettle. I was so angry I was demented, searching every

[82] The meetings arranged to discuss whether a brother or sister will be publicly reproved or disfellowshipped are called judicial committee meetings, as elders, like the Governing Body, believe they have court-like rights over people's lives.

cragged mountain and every dark ravine just to understand. I started friendships and ended them; I started relationships and then tore fast away; I bucked and ducked anything or anyone that might hold me down.

I dreamt, sweating and gasping, and in those dreams I was tearing skin from faces, breaking heads against pavements, shaking and slamming into death anyone who tried to silence me with words I'd heard too many times: be quiet; be nice; be a good girl.

I dreamt I was trying to speak the truth of how I felt, of the torture of being silenced, but the people just shook their heads, so I wrote their names in red on a white wall: they would be next, the elders judging and lying, and lifelong friends quick with gossip to each other's houses. Let me at you, so I can gouge you and yank the hair from your heads.

I dreamt I was in a room with no window, trapped on a bed against a wall and choking on cement that clogged my throat. I was crying, beating the walls with my hands, but no one came. No one ever comes.

I make tea and look out of the window. Rainwater is drying on the path, the blue sky reflected back at itself as birds criss-cross both. Our lives are a mirror. We see in others that which we are, and birds of all feathers cross our paths. We are both water and sky, and all the birds too. Sometimes the sparrow, sometimes the sparrow hawk; sometimes the songbird, sometimes the bird of prey. Needing both to fly and rest, and other times to dry under a blue sky.

A gathering for us – Mum, my brother and sister, and me – is an odd thing; a bringing together of four autobiographies; an assembly of mirrors. And none of us can really bear the pain of what we see reflected back at ourselves.

Our mother, always watching us: Are they okay? Have I loved them enough? I should have left that man. I should have got them out of that religion. Do they judge me? Are they angry? If I keep on loving them, listening to them, it'll be okay…please, let it be okay.

My brother, watching his sisters, his mother: Are we all mad? We could not have had that life and stayed sane. It's too painful to be together. Best we don't go too deep. Stay on the surface and love each other. It's all we can do.

My sister, watching and angry: She should have got us out. I am the outsider. They've always had each other. It's okay for them. Why didn't she leave? Why didn't she save us? I love them all so much. Why does being together make me so afraid?

Me, hardly able to watch: Stay still. Love them where they are, for who they are. I can't bear to be here. Stay with them all. I need to leave. Stay and be loved, and love. Do they love me? I'm not sure. I don't think they do. I'll have to love them from over here. It's safer here.

Music plays, the Beatles, downloaded now as the beat-up albums are in the attic, and we dance around Mum's kitchen, and the din is here, there and everywhere, bouncing in the teacups and doing somersaults across the rug. She knows every word, and so do I, raised as I was on every song the Fab Four ever wrote. *Love, love me do; you know I love you.* Our family humour is different and the same. Rude, and Mum raises an eyebrow. An in-house joke, and the roof rises. Vast copper pans of food get admired and stirred; wine is refused or passed around; juice for the great-grandchildren and water for the dogs.

It takes as long to leave as the entire evening passed, with coats and unfinished conversations finishing half-in half-out of rooms. New boyfriends and girlfriends perch and hover, and we wonder what they're wondering about us all, loud and loving and still dancing as someone breaks into song and those not in voice laugh along.

But we all know how it shaped who we became, the thing we all were. And I think we are all afraid still, in our way, that we will be killed by a vengeful god for turning our backs on him, for leaving the safety of the flock for the depravity of the world. I don't think we'll ever really be able to stop seeing the signs in every war and earthquake and food shortage and pestilence, the things which must occur, 'and then the end will come'. I don't think we'll ever forget the power of the Truth, the feel of it as we sang in stadiums, set apart, better than, bonded as brothers and sisters in the faith awaiting our instructions from the Governing Body. But equally we know these truths were toxic. They ate into our deepest selves masquerading as faith, as love, as loyalty.

Don't tell me it wasn't that bad. Don't tell me we did have some good times, though, didn't we. There are poisons that taste a little sweet...

Look in the mirror of each other and see just how we've faired from the near-lethal drip-drip of the promise of sweet salvation, and notice how we laugh to salve the lingering splinters of hurt.

> 'Some things are so bizarre, painful, and dreadful, all one can do is to laugh to maintain one's sanity.'

I'm not sure how to wrap this up. I haven't set out to tell you anything new, so maybe that's why I can't seem to create the 'that equals that' sentence, the 'because thus is so, then thus is so' that you might have been hoping to take away with you as some kind of definitive conclusion of all matters. The truth is, there is no such thing anyway, and it's insane to claim there is. If cornered, I would simply say: there is nothing to be achieved other than drowning by clinging to the water; let it hold you and, when you are ready, don't be afraid to dive below the surface.

I honestly felt like I had the truth; that no matter what, this truth would free me. But it pinned me down. It cornered and distorted and annihilated, like a bully first backs a victim to a wall, then begins a system of coercion, then goes in for the blow. I shall now use the word betrayal.

In Inferno, the first part of Dante's *The Divine Comedy*, he portrays betrayal, or Treachery, as the Ninth Circle of Hell, or the most despicable of acts after Limbo, Lust, Gluttony, Greed, Anger, Heresy, Violence and Fraud. From a study of Inferno:

> 'Treachery in its own right is wasteful to Life itself. It is more serious than the other previous sins due to the sinners' assumption of being able to claim absolute authority over any living being […] Treachery was a frozen landscape ringed by the Classical and Biblical Giants who symbolized pride and other spiritual flaws lying behind acts of treachery…'[83]

Could the Witnesses, or any other religious body hellbent on being the 'absolute authority' of matters of faith and belief – surely a case of the utmost arrogance, if ever there was one – be considered guilty of treachery? It matters not to the men who peddle nonsense and lies as truth that those who put their trust in them are being lied to; it matters not that when the

[83] www.dantesinferno.fandom.com

once-believers are cast aside as non-believers they flounder and hurt, wondering how they could have devoted so many years to a truth that simply wasn't.

It felt like such a deep betrayal of my love, my trust and my loyalty when I began to see the Witness truth for what it was – a dogmatic manmade construct designed to instil fear of losing faith in the Organisation (and therefore Jehovah God as its authority) as a death sentence, thereby pinning me to the wall – that for so very long I felt only helplessness.

I would watch as a visitor, or 'interested person' as they were called, would be encouraged, unsure and a little out of their comfort zone, into a Kingdom Hall for the first time. They would be greeted with much enthusiasm, led to a seat, assured of their most welcome presence. They would see the clean, well-dressed, polite men and women, with their children all in a smiling row, and the meeting would begin with rousing song and earnest prayer. They would hear the quiet rustle of Bible pages, sense the hush of reverence for its final say, feel the commitment of multiple minds to a purpose: to preach this beautiful truth surrounded by your faithful, trusted brothers and sisters until the end comes and paradise follows. What human, a little or a lot broken (as we all are in our way) wouldn't want to belong to that? Underpinning every new membership to a club or a support group (or a religion or a cult) is the intrinsic desire to be accepted, to belong to something. It doesn't matter whether it's Alcoholics Anonymous or golf or God, we seem to need to gather together and identify with something, learn the lingo, perfect the swing, sing the hymn. There's nothing inherently wrong with that; it's what we do to salve the otherwise lonely thrashing about in just what life is without belonging.

But what these often vulnerable people don't realise – and from what I witnessed, those who entered the Witness world out of choice rather than being born into it were all vulnerable in some way – is that this initial meeting, this warm greeting and most welcome respite from the thrashing about, is the first unwitting step towards the bully's wall. Before long comes the coercion. And then the blow. But consider this: the wall is not a literal wall, but the Truth itself, sure and strong; the coercion is not constructed of insults, but a series of initiations and accolades; and the blow is: now you're in, you'll die if you leave. Imagine that. And imagine this: You are invited along to a Kingdom Hall, and you accept for whatever reason. You are welcomed, and you are shown to a seat. But before you are permitted to sit you are taken outside, to the back of the hall. As far as your eye can see there are unmarked gravestones in rows upon rows longer than even those in Ypres Salient on the Western Front. Each stands at the head of the grave-diggers' as yet unfilled holes.

You turn to the elder who has led you out here, who has his hand lightly on your elbow. "What is this place?" you ask.

"Ah," he says, and there's a particular pride in his voice, "these are the graves we've prepared for those who disagree with us."

Imagine if this was real, in that it existed not merely as a belief in the minds of each and every Witness – for this is how they are trained to view those of the human race who don't worship Jehovah – but was a literal and prepared place at the back of every single Kingdom Hall across the planet. One of two things would happen: you would run, right then, and fast; or you would stay, for the fear would already have gripped you far tighter than the hand lightly on your elbow.

The prime objective of a bully? To take away a person's self-belief and self-expression and to put the fear of God, or them, in them. In this context, if you run you will be deemed 'too self-willed for the Truth'. If you stay, nothing you think or feel from that moment onwards will have any merit if it doesn't line up with Jehovah's purpose and truth as revealed by his only true witness on Earth – the Governing Body. In fear your head will nod, and you will await instructions, even if they defy all human logic and compassion. You will close your heart to unbelievers and you will shun family and friends. You will follow first the brother or sister who brought you here, and believe them; and then the elders and overseers on platforms who confirm what that brother or sister has told you.

You could be forgiven for thinking it is Jehovah God, your creator, you are faithfully following, and his ways and truth you are obeying when you don't celebrate your child's birthday, or answer the cry of help from an unbelieving friend. You may think it's Jehovah's ways you are following when you observe children being taught not to believe or trust in themselves and their hopes and dreams, but to put their faith fully in Jehovah alone to guide them. And you may come to believe, when you see families ripped to pieces, sick people told what treatment they can and can't have, and the depressed told they are not faithful enough, that these too are Jehovah's ways, his higher wisdom, for we are all imperfect and therefore incapable of making our own decisions. They are not. They are the instructions of men who must continue to flog a truth as far from truth as planet Earth from the very edges of the known universe, because to admit otherwise would result in exposure as the merciless, treacherous liars they are.

But the people will nod and follow the instructions, thinking they have chosen this life as part of their God-given freewill, unaware for the most part that some of the deepest psychological fears known to humans – of being alone and our own mortality – have been triggered by the passive bullying of elders claiming to be the spokesmen of this higher wisdom. But why? Why stay? Because those who nod their heads and follow instructions will eventually receive the mighty accolades of 'a fine sister', 'a strong brother', 'a credit to the Truth'. And if they don't nod their heads and follow instructions, they too will be shunned as they have been taught to shun, and labelled 'apostate'.

It has to be asked: Is this really freewill? Or the instant, clawing fear of being lowered into one of those as yet unmarked graves? Yet I know why people stay, which is why I have no final thing to say. People need AA or golf or God. They need to belong.

Seems God, the creator or energy in all that we see and are, is being lied about though, on an astronomical scale. If you're happy being lied to, then stay; if not, flee. It will be traumatic, and break you in ways that will make you wish you stayed, but consider this… If you love God, and need his presence in your life, you have the exhilarating choice to clear his name by refusing to believe and spread the lies written in his name, and instead love him with the freedom you were born with, the freedom he created you with. It will also free you to be you, to discover who and what and why you are. And, goodness, the laughter and the tears and the joy and the satisfaction in that.

It is not wrong to ask questions, to delve, to shelve that which no longer makes sense. What is wrong is to corner and coerce and deal blows that few have the strength to field for fear of fear itself, in the end; to label as 'apostate', an 'enemy of God', a person who expresses a different viewpoint to that which is being forced upon you as 'this is the way it is, or else you will suffer the consequences'.

I first read *Crisis of Conscience* by ex-Governing Body member Raymond Franz twenty years ago. I recently reread it. It is a beautifully written book, and testament to the warmth and compassion of its author for humankind, and his deep love of truth. He wrote with an openness, and a fervour, on many of the subjects I have touched on here, and with an astounding depth of knowledge.

He talks about the outrageous claims the Governing Body made on the deeply personal way married couples enjoyed each other's bodies, humiliating those who, consumed with guilt, felt compelled to confess because of fear of Jehovah's disapproval, and disfellowshipping those who continued to enjoy oral sex as part of their foreplay. For some, because of injury or surgery, this was the only way they could pleasure each other, and one of the most shocking examples of utter compliance with the Governing Body in relation to oral sex I have ever read is this (my italics): '*I am scared, I am hurt* [...] *I know you will tell me what to do.*' All of the cases he cites are heartbreaking. (p. 57-67)

He dissects the chronology of 1914 and 1975, along with other key Witness dates, incredulous that although these dates have absolutely no scriptural substantiation, they were still presented as fact. (1914 still is.) More shocking was the Governing Body's opinion that any brother or sister taken in by the furore of 1975 had 'reached false conclusions on [their] own', and neither acknowledged nor apologised for the catastrophic effect on millions of people's lives when 1975 came and went. (p. 277-279, 282-287, 337-338)

He reveals some of the life-changing decisions made about brothers and sisters they had never met – 'whether one qualifies as an elder if he approves of his son or daughter taking higher education; whether one qualifies as an elder if he does shift work and sometimes (while on night shift) misses congregational meetings; whether elders can accept circumstantial evidence of adultery, or the testimony of a wife that her husband confessed adultery to her, and whether this is sufficient to a allow for a Scriptural divorce and remarriage' – and the dismissive, disinterested attitudes of the men making those decisions in a matter of minutes that would affect the lives involved for years. (p. 55-56)

He talks about the illegal movement of money, so as to gain a better return on the American dollar, and the methods employed to avoid paying heavy import taxes on the transporting of equipment into certain countries. (p. 56)

In the chapter entitled 'Double Standards' he exposes the shocking hypocrisy of a Governing Body imposing rules in Malawi and Mexico in the sixties and seventies that resulted in the gang-raping, beating, torturing and killing of faithful brothers and sisters and their children in the latter, and their safety and protection in the former. There was neither acknowledgment nor apology to the surviving families. (p. 173-186)

The effect *Crisis of Conscience* had this second time was more profound than the first. The first time I was still in shock, I think, after leaving, and certainly too heartbroken to absorb many of the finer points. This time I was able to analyse each of his discussions much recovered, and I echo Raymond's own summary about this group of cruel, dogmatic, unloving men who he simply could not work with any longer:

> 'I could not personally comprehend how grown men could fail to be repelled […] could not be deeply moved by its effect on people's lives […] How those responsible – genuinely and primarily responsible – for all this can approach God in prayer at night and say, "Show us mercy as we have shown mercy to others," is difficult for me to understand.'

Raymond Franz never doubted the existence of God, or Jesus, or what he considered to be the sacred words of the Bible in his hand. No, he needed answers from the men who twisted and grossly misrepresented scripture to suit their, by now, pathological attachment to being right over being truthful. He needed to know where their love was, their mercy. This gentle, loving man was disfellowshipped after decades of faithful service, accused of apostasy: the crime of free thought.

Watch the despicable YouTube clip below[84] entitled 'By Condemning "Despicable Apostates", has the Governing Body Condemned Themselves?' and see current member of the Body, Anthony Morris III[85], in full, sickening swing on becoming an enemy of God. Listen to the laughter of his audience as he demonstrates God's view of his enemies by lighting a match and

---

[84] https://youtu.be/jebv0TuLqeg

[85] A further shocking example of Anthony Morris III. https://tonyortega.org/2019/04/09/an-ex-jehovahs-witness-explains-why-the-bottlegate-video-is-so-crucial/

– poof! – extinguishing it. It made me cry. It made me want to write something unpublishable.

Like Raymond, who watched helpless and heartbroken as one by one his dearest and most faithful friends were disfellowshipped for the crime of free thought, I too have sat with friends sobbing because of the terrible hurt inflicted by elders and overseers who have labelled them as apostates, enemies of God, because they've dared to question one of the Governing Body's truths. Like Raymond, not one of them ever received an apology. No one ever receives an apology.

I've listened to podcasts and watched amateur videos and professional TED talks on truth and untruth from those on the receiving end of the latter and in the throes of searching for the former. I've read the outpourings of support groups for ex-Witnesses (with tens of thousands of members) who write about their PTSD, severe depression and suicide attempts.[86] I've read tragic stories from friends of those who succeeded.[87]

I've watched documentaries – in particular the 'Cults' episode on *Explained* on Netflix – and cried with those crying into the camera for their 'hijacked life', their 'lost childhood' and 'loss of self-worth and confidence' at the hands of men who claim the right to impart higher wisdom as imparted by God.

I've heard the foaming monologues of those who believe the Witnesses should be stripped of their charitable status for failing to utter one charitable word or extend one charitable act towards those suffering in their ranks, for as undeniably

[86] The figures are impossible to confirm as the Governing Body closes rank around suicide much as it does around abuse, but it is claimed the suicide rate amongst ex-Witnesses is five to ten percent higher than national averages.

[87] https://eu.freep.com/story/news/local/michigan/2018/03/18/jehovahs-witnesses-murder-suicide-keego-harbor/409695002/

unethical as most charities are, their corruption is at least balanced by helping their fellowman, whoever their god or lack of. As a non-stock, not-for-profit organisation, what do the Witnesses spend the millions of tax-free donations on, aside from providing a meagre allowance for pioneers, missionaries and Bethel workers? All Bethel workers must take a 'vow of poverty', and turn over any supplementary income they earn on their day off – other than that required for additional basic human needs (which their paltry allowance from the Society doesn't cover) – to the Society. This makes Morris III's 'Bottlegate' shopping trip, caught on camera, even more offensive.

It is common knowledge that vast swathes of the headquarters at Brooklyn have been sold in recent years for nearly $800 million. What have the Governing Body, this fluctuating number of men (who have never numbered more than eighteen, and currently stand at eight) done with that vast sum of money other than purchase new headquarters in Warwick, New York?

It is less common knowledge, however, that for ten years, between 1991 and 2001, the Governing Body were active members of the United Nations as an NGO – a Non-Governmental Organisation – obediently publishing (heavily cloaked) pro-UN information through the pages of the *Watchtower* and *Awake!* magazines and attending meetings with United Nations officials and other NGO members. This is a worldly organisation the Governing Body have for decades branded as the true representation of political evil on Earth, Satan's No 1 tool to mislead the nations, as depicted by the many-headed scarlet beast of Revelation. Tami Dickerson's book, *Jehovah's Witnesses and The United Nations: How the Watchtower Society fooled millions*, is superbly and intricately researched.

As a devout Witness, Tami initially set out to prove what she considered to be a wicked anti-Witness rumour wrong. This is what she discovered:

> 'Finally, after exhausting all possible leads I had no choice but to face the facts – every piece of evidence and verifiable documentation led to only one conclusion: This offensive "rumor" was actually the truth.'

Part of the documentation she discovered revealed 'active participation' by Witness members at United Nations events, conferences and interviews on items such as 'Safe Blood Starts With Me! Blood Saves Lives!' She quotes from a commemorative book published shortly after (her underline):

> '"Of particular note was the presence of Jehovah's Witnesses at the event [...] All participants expressed their gratitude to the humanitarian actions of voluntary blood donors."'

Is it a coincidence that shortly before the Governing Body had revealed a 'new truth' concerning the use of blood in medical interventions, as discussed in the same article in *The Guardian*, 8 October 2001, that first exposed their alliance with the UN (my underline):

> '...God had revealed to them that transfusions of some blood components might be acceptable, providing there was later repentance...'

Upon exposure of their playing nicely with the scarlet beast, the Governing Body immediately withdrew their registration, and wrote that they'd only joined so they could access the United Nations' library...

Blood transfusions, the two-witness rule, rules about foreplay, the absolute insistence of dates being scripturally correct... These outrageous truths, enforced by a body of men through the pages of the *Watchtower*, men as far removed from love and truth and human compassion as is possible, have destroyed *countless* lives. The general public are not privy to the Witness-only version of the *Watchtower* published for this purpose, no, they are offered a 'soft' *Watchtower*, a Public Edition version intended to dupe and lure those floundering and vulnerable and in need of a bit of faith.

And what in God's name will they write next to tailor world events to fit their truth? Are they secretly still in bed with the scarlet beast, the United Nations, so together they can engineer the persecution of the common 'Tom, Dick and Harry'[88] brothers and sisters to fit the Great Tribulation model? I acknowledge this is a bold thing to say, but it is my feeling these men will stop at nothing to prove their rightness. The whole show is well and truly out of control.

Like Raymond, I know people who for decades gave their hearts, their souls, their everything to the Witnesses; good people who would have parted with their last coin if it meant they could honour Jehovah by helping to purchase a new carpet for their local Kingdom Hall or a smarter fence for the car park. I've sat and listened to their prayers as they've begged for more self-control, for a purer mind, for fewer sinful thoughts, on the verge of weeping for not being good enough in Jehovah's eyes (in

[88] As uttered by one of the Society's presidents. (p. 323 of *Crisis of Conscience*)

their eyes), of failing the test of a Witness worthy of the 'fine gifts' Jehovah bestows on his faithful followers. I've listened to their honest, brave talks – like the gentle lady Sheryl Bogolin who, realising she had got it so, so wrong, became depressed, ashamed at how she had treated dear friends and family because of being 'misguided' for years of her life. She recorded a most beautiful podcast on YouTube called '61 years of faithful service.'[89]

I've been in the company of those determined to defend the Truth to the death, even defending elders who'd committed vile acts – 'for all are weak and fall short of the glory of God, and all are justified freely by his grace…' (Romans 3:23 KJV) – and lied and destroyed lives whilst expecting that 'grace' in bucketloads. I've heard and read of numerous cases brought against the Witnesses, notably of sexual abuse, that have not-so-mysteriously disappeared without trial, and the monies paid for that silence. I've seen the 'for all are weak' card played over and over as an excuse, as a reason to deny all accountability, as a complete cop-out to accepting the fact that a terrible act has been committed. Read the 2 September 2021 article from the *Guardian* online, which cites the Witnesses' defence of a civil claim brought against them for the five-year abuse of a young girl by a ministerial servant. She was four years old when the abuse began. The full IICSA (Independent Inquiry Child Sex Abuse, 2021) report can also be read online. In recent weeks several other cases of child abuse within the Witnesses have been published and covered on international news channels, which I read with horror and rage. And I wonder what the outcome was of the 2017 $66 million class-action lawsuit brought against the

[89] https://podtail.com/en/podcast/beroean-pickets-jw-org-reviewer/why-i-left-the-watchtower-organization-after-61-ye/

Witnesses in Canada (alone) for sexual abuse?[90] These men are not 'weak', they are despicable.

I was friends with those who paid lip service to the Truth, whilst quite freely drinking and smoking and fornicating behind closed doors, and who figured 'whatever', for want of a better word.

I've heard children sobbing as they're being thrashed by their parents for not sitting still at the meeting. I've seen the light go out in their eyes, eventually, as they fall in line, frightened and silenced by a truth far bigger than the dreams they dared to have of being anything other than an obedient Jehovah's Witness. The Witnesses are now baptising these 'in-born' children, some as young as six years old, to counter the decrease in numbers of active adult members.[91] The videos[92] created by the Society to specifically target these young minds[93] are deeply disturbing. Hitler would be proud.

I know those who've left their religion or cult and why, and I know those who've stayed and why, so I'm not telling you to pack up your Bible (or any other religious book) and abandon your faith. What I am saying is that if what those books are telling you is causing hurt and separation – or the men who quote heavily from those books are telling you in order to shore up their version of truth – then can it really be a truth worth defending at all costs? Indeed, is anything that is a manmade construct of whatever belief and faith is worth defending at all

---

[90] See the heading 'The Witnesses and sexual abuse' in the list of online sources at the end of the book.

[91] https://www.quora.com/Why-are-many-Jehovah-s-Witnesses-children-being-baptized

[92] https://www.youtube.com/watch?v=E8pL-LnqNyw

[93] https://tonyortega.org/2019/04/09/an-ex-jehovahs-witness-explains-why-the-bottlegate-video-is-so-crucial/

costs? Why is it we become so attached to these constructs, to the point where we defend and judge and attack? Or frighten and silence children who never get the chance to explore who they are away from the only truth they've ever known? Or consider anyone 'less than' because they do not believe what we believe, to the point where we will dismiss or diminish them as living, breathing, worthy human beings?

For the vast majority of Witnesses it is not their fault they behave the way they do. They are the victims of sustained propaganda, a brainwashing so convincing they will reject all natural human instincts to uphold the dogmatic rules and instructions penned in a *Watchtower*. As Sam Fade states, they are quite literally brain damaged. A deeply sinister aspect of brainwashing is that the victims are so damaged they don't even realise they have fallen victim. How else would you explain the unshakable adherence to men, the tolerance of hypocrisy and law-breaking, the trust in ever-changing dates and truths as real and true, the complete inability to consider any other viewpoint other than their own as valid, the cruelty of shunning loved ones who can no longer cope and leave? The men at the self-appointed top, however, they know exactly what they're doing, and have done for decades… Perhaps it is time the whitewash was washed from the tomb of lies they have dedicated decades to constructing and hiding behind.

We are born with an inherent abhorrence of absolute control and inexcusable cruelty: we remove dictators and gather together against those who beat animals or women or children. Why do we not do the same with religious control and cruelty? Why are we so disabled by its power? Is it because we essentially believe it has something, anything at all, to do with God, and therefore must acquiesce?

To requote: '*A belief is only a thought we keep thinking.*' Beliefs are not real. They exist only in the chattering ether that is the human mind wishing to understand that which it doesn't understand. And they are neither a reason nor an excuse for abuse of any kind – religious, cultural, social, sexual, in short, anything that takes away a human being's smile, lifeforce, life.

The Witnesses may well get their Armageddon, but I don't think it will be the Armageddon of their dreams. Something is emerging. There is a growing sense of wanting something better; huge changes in consciousness towards being better; whole movements for understanding and including, and others for the end of judgement and mistreatment. There may yet be difficult times, and world events and human behaviour we struggle to comprehend, but as the man who opened that shiny black door said to me, 'There are some beautiful things happening in the world, despite the unfortunate pockets of war and other troubles, and some beautiful people doing them. Take a look at that, just to see. I think you'll be surprised. And I think it will help you understand the wider, bigger picture.'

I have never forgotten the impact of those words. And I have never stopped believing we are capable of choosing the wider, bigger picture instead of the narrow, hurtful alternative. It is both indefensible and unsustainable to mislead, to coerce, to lie. Sooner or later the lie will collapse, exposing the bones of those no longer permitted to whitewash or hide.

The examined life, to come full circle to Socrates, is a thing of beauty, the thing that marries wisdom with humility. What we have discussed here, this thing called belief – specifically religious belief, but equally any belief that hurts and divides – is not wisdom married with humility, it is opinion married with misplaced superiority. Wisdom married with humility is the realisation there is no man nor book nor way that will ever truly represent what truth is, because such a thing simply doesn't exist, if we are strong enough to face that truth. The only workable truth is that we're all here, and we all have the opportunity to examine, to be better, to change, comfortable with knowing it is the examination that is the path to personal and collective wisdom, not the proving, and certainly not the commitment to disproving all else but our own truth as truth.

Imagine the playground as a playground not a battle-ground, where the roundabouts are glorious discussions around tables with open minds and light hearts ready to embrace the length and breadth of just what it is to be a believing or a non-believing human being, and where the swings are the playthings of the debate, with absolutely no need whatsoever to be right, humbled by the sharing and wiser for it.

Is it possible, do you think, to do that?

Should we want for anything less?

Epilogue

I'm lying on a bed in a warm, quiet room where the vibrations of Tibetan singing bowls can still be felt. She's by my side, the healer, concentrating, her hands moving above my body. I close my eyes, try to relax into what is happening.

For a long time I have been curious about the power of healing, despite the echo of long-ago fear and even the immediate, persistent thoughts of whether it's real. And yet I'm willing to experience this, to surrender to it, it being something I have chosen to explore.

"Something…there's something…" she says. "A little girl, you're a little girl, and you're frightened. You're very anxious. Can I look a bit deeper?"

And quite unexpectedly I am fully alert.

"There's something here…a blockage…it's been here a long time…may I take a look?"

I open my eyes. Her hands are circling over my left side, over my spleen. She pauses, and I nod.

"You're a little girl, about six…and you're frightened. The blockage is here. Something happened…it's been with you such a long time. Do I have your permission to look further?"

My heart is thumping, my breath shallow. I know about that little girl. I just don't know how she knows. And why now?

It's too much. But I must listen. I must surrender to this. I nod, and close my eyes again.

"You're about six or seven, and you're in a room. You're very anxious. Something happened in there. I don't know what it is but it's still here, and you've been carrying it… I'd like to help you with it. Do I have your permission?"

"Yes. Please." I can hardly breathe now. My body is vibrating, my head too.

"It's here, right here…"

There is a sensation I am unable to describe, and a sudden weakness, a complete inability to think or move. My left side is throbbing, but not with pain, with an odd emptiness. She covers me with a blanket and tells me to lay still, to breathe, to let go of all thought, to let my body adjust. Physically and mentally I have no choice. I cannot form thoughts or lift my head. I don't even have the desire. There is just a deep, deep peace.

I haven't thought about that little girl for decades, trapped in that room, frightened and feeling sick. But it would seem for decades I have carried her fear in my side, as if I were still her, still there. I know I am still her, just me now, and the room is a story from so long ago, so why…?

When I get home I look up thrombocytopenia, a condition characterised by abnormally low levels of platelets, which I have had for years. It is the spleen that regulates platelets and can sometimes harbour and/or destroy them. The body keeps the score.

And then I open my notebook, where I have been making notes for my life writing assignment 'To Go Beneath the Water' – '*I am six years old and sat between my mother and a woman with fidgeting hands. We're at a Bible study meeting in a room that is too hot…*' – and we cry together, me and the little girl, and I'm so grateful I can tell her it's okay now. We're okay now.

The Rise and Fall

What is there left to think about, when the thinking's all been done
Who is there left who loves, when fear's been on the run
Whose heart dares to trust, when doubt has had its say
Whose soul doesn't bleed, when hurt has had its way
Who stands at the edge and doesn't see the drop
Who turns to dark black sky and prays for life to stop

Stand tall and unashamed
Of tears that come to fall
Take a breath and bravely
Embrace the rise and fall

See the look that holds the hand held in a room
Where noise comes too quickly, and peace leaves too soon
Return to yourself then, be there for a while
The people's cries will abate as time revolves its time
Step quietly in the moment you found inside your mind
See all your befores and afters, the things you left behind

But there's a whisper now from over there, the sweetest, softest call
That changes come and changes go, or never change at all

Stand brave and unashamed
Of tears that come to fall
Take a breath and bravely
Embrace the rise and fall

K L Miller

Bibliography and Sources

Books

Adams, D. (1994) *The Hitchhiker's Guide to the Galaxy*, Weidenfeld & Nicolson, UK

Bach, R. (1970) *Jonathan Livingstone Seagull*, Macmillan Inc
bin Laden, C (2004) *Inside the Kingdom*, Virago Press

Bolte Taylor, J. (2006) *My Stroke of Insight: A Brain Scientist's Personal Journey*, Viking

Byrne, R. (2006) *The Secret,* Atria Publishing Group

Coelho, P. (1988) *The Alchemist,* first published in Portuguese by Harper Collins

Dawkins, R. (2006) *The God Delusion,* Houghton Mifflin, New York

Dickerson, T. (2011) *Jehovah's Witnesses and The United Nations: How the Watchtower Society fooled millions.* Available on Amazon

Estés, C.P. (1992) *Women Who Run with The Wolves,* Rider, UK

Franz, R. (1983) *Crisis of Conscience*, NuLife Press, USA

Hicks, E. & J. (2007) *The Law of Attraction*, Hay House Inc

Holloway, R. (2017) *The Little History of Religion*, London, Yale University Press

Kolk, Bessel (van der). (2014) *The Body Keeps the Score*, Viking Penguin, USA, Penguin Books, UK

Kozlowski, L. (2020) *Trauma Bonding,* published by Escape the Narcissist

Luna, A. and Sol, M. (2019) *The Spiritual Awakening Process* published by Amazon UK

Mendez, P. (2020) *Rainbow Milk*, Dialogue Books, UK

Obama, M. (2018) *Becoming*, Crown, USA, and Penguin Random House, UK

O'Brien, R. C. (1975) *Z for Zacharia*, Heinemann Educational Publishers, Oxford, UK

Peck, Scott M. (1978) *The Road Less Travelled*, Simon and Schuster (USA) and Hutchinson & Co (UK) (1983)

Russell, B. (1950) *Unpopular Essays,* George Allen & Unwin Ltd, London, UK

Schopenhauer, A. (1890) *The Essays of Arthur Schopenhauer; Religion, a Dialogue, Etc.*, Anodos Books, Dumfries & Galloway, Scotland (2017)

The New World Translation of the Holy Bible, The Watch Tower Bible & Tract Society, Pennsylvania, USA

Tolle, E. (2005) *A New Earth: Awakening to Your Life's Purpose,* Penguin Group (USA) and Michael Joseph

Tolle, E. (2003) *Stillness Speaks: A Guide to Spiritual Enlightenment* [2016 edition], Yellow Kite Books

Tolle, E. (1997) *The Power of Now,* Namaste Publishing

Films and Documentaries

Apostasy, written and directed by Kokotajlo, D. (2017) originally screened at Toronto International Film Festival, now streamed on YouTube, Amazon Prime, iPlayer, Curzon

Becoming, Michelle Obama, streamed on Netflix

I Am Not Your Guru, Tony Robbins, streamed on Netflix

I-Origins (2014), originally screened in Russia, now streamed on Netflix

Finding Joe (2011), streamed on Amazon Prime Video

Online Sources, Interviews, TED talks and Articles

Alan Watts on faith
https://youtu.be/sfS6jZgjMBI

Alan Watts on honesty
https://youtu.be/O219t16U4Qg

Apostasy
https://www.eco nomist.com/prospero/2018/07/25/apostasy-is-a-heartbreaking-look-at-life-as-a-jehovahs-witness

'By Condemning "Despicable Apostates", has the Governing Body Condemned Themselves?'
https://youtu.be/jebv0TuLqeg

Cavorting with the Devil: Leaving the Jehovah's Witnesses
https://www.lancaster.ac.uk/fass/resources/sociology-online-papers/papers/holden-cavorting-with-the-devil.pdf

Child baptism within the Witnesses
https://www.quora.com/Why-are-many-Jehovah-s-Witnesses-children-being-baptized

Child brainwashing within the Witnesses
https://www.youtube.com/watch?v=E8pL-LnqNyw
https://tonyortega.org/2019/04/09/an-ex-jehovahs-witness-explains-why-the-bottlegate-video-is-so-crucial/

Great Tribulation
https://www.jw.org/en/bible-teachings/questions/great-tribulation/

Interview with John Cedars
https://www.youtube.com/watch?v=oK7h5czSiYA

Interview with Dan Kokotajlo
https://www.theguardian.com/film/2018/jul/15/apostasy- director-daniel-kokotajlo-liberating-to-leave-jehovahs-witnesses- interview

Jill Bolte Taylor on right and left brain functions and processing
https://www.youtube.com/watch?v=PezzZ_ccgQ

Reid (2012, pg. 46) on Thoreau
www.plato.stanford.edu/

Religious fundamentalism and brain damage
https://www.salon.com/2019/01/08/a-link-between- brain-damage-and-religious-fundamentalism-has-now-been- established-by-scientists_partner/

Richard Dawkins on religious indoctrination of children
https://www.richarddawkins.net/2015/02/dont-force- your-religious-opinions-on-your-children/

Sheryl Bogolin on 61 years of faithful service
https://podtail.com/en/podcast/beroean-pickets-jw-org-reviewer/why-i-left-the-watchtower-organization-after-61-ye/

Study of Dante's Inferno
www.dantesinferno.fandom.com

Support for ex-JWs
www.exjwsupport.co.uk
https://jwvictims.org

The Witnesses and abuse of women
https://jwvictims.org/2018/09/17/dangerous-advice-to-domestic-violence-victims-with-a-disturbing-twist/

The Witnesses and advice to wives of adulterous husbands
https://jwvictims.org/2020/01/12/watchtowers-blatant-misogyny-in-advice-for-innocent-wives/

The Witnesses and blood transfusions
https://www.youtube.com/watch?v=U94nUZD05zo

The Witnesses and child molestation
https://www.nbcnews.com/id/wbna21917798

The Witnesses and damage to brain development in children
https://freedomofmind.com/how-jehovahs-witness-teachings-can-damage-brain-development-in-children/

The Witnesses and sexual abuse
https://www.theguardian.com/society/2021/sep/02/millions-children-religious-groups-vulnerable-abuse-england-and-wales

https://www.iicsa.org.uk/document/child-protection-religious-organisations-and-settings-investigation-report-september-2021

https://news.sky.com/story/there-was-no-reprimand-nothing-changed-survivors-criticise-jehovahs-witness-elders-for-failing-to-act-over-child-sexual-abuse-claims-12396672

https://apple.news/Ah198-WQ-TBW51TKXycnPrg

https://toronto.citynews.ca/2017/10/02/66m-class-action-sex-abuse-suit-filed-jehovahs-witnesses/

https://revealnews.org/blog/jehovahs-witnesses-sued-in-canda-for-history-of-sex-abuse-cover-up/

The Witnesses and suicide
https://www.openmindsfoundation.org/shunning-suicide-jehovahs-witnesses-alienations-deadly-toll/

https://eu.freep.com/story/news/local/michigan/2018/03/18/jehovahs-witnesses-murder-suicide-keego-harbor/409695002/

https://www.jehovahs-witness.com/topic/5712468550615040/what-current-suicide-mental-illness-rate-among-jws-previous-members

The Witnesses and the two-witness rule
https://aoadvocates.com/jehovahs-witnesses-new

https://lawandreligionuk.com/2020/02/14/jehovahs-witnesses-and-the-two-witness-rule-a-comment-on-bxb/

The Human Library
www.humanlibrary.org

Trauma bonding
https://www.harleytherapy.co.uk/counselling/what-is-trauma-bonding.htm

http://abusewarrior.com/toxic-relationships/narcissistic-abuse/signs-of-trauma-bonding/

'What Shall We Tell the Children?' by Nicholas Humphrey
https://www.youtube.com/watch?v=yfr6SkaBuq0 www.jw.org

Children's Rights

https://en.wikipedia.org/wiki/Save_the_Children
https://www.savethechildren.org.uk/
https://www.nspcc.org.uk/
https://adc.bmj.com/content/90/7/715

1975

https://www.jwfacts.com/watchtower/1975.php

Printed in Great Britain
by Amazon

75731323R00170